Events and
Movements in
Modern
JUDAISM

Events and Movements in Modern JUDAISM

*Edited by Raphael Patai
and Emanuel S. Goldsmith*

PARAGON HOUSE

First Edition, 1995

Published in the United States by

Paragon House
370 Lexington Avenue
New York, NY 10017

Copyright 1995 by Paragon House

Library of Congress Cataloging-in-Publication Data

Events and movements in Modern Judaism / edited by Raphael Patai and Emanuel S. Goldsmith.
    p.   cm.
    "Papers presented at two conferences on 'Influences in the Reconfiguration of Modern Judaism' "—Introduction.
    Includes bibliographical references.
    ISBN 1-55778-707-7
    1. Judaism—20th century—Congresses. 2. Jews—Intellectual life—Congresses. I. Patai, Raphael. II. Goldsmith, Emanuel S.
    BM30.E88   1996
    296'.09'04—dc20   95-18830
                                                              CIP

Contents

Introduction

This volume, *Events and Movements in Modern Judaism*, is the second containing papers presented at two conferences on "Influences in the Reconfiguration of Modern Judaism," sponsored by the Council for the World's Religions and held in Stanstad, Switzerland, on September 1–5, 1988, and in Toledo, Spain on November 9–13, 1989, with the participation of Jewish scholars from the United States, England, France, Israel, and Australia. Raphael Patai served as convenor and chairman of the conferences.

The first volume, *Thinkers and Teachers of Modern Judaism*, edited by Raphael Patai and Emanuel S. Goldsmith, was published by Paragon House in 1994. It contains papers dealing with the following personalities who have contributed to the reshaping of Jewish ideas and values in modern times: Ahad Ha-am, Abraham Isaac Kook, Asher Zelig Margaliot, Franz Rosenzweig, Martin Buber, Leo Baeck, Joseph Soloveitchik, Abraham Joshua Heschel, Mordecai M. Kaplan, Primo Levi, H. Leivick, and Yehuda Amichai.

The present volume contains seventeen papers focusing on the major events and movements that had a share in the reconfiguration of modern Judaism. Acquaintance with these issues is essential for an understanding of where Judaism stands today in its spiritual coming-to-terms with the Holocaust, its varieties along the Orthodox-Liberal range of religious thought and observance, its methods of religious teaching, its movement toward modernization, its admission of women to equal participation with men in religious life, its attitude to Israel and Zionism and the reintegration of Oriental Jewry, and, last but not least, its new developments on the American scene.

This volume begins with Richard L. Rubenstein's paper on the year 1881 which marked the beginning of a new era for Russian Jewry as well as for both the Jews of America and for what was then the very small Jewish community of Palestine. This is followed by Samuel Z. Klausner's study of the implications of the Holocaust for Jewish literature and thought as well as for Jewish community organization.

Three essays deal specifically with the effects of modernization on Jewish life. Calvin Goldscheider discusses demographic trends and the changes they have precipitated in Judaism and the Jewish people. Joseph R. Rosenbloom presents a survey and analysis of Jewish adjustment to changing conditions from the beginnings of Jewish history to modern times. Benjamin Uffenheimer concentrates on the theological and political significance of modern Jewish studies and biblical research.

The current resurgence of Orthodox and neo-Orthodox Judaism in Israel and the countries of the Diaspora is the subject of three papers. Samuel C. Heilman relates the revival of Orthodoxy to sociological and psychological understandings of the numinous. Michael G. Berenbaum comments on the challenge of American pluralism for Orthodox theory and practice. Charles Selengut discusses theological issues theological issues and emphases in Orthodox thought.

In the two essays on trends in liberal Judaism both practical and theoretical problems are analyzed. John D. Rayner reviews liturgical developments in the Liberal and Reform Jewish movements in England, while William E. Kaufman comments on theological trends in Reform, Conservative and Reconstructionist Judaism in the United States.

Three papers comprise the section on Israel, Zionism and the Middle East. Saul Patai offers an analysis of the conflict between Orthodox and secular Jews in Israel. The implications of the establishment of Israel for the Zionist movement and for Jewish life in the Diaspora is the subject of David M. Gordis' paper. Guy Haskell discusses the reintegration of the Jews of the Middle East into world Jewry especially since the establishment of the State of Israel.

In his paper on the current situation of American Jewry, Michael G. Berenbaum addresses social, political and spiritual issues. Riv-Ellen Prell presents an analysis of the factors leading to the establishment of the various types of *havurot* or fellowships, and the implications of this new trend for American Jewish life.

The volume concludes with two studies of gender issues in contemporary Jewish polity, culture and religion by Sheldon R. Isenberg and Livia Bitton-Jackson.

The common denominator in all the papers contained in both volumes is that they all deal with change. They leave little doubt that change, seeking and reaching new understandings, is the most significant feature that has characterized Judaism following the *Sho'ah*. The Nazi Holocaust succeeded in reducing the number of Jews by one third. It did not succeed in muting the age-old creativity of the Jewish religious spirit.

Once again the editors wish to express their gratitude to Frank Kaufmann, Executive Director of the Conferences, to the Council for the World's Religions, for making them possible, and to the participants for their cooperation and enthusiasm. It is the sincere hope of the editors that these volumes will contribute to the illumination of current Jewish issues and to the strengthening of Jewish life.

Raphael Patai
Emanuel S. Goldsmith

Tu Bi-Shevat, 5755
January 15, 1995

Contributors and Editors ✡

Michael G. Berenbaum is Project Director of the United States Holocaust Memorial Museum and Hyman Goldman Adjunct Professor of Theology at Georgetown University. He is the author of *The Vision of the Void, After Tragedy and Triumph,* and *The World Must Know,* and co-editor of *Holocaust: Religious and Philosophical Implications.*

Livia Bitton-Jackson is Professor of Hebrew at Lehman College of the City University of New York and author of *The Jewess as a Fictional Sex Symbol, Elli: Coming of Age in the Holocaust* and *Madonna or Courtesan? The Jewish Woman in Christian Literature.*

Calvin Goldscheider is Professor of Sociology and Judaic Studies at Brown University and author of *Jewish Continuity and Change, Population, Modernization, and Social Structure* and *Urban Migrants in Less Developed Nations.* He is also the co-author of *The Transformation of the Jews.*

Emanuel S. Goldsmith is Professor of Yiddish Language and Literature and Jewish Studies at Queens College of the City University of New York. He is the author of *Modern Yiddish Culture: The Story of the Yiddish Language Movement* and co-author of *The Ameri-*

can Judaism of Mordecai M. Kaplan, and *Dynamic Judaism: The Essential Writings of Mordecai M. Kaplan.*

David M. Gordis is President of the Hebrew College in Brookline, Massachusetts and director of the Wilstein Institute of Jewish Policy Studies. He is the editor of *Crime, Punishment and Deterrence: An American Jewish Exploration* and co-editor of *Jewish Identity in America.*

Guy H. Haskell teaches Judaic Studies at Emory University. He is the author of *From Sofia to Jaffa: The Jews of Bulgaria and Israel* and general editor of *Jewish Folklore and Ethnology Review.*

Sheldon R. Isenberg is Associate Professor of Religion at the University of Florida and author of numerous studies including "Aging in Judaism" in *The Handbook of Aging and the Humanities.*

Samuel Heilman is Professor of Sociology at Queens College and the Graduate Center of the City University of New York. His books include *Defenders of the Faith, Synagogue Life, The Gate Behind the Wall* and *A Walker in Jerusalem.*

William E. Kaufman is Rabbi of Temple Beth El in Fall River, Massachusetts and Adjunct Professor of Philosophy at Rhode Island College. He is the author of *Contemporary Jewish Philosophies, Journeys: An Introductory Guide to Jewish Mysticism,* and *The Case for God.* He is also the co-author of *A Question of Faith.*

Samuel Z. Klausner is Professor of Sociology at the University of Pennsylvania and the author of *The Quest for Self-Control: Classical Philosophies and Scientific Research,* and other works.

Raphael Patai, anthropologist and folklorist, has written and edited over seventy books including *The Jewish Mind, The Hebrew Goddess, The Jewish Alchemists,* and *Hebrew Myths* (with Robert Graves). In 1983 Fairleigh Dickinson University Press published *Fields of Offerings: Studies in Honor of Raphael Patai,* edited by Victor D. Sanua.

Saul Patai, a resident of Jerusalem since 1938, is Professor Emeritus of Chemistry at the Hebrew University of Jerusalem and editor of the encyclopedic 75-volume *Chemistry of Functional Groups.*

Riv–Ellen Prell is Associate Professor of Anthropology at the University of Minnesota and the author of *Prayer & Community: The*

Havurah in American Judaism and of a number of anthropological and ethnographic studies on Jewish themes.

John D. Rayner is Rabbi Emeritus of the Liberal Jewish Synagogue, St. John's Wood in London, England and the co-author of *The Jewish People: Their History and Their Religion*. He also co-authored *Judaism for Today, Service of the Heart* and *Gate of Repentance*.

Joseph R. Rosenbloom is Adjunct Professor of Classics at Washington University in St. Louis. His publications include *Conversion to Judaism: From the Biblical Period to the Present*.

Richard L. Rubenstein is the Robert D. Lawton Distinguished Professor of Religion at Florida State University. His many books include *After Auschwitz, The Religious Imagination, Power Struggle,* and *Approaches to Auschwitz* (co-author).

Charles Selengut is Professor of Sociology at the Community College of Morris in Randolph, New Jersey. His publications include *Seeing Society* and *By Torah Alone: Yeshivah Fundamentalism in Jewish Society*.

Benjamin Uffenheimer is Professor Emeritus of Bible at Tel Aviv University. He is the author of *Ancient Prophecy in Israel, Prophetic Experience,* and *The Visions of Zecharia: From Prophecy to Apocalyptic*.

1. 1881: Watershed Year of Modern Jewish History

Richard L. Rubenstein

Although it is always difficult to pinpoint a date as initiating a new historical trend, there is considerable agreement that 1881 was such a year for the Jewish communities of the Russian Empire. Because of the long-range impact of the fate of eastern European Jews on their co-religionists in western Europe and North America, 1881 can be seen as a watershed year for them as well.

The situation of the Jews of Russia had been deteriorating through-out the decades of the seventies. The reign of Tsar Alexander II (1855–81) appeared to have begun auspiciously. On the day of his coronation, August 26, 1856, juvenile conscription, one of the most degrading aspects of the *rekrutshchina* or conscription system intro-duced by Tsar Nicholas I (1825–55) in 1827, was abolished.[1] On December 2, 1857, Jews were once again permitted to be domiciled in frontier provinces adjacent to Prussia, Austria, and Bessarabia. Thereafter, many, but by no means all, of the disabilities affecting Jews were ameliorated.[2]

The new, more liberal policies toward the Jews initiated by the new tsar were part of a larger trend toward the rationalization of Russia's

1

economy and political structure initiated by Peter the Great.[3] The
policies appeared to confirm the optimism of those Jews who favored
secularization, modernization, and some degree of Russification. It
was the hope of both the Russified and the Hebraic parties among the
modernizers that internal Jewish reform would be met by political
emancipation. The modernizing mood was perhaps expressed most
characteristically in the celebrated poem of Yehudah Leib Gordon,
Hakitza Ami ("Awake My People," 1866). It reads in part:

> Awake, my people! How long will you slumber?
> The night has passed, the sun shines bright. . . .
>
> This land of Eden [Russia] now opens its gates to you,
> Her sons now call you "brother."
>
> How long will you dwell among them as a guest,
> And why do you now affront them?
>
> Already they have removed the weight of suffering from your shoulder,
> They have lifted off the yoke from your neck
> They have erased from their hearts gratuitous hatred and folly,
> They give you their hand, they greet you with peace . . .
>
> Open your heart to wisdom and knowledge
> Become an enlightened people, and speak their language. . . .

In spite of the optimism concerning the Jewish future, some troubling developments had already taken place. In 1871 there had been a
pogrom in Odessa that anticipated the developments of 1881. Like
Manchester, Odessa was a city without an indigenous feudal tradition
and, hence, more hospitable to capitalist development than cities like
Moscow and Kiev. Odessa had been founded on a site which until
1789 had been occupied by the Turkish fortress of Khadzhi-Bei. As a
free port and seat of the governors of Novorossia (New Russia) and
Bessarabia, it was the most secularized, economically liberal city in
eastern Europe. The Russian authorities were interested in develop-

ing this outpost. Unlike Moscow and St. Petersburg, where the right
of domicile was accorded only exceptionally to a miniscule number of
Jews, Jews were permitted to settle in Odessa. In 1855 they numbered 17,000, or 21.7 percent of the population; in 1895, 139,984, or
34.65 percent. From the 1880s to the Russian Revolution, Odessa had
the second largest Jewish population in Russia, Warsaw having the
largest.[4] As the most westernized city in the empire, Odessa was the
leading intellectual and literary center of the Hebrew Enlightenment.

Compared with the rest of Russia, Odessa was a relatively open and
liberal city. Its non-Jewish population had a higher level of education
than that of the rest of Russia. At the same time, as a bourgeois port
and one of Russia's most important gateways to the West, Odessa
represented everything that the Slavophiles found wanting in the
"new" Russia.[5]

Although the 1871 pogrom was mild in comparison to the 1881
pogroms, it did foreshadow things to come. Directed primarily against
Jewish artisans and small merchants, it revealed that secularized Jews
were at least as likely to be targets of overt anti-Semitic aggression as
Orthodox Jews. It also revealed that modernization, secularization,
and even professional status did not prevent Jews from being tar-
geted. One of the nastier aspects of the Odessa pogrom, again fore-
shadowing things to come, was the tendency to blame the victims.
Both revolutionaries and conservative political spokesmen were inclined to see the violence as a response of the "people" to Jewish
exploitation. Among others, this view was forcefully expressed by
Mikhail Dragomanov, a leading Ukrainian nationalist intellectual.[6]

A crucial turning point for Russia as well as the other industrializing
nations of Europe and European derivation came with the onset of
the Great Depression of 1873. The depression began in Germany,
Austria-Hungary, and the United States and lasted until 1896. It
afflicted all of industrializing Europe, North America, and Australia.
In the midst of the depression, there were two periods during which
conditions improved, 1879–82 and 1886–89.[7] The depression was
somewhat milder in France and England and elsewhere.

At the risk of oversimplification, the Great Depression can be seen
as a consequence of the extraordinary industrial and technological

progress which had been made in the countries of northern Europe and North America. During the depression years productivity increased dramatically, but prices and profits fell. The period was experienced as a severe depression because of the price deflation, which was largely due to scientific and technological progress in industry, agriculture, communications, and transportation. In a continent with an exploding population, itself a phenomenon related to modernization and rationalization, ever fewer peasants were needed to work the land which yielded an ever more abundant crop. At the same time, reduced transportation costs made it possible to import cheap grain and other foodstuffs from overseas. For example, between 1873 and 1896 food prices in Great Britain dropped by 40 percent.[8] The situation was no different elsewhere in Europe.

In Poland and Russia, the destruction of the traditional rural economy was accelerated by the land reforms which began in 1846 in Poland and 1861 in Russia. As a result of these reforms, some forty-eight million serfs were emancipated. Although the rhetoric employed by the advocates of emancipation stressed the humanitarian need to "liberate" the serfs and the inhumanity of the serf system, the emancipation must be seen as a modernizing and rationalizing measure. Emancipation had the effect of throwing tens of millions of peasants into an impersonal money economy, a development for which they were wholly unprepared, while fostering the severance of whatever traditional bonds of mutual responsibility existed between lord and peasant.[9] The majority of the peasants were among the least competent agriculturalists in all of Europe; they were also illiterate. After emancipation some peasants prospered; most were proletarianized or rendered redundant in a society afflicted with large-scale unemployment. Moreover, as the population exploded, the old balance between land and population disappeared. Even peasant families who succeeded in retaining their small holdings were unable to provide land for their offspring. In the premodern period, the population was sufficiently stable so that adequate land could be found for younger as well as firstborn peasant sons. After emancipation, at first thousands and then millions of peasants were threatened with the most disastrous form of economic and social degradation a peasant could experience, loss of land.

To forestall this development, peasants resorted to subdivision to provide land for their offspring. However, subdivision had obvious limits. The peasant population was increasing while the per capita availability of land was diminishing. Unable to find work at home, millions of landless peasants turned to the towns and cities, first of their native lands and then of western Europe and the United States. In eastern Europe the industrial base was too fragile to provide for sustained employment for more than a small number of the newly urbanized, landless peasants. At the same time, the growth of the cities further facilitated the consolidation of small peasant holdings by creating a vastly enlarged demand for agriculture that could not be met by uneconomic small holdings, especially in view of the competition of overseas food sources. As was the case elsewhere, the movement toward consolidation became irreversible. And, while it enriched the larger and more enterprising farmers, it further disrupted the ancient social ecology of village life.

The destruction of the old economy had disastrous effects on Jewish life in the villages of the Pale of Settlement. Under the older, traditional economy the Jews had been a "middleman minority."[10] Their economic and social location resembled that of other middleman minorities such as the Chinese in Southeast Asia, the Armenians in parts of the Middle East and Turkey, and Indians and Pakistanis in Kenya and Uganda. Middleman minorities are usually permitted domicile in order to do work that for one reason or another is not being done by members of the indigenous population.

Of considerable importance is the fact that in premodern societies it is neither socially nor economically functional for middleman minorities to share a common religion with the indigenous majority. Successful commerce requires impersonal, objective attitudes. These are less likely to develop in traditional societies between persons with religiously legitimated kinship bonds. The flow of finance and commerce often requires a depersonalized in-group/out-group double standard. In European Christian society, the Jews have historically been the most conspicuous, and the most hated, middleman minority.

From the sixteenth century onward, there was a general pattern of migration of Jews from the more advanced economies of western Europe to the more primitive economies of eastern Europe. As the

Western economies became increasingly rationalized, the Jewish minority was increasingly displaced by the non-Jewish bourgeoisie. Insofar as there was a Jewish artisan class, it too tended to be displaced. As Jews became redundant in the West, they turned to the East where the role of a nonindigenous class of middlemen was still needed. Having remained feudal and agrarian for a far longer period than the West, eastern Europe offered Jews opportunities for a viable existence which the masses had lost in the West. This window of opportunity began to close in the second half of the nineteenth century under the impact of the emancipation of the serfs, urbanization, and industrialization. The Jews of eastern Europe now found themselves domiciled in lands in which the alien character of both their religious and their ethnic traditions intensified the normal hostility felt toward the stranger perceived to be functionless.

The Jews did not become functionless because of want of ability, skill, or willingness to work, but because an increasingly desperate sector of the majority saw its best possibility of sustaining itself by doing the work the Jews had been doing and barring the Jews from access to whatever new opportunities the changing economy might offer. Before the modern period the Jews had been a complementary economic class; with the onset of modernization they became a class of competitors. Under the circumstances, the Russian government could find little reason to protect the interests of so alien a minority when they were in conflict with those of insecure members of the indigenous majority.

The Emancipation of the peasants in 1861 had other, long-range, negative structural consequences for the Jews as well as other minorities, the Jews being the worst sufferers. An important result of Emancipation was "the abolition of the serf-owning landlord as the effective viceroy, magistrate, administrator, of the rural population."[11] The need to control this mass led to the rapid growth of the state bureaucracy, many of whose recruits came from the landowning families which had been hurt badly by Emancipation. The bureaucracy was also enlarged as a result of the rapid growth of commerce and industry in the final quarter of the nineteenth century. In the century's final decade Russia had achieved an annual rate of growth of more than eight percent, the highest in the world, and remained above six percent, the highest in Europe, until the beginning of the Great War.[12]

As was so often the case, the bureaucracy sought order through the establishment of uniform rules and procedures amidst inherently destabilizing socioeconomic developments. Elsewhere I have argued that modernization often involves homogenization which governments have attempted to achieve through centrally administered uniform compulsory education and the segregation, expulsion, or extermination of those groups that cannot be assimilated to the majority.[13]

The tendency toward homogenization was evident in both the attitudes and policies of the new tsar, Alexander III (1881–94). Before his reign, the tsar's non-Russian subjects, who in the 1880s numbered fifty million, saw the tsar as their protector against Russian officialdom. With the exception of the Jews, this protection was usually forthcoming. The tsars regarded all of their subjects as equally subject to their will. Monarchy thus functioned as a supranational institution. This attitude was not shared by Alexander III, who regarded only his fifty million Great Russian subjects as worthy of trust. The monarch's nationalist feelings were in accord with the homogenizing policies of the bureaucracy which pursued a policy of uncompromising Russification. Since tsarist Russia was essentially a sacralized polity, Russification involved insistence upon tsarist absolutism and Russian Orthodoxy as the only true faith. A policy of official hostility was directed against all non-Orthodox believers, especially Baptists, Roman Catholics, Old Believers, and Uniats.

The policy of religious and ethnic intolerance has often been regarded as in tension with the rationalizing thrust of both the Enlightenment and modernization. In reality, both were expressions of bureaucratic rationalization and modernization. Homogenization served administrative convenience, and homogenizing ideologies provided the appropriate legitimation. These tendencies were evident in the career of Konstantin Petrovich Pobedonostov (1827–1904), Procurator of the Holy Synod from 1880 until his death. An unwavering believer in tsarist absolutism who fostered a policy of

uncompromising Russification, more than any other official
Pobedonostov was responsible for the policies toward minorities
during the reign of Alexander III and the first part of that of
Nicholas II (1894–1917). Nevertheless, Pobedonostov can be seen
as a modernizing bureaucrat.

Inevitably, those most grievously affected by the policy of Russification were the Jews. In eastern Europe the destruction of the old
feudal economy had disastrous effects on Jewish life. As peasants with
larger holdings prospered, they began to displace the Jews from their
traditional economic roles. Goaded by necessity, still other non-Jews
abandoned their distaste for trade and commerce and became direct
competitors of the Jews. An indigenous petite bourgeoisie arose
which successfully looked to government and social pressure to assist
it in its competition with the Jews. At the same time, a very large
sector of the Jewish population was experiencing downward economic mobility and found itself competing with an equally desperate
non-Jewish proletariat.

Introduction of machinery into the processes of production caused
a further deterioration of the economic condition of Jewish artisans.
Before industrialization, the artisans were found in fields which required some skill but little capital. These included work as tailors,
bookbinders, cigarmakers, watchsmiths, and gold-and silversmiths.
With the introduction of machines these fields required ever less skill
and ever more capital. In Poland those Jews who had sufficient capital
to become factory owners preferred unskilled Polish workers to de-
classed Jewish artisans and petty merchants. Hopelessly under-
capitalized, the majority of Jewish artisans and petty merchants were
proletarianized during a period of high unemployment when a non-
Jewish working class was available. Moreover, employment in heavy
industry, one of the most promising sources of job creation, was
largely barred to Jews by state policy and worker resistance.[14]

The decisive blow came in April of 1881. On March 1, 1881, Tsar
Alexander II was assassinated by members of a revolutionary terrorist
group, Narodnaya Volya (People's Will). There had been a number of
assassination attempts before the conspirators finally succeeded, the
most shocking being the explosion in the Winter Palace in St. Peters-

burg, February 5, 1880. A workman by the name of Khalturin placed a bomb of one hundred pounds under the room in which the tsar dined. When the bomb went off, ten members of the palace guard were killed and another thirty-three wounded. Alexander had unexpectedly delayed entering the room and thus escaped. However, the attempt sent shock waves through the regime. The fact that a terrorist group had successfully penetrated the Winter Palace exaggerated its power and size in the eyes of the tsar and the police. Moreover, the educated classes exhibited considerable passive sympathy for the terrorists and hostility to the regime.[15] There had also been an attempt on the tsar which involved blowing up his railway coach as it traveled from the Crimea to St. Petersburg.

The police had adequate warning that something was afoot before the final blow struck. On February 27, A.I. Zhelyabov, one of the terrorist leaders, was arrested by the police. Although he refused to inform on his comrades, Zhelyabov insisted that the tsar was about to be killed no matter how many conspirators were arrested. He was not believed, but he was, of course correct. A bomb was thrown by N. Rysakov, one of the conspirators, which exploded under the axle of the tsar's carriage. Alexander did not seek to get away from the scene quickly as he was urged to do by his escorts. Instead, he went back on foot to look at Rysakov who had been captured by the police. This gave the conspirators their second chance. The fatal bomb was thrown at the tsar who died two hours later.

One of the participants, Gessia Gelfman, was of Jewish origin. Her presence among the terrorists was enough to trigger the release of a massive, popular anti-Semitic explosion. Anti-Semitism had already been stimulated by the unsatisfactory peace treaty imposed upon Russia at the Congress of Berlin after the Russo-Turkish War of 1877–78 in which Disraeli played an important role in limiting Russian ambitions against Turkey, as well as by press defamation and the generally depressed economic conditions. The objective conditions making for an anti-Semitic outbreak were already present without the assassination and Gelfman. These were nothing more than matches applied to a waiting fuse.

The first pogrom took place in Elizavetgrad (now Kirovograd) in the Ukraine on April 15, 1881. The details of the pogroms are too well known to require repetition in this context. We must, however, note that by the end of 1881, 215 communities had been victimized, hundreds of Jews were killed, mutilated, and raped. More than twenty thousand lost their homes and one hundred thousand their livelihood. The violence continued until 1884 and there was another wave of pogroms between 1903 and 1906, beginning in Kishinev.[16]

In his analysis of the pogroms, Stephen M. Berk points to the deteriorating condition of peasants and workers throughout the empire as a principal economic factor. By the end of the decade of the seventies, less than half of the peasants had plots sufficient to sustain their families. This led millions of peasants unsuccessfully to attempt to rent more land or to hire themselves as farm laborers. This did not solve their problems as land rents increased more rapidly than wages or the price of wheat.

There was, however, a massive migration of peasants from the land to the cities. According to Berk, between 1860 and 1870, the government issued fewer than thirteen million internal passports; in the crucial decade of the seventies thirty-seven million were issued.[17] Peasants from the northern and central regions of the empire migrated south in search of work. The railroads were able to engage some of these wanderers, but the vast majority were itinerants in search of any kind of work they could find. Their situation was not unlike that of contemporary undocumented aliens in the United States. With almost no bargaining power, the migratory workers, known as *bosiaki* (the barefoot brigade) were compelled to take any kind of work, no matter how harsh the conditions, that was available.

The presence of so large a mass of bitter, desperate people also constituted a threat to the indigenous artisans, workers, and merchants of the South who were trying to cope with the effects of the Great Depression. The normal competition between Jews and non-Jews was thus envenomed by the instability, diminishing opportunities, and basic poverty of the region. Not surprisingly, both the migratory workers and the urban non-Jews saw the Jews as the cause of their misfortunes.

According to Berk, the pogroms were primarily a Ukrainian phenomenon which invariably began in the cities or large towns and thereafter spread to the countryside. Berk has characterized the core group of *pogromshchiki* as comprised of "the *meshchanstvo* or petty bourgeoisie, including shopkeepers, butchers, clerks, joiners, tanners, carpenters, and artisan elements of all types."[18] Railroad workers were especially active both in participating in the pogroms and in spreading word about it, which stimulated further pogroms. According to Berk, the peasants were not primarily responsible for the pogroms which, he asserts, were "in terms of origin and severity, primarily urban events," beginning in the cities and only later spreading to the villages. Hearing that Jewish property was available for the taking, the peasants generally entered the cities toward the end of the pogroms to gather up their share. Nor were the pogroms nearly as violent in the peasant villages as in the cities.[19] Although located primarily in the south, there was a large Great Russian component among the *pogromshchiki*. The Russians were an important part of the migratory workers, the *bosiaki*.

Berk's findings are important because they tend to confirm the fact that a very large proportion of those who actively participated in the pogroms were persons rendered vocationally surplus by the modernization process. This in turn tends to confirm the view that modern anti-Semitism is a modernization phenomenon and does not need the Marxist burden. Too much is claimed for the "class Marxists" when we find all sectors of Russian society justifying pogroms, including government and intellectuals. The government instigated the pogroms. Police permitted them, and intellectuals justified them. As long as the Jews remained a complementary economic population fulfilling middleman-minority roles, the alien character of their religious and ethnic roots could be grudgingly tolerated. With the modernization and industrialization of the Russian Empire it had already entered "the take-off period" of modernization and by the next decade would have the highest annual growth rate of any industrial power—the Russian government was confronted with millions of desperate citizens who were prepared wholly to displace the Jews. And, the success of the Narodnaya Volya in assassinating not only the tsar but other high officials with the sympathy of the educated classes was enough to convince high officials of the need to reconcile the "people" to the regime. Under the circumstances, the Jews, who were almost universally regarded as exploiters of the people, could easily be done without. In January 1882 Count N.P. Ignatiev had repeated the words of the Kiev public prosecutor, who had attacked the Jews at a trial of a group of *pogromshchiki*, saying "The western frontier is open to the Jews; why don't they cross it for their own good?"[20]

The question of the regime's complicity in the pogroms has never been completely resolved. Berk has concluded that the pogroms were spontaneous. They usually spread from a large city to the surrounding area, after which there would be a break for several days, and then another pogrom would start in another large town. In spite of the unwillingness of the police and military to stop the violence and even on occasion their willingness to join in, Berk argues that "not a single document has come to light" indicating official government instigation of the pogroms.[21]

The question of responsibility for instigation was less important than the response of the Russian government and educated classes to the events. As is well-known, that response was one of sympathy for the perpetrators and harsh contempt for the victims. To the extent that perpetrators were arrested and lightly punished, the motive of the regime was distrust of disorder and popular spontaneity rather than any sense of injustice to be rectified. Pobedonostov, ever the man of law and order, expressed his opposition to the pogroms in June 1881 in a letter addressed to the new tsar. Several months later in 1882 he denounced the Ministry of the Interior, headed by Ignatiev, for permitting the riots to take place. The most important government official responsible for containing the pogroms was Count Dmitri Tolstoi. Ironically, opposition to the pogroms was most effective among ultraconservatives like Pobedonostov and Tolstoi.

Nevertheless, as was the case in the aftermath of *Kristallnacht*, the law-and-order bureaucrats were infinitely more dangerous than the hoodlum rioters. The official response to the pogroms was given legal expression in the infamous "Temporary Edicts" promulgated in May 1882. The May Laws were designed both to injure and to insult, and succeeded in doing both.

By 1882 it was clear that the ultimate aim of Russian policy in the aftermath of 1881 was the total elimination of the Jews as a demographic presence in the empire. The objective was thoroughly modern. Elimination through discrimination, expulsion, population exchange, ghettoization, or outright extermination have become the methods employed by states in the modern period in dealing with unwanted minorities. It remains to be seen whether the Israeli government will be able to avoid some policy of population elimination such as expulsion toward its unwanted population if present trends continue. Certainly, there is little doubt concerning the population consequences of an Israeli military defeat. In the case of Pobedonostov, what remained of the medieval view was his conviction that religious conversion could take care of a part of the problem. This was expressed in his oft-quoted "solution" to the Jewish problem. "One-third will die, one-third will leave the country, and the last third will be completely assimilated within the surrounding population."[22]

Elsewhere, I have argued that there is an element of political rationality in state-sponsored or state-instigated pogroms.[23] Their calculated denial of the normal protection of the law to the target population is a breach of the social contract which transforms the victims into outlaws whom the dominant majority are at liberty to injure or kill at will. Of necessity, such periods of lawlessness must be strictly limited. Where the regime aims at systematic lawlessness and/or the demographic elimination of the target population, popular violence must be followed up and reinforced by bureaucratic violence. This was the case with the enactment of the May Laws of 1882.

The pogroms and the subsequent bureaucratic violence had the desired effect. Although inefficient and more or less nonracist when compared to the German program of state-sponsored population elimination, they resulted in the emigration of more than four million Jews between 1881 and 1930. Never before had so large a proportion of the Jewish people emigrated from one country in so short a time. Not surprisingly, the first to migrate included a very high proportion of modernized and secularized Jews. Having been both more exposed to and more optimistic concerning the benefits of moderate Russification, they were in the best position tragically to read the signs of the times.

There were basically four responses to the events of 1881: as noted, emigration to the West was the preponderant response; the other responses included the beginnings of modern Zionism with the founding of the BILU and Hibbat Zion movements, ultimately culminating in the founding of the state of Israel; revolutionary politics within Russia leading to the founding of the Bund and a highly visible participation of Jews in the Bolshevik movement; and, on the part of a portion of the population, paralysis and immobilism, with its tragic completion of the process begun in 1881, the Holocaust of 1939–45.

Large numbers of Jews had no intention of emigrating from their place of birth even when the character of the regime was no longer clouded in even a remnant of ambiguity. For many of the brightest and the most energetic, revolution was the only answer. As noted above, the state had abrogated the social contract, the essence of which is obedience to the sovereign's laws in exchange for the sovereign's protection. In tsarist Russia, however, the sovereign and his agents had become the chief perpetrators of injury both by their overt sympathy with the rioters and their subsequent bureaucratic violence. Whatever legitimacy the regime had previously commanded in Jewish eyes was understandably a thing of the past, especially for the young whose future still lay ahead of them. When in 1881 Ignatiev, who was all too willing to encourage lawlessness against the Jews, charged that the Jews were responsible for terrorism, he was in error. At the time, there were almost no Jews among the revolutionaries. According to Edmund Crankshaw, ". . . the whole revolutionary movement until the 1890s was Russian to the core."[24] It was only in the 1890s that Jewish workers and intellectuals were attracted to Marxism and founded the Bund as a Jewish Social Democratic Party. In addition, a very important group of young Jews including Lev Bronstein, later to be known as Leon Trotsky, joined the group that was to become the Bolsheviks.

The turn of a highly visible group of young Jews to revolution was to have disastrous consequences on Jewry in the 1920s, especially in Central Europe and in the halls of the Vatican, where Bolshevism was widely regarded as a Jewish assault on Christian civilization. The importance of this perception for the ultimate fate of Europe's Jews cannot be overestimated.

Emigration to the West also had problematic effects for the Jewish situation. Because of its multiethnic and multinational character, the United States was ultimately able more or less to integrate the huge transfer of population, but, as we know, this was not without stress and the rise of nativistic movements fearful of what a large body of Jews would do to America's fundamentally Christian culture. Moreover, the nativistic response could be given the voice of literary sophistication by such luminaries as Henry Adams and Henry James as well as cruder mass expression.

Emigration did, however, exacerbate nativistic and racist feelings in the more homogenous countries of western Europe. I have dealt with this issue in detail elsewhere.[25] In the present context, it is sufficient to note Heinrich von Treitschke's comment that "year after year there pours in from the inexhaustible Polish reservoir a host of ambitious pants-selling youngsters, whose children will some day control . . . the stock exchanges and the newspapers."[26] Trietschke's essay, "A Word About Our Jewry," gave anti-Semitism academic respectability in late-nineteenth-century Germany. It was the emigration of the Jews of the Russian Empire that moved him to write as he did. It was the tragedy of the emigrating Jews that they moved to the West just at the point at which the homogenizing tendencies of modernization and bureaucratic centralization were intensifying the hazards of the stranger and the resident alien.

A principal reason for paralysis was the fear of the traditionally minded, and even some of the less traditional, that emigration to the United States would result in the eventual disappearance of large numbers of Jews as Jews. This is not the occasion to discuss the complex question of intermarriage and conversion among American Jews. Nevertheless, it is this observer's opinion that there was considerable substance to the apprehensions concerning the eventual disappearance of large numbers of Jews within the larger non-Jewish population.

It was only the Zionist movement that held that, at the heart of the Jewish problem, was the simple presence of Jews, not because they were compelled to become a middleman minority or because of any conceivable truth in the defamations hurled at them by anti-Semites, but simply because they were the stranger par excellence. Whereas other peoples were ethnic or racial strangers, the Jews alone were both ethnic strangers and the one people who by their very existence challenged the fundamental Christian truth that "Christ is Lord." Put differently, the Jews were the disconfirming other par excellence. Although the full dimension of this perception was expressed neither by Pinsker nor Herzl, they intuited the full dimension of the peril and called the Jewish people to an existence in which they would no longer be an alien presence.

There were, however, two aspects of the alien character of Jewish existence which the early Zionists and even the founders of the State of Israel did not fully comprehend: (a) Jews had become an alien presence as a consequence of military defeats in the Judeo-Roman Wars of 66–70 C.E. and 131–35 C.E., and could only by military victory achieve dominance over a territory in which they would no longer be strangers (to date, that victory has eluded the State of Israel); and (b) in an age of instantaneous global communication and jet transportation, a territorial solution does not end the perils of the alien character of Jewish existence. The real significance of the United Nations' infamous "Zionism is racism" resolution (now repealed) was to ratify once again the universally alien character of the Jew.

NOTES

1. An abbreviated version of Nicholas I's "Statutes Regarding the Military Service of Jews" (August 26, 1827) is to be found in Paul R. Mendes-Flohr and Yehuda Reinharz, eds., *The Jew in the Modern World: A Documentary History* (New York: Oxford University Press, 1980), 305–6.

2. See Stephen M. Berk, *Year of Hope: Year of Crisis: Russian Jewry and the Pogroms of 1881–1882* (Westport, Ct.: Greenwood Press, 1985), 8–9.

3. See James H. Billington, *The Icon and the Axe: An Interpretive History of Russian Culture* (New York: Vintage Books, 1970), 163–203.

4. See article "Odessa," *Encyclopaedia Judaica* (Jerusalem: Keter Publishing House, 1972), vol. 12. 1319–25.

5. On the Slavophiles, see Hans Rogger, "Russia," in Hanz Rogger and Eugen Weber, eds., *The European Right* (Berkeley: University of California Press, 1966), 443–99.

6. Berk, *Year of Hope*, 71.

7. Hans Rosenberg, "Political Consequences of the Great Depression of 1873–1896 in Central Europe," in James J. Sheehan, ed., *Imperial Germany*. (New York: New Viewpoints, 1976).

8. Eric Hobsbawm, *op. cit.*, 37.

9. See Edward Crankshaw, *The Shadow of the Winter Palace: The Drift to Revolution 1825–1917* (Harmondsworth, Middlesex: Penguin Books, 1976), 196–209.

10. On the subject of middleman minorities, see Walter Zenner, "Middleman Minorities and Genocide," in *Genocide and the Modern Age: Etiology and Case Studies of Mass Death* (Westport, Ct.: Greenwood Press, 1987), 254–81.

11. Crankshaw, *Winter Palace*, 331.

12. John P. McKay, *Pioneers for Profit: Foreign Entrepreneurship and Russian Industrialization 1885–1913* (Chicago: University of Chicago Press, 1970), 4–5.

13. See Richard L. Rubenstein, *The Age of Triage: Fear and Hope in An Overcrowded World* (Boston: Beacon Press, 1963), 17.

14. See Abram Leon, *The Jewish Question: A Marxist Interpretation* (New York: Pathfinder Press, 1970), 206–7.

15. Crankshaw, *Winter Palace*, 297.

16. See Berk, *Year of Hope*, 36–55, for a succinct discussion and analysis of the pogroms. See also Louis Greenberg, *The Jews in Russia*, 2nd ed. (New York: Schocken Books, 1976), 1–75, and article "Pogroms," in *Encyclopaedia Judaica*, vol. 13, 695–8. See also David Vital, *The Origins of Zionism* (Oxford University Press, 1975), 52.

17. Berk, *Year of Hope*, 42.

18. Ibid., 39.

19. Ibid.

20. Vital, *Origins of Zionism*, 70.

21. Berk, *Year of Hope*, 41.

22. Article, "Pobedonostov," in *Encyclopaedia Judaica*, vol. 13, 663.

23. Rubenstein, *Age of Triage*, 140–41.

24. Crankshaw, *Winter Palace*, 334.
25. Rubenstein, *Age of Triage*, 144–66.
26. Heinrich von Treitschke, "A Word About Our Jewry" in Paul R. Mendes-Flohr and Yehuda Reinharz, eds., *The Jew in the Modern World: A Documentary History* (New York: Oxford University Press, 1980), 261.

2. The Holocaust and Jewish Social Policy

Samuel Z. Klausner

Today, an extensive literature, mostly, but not exclusively, Jewish, interprets the motives, design, and implementation of the Nazi mass murder of Jews, the Holocaust. Jewish interpretations include literature by and diaries of victims and martyrs; autobiographies of survivors and children of survivors; local histories or *yizkerbicher;* comprehensive social histories; novels and poems in Hebrew, Yiddish, and other languages. The Holocaust is interpreted in music, visual and performing arts, and liturgical compositions by survivors, victims, and those who memorialize them. Theologians and philosophers have struggled to offer a moral meaning of the events, and political analysts and leaders derive policy lessons.

This paper examines a small sample of theological and philosophical reflections on the Holocaust. We then ask what Jewish social policy implications, if any, derive from these writings? Marxist theory and praxis are more closely bonded intellectually than are theology and social policy in our more "bourgeois" tradition. Yet, contemporary theology is written as a guide for religion, a way of living. The classic philosophers were teaching "how to live."

Theology, God-talk, is a discussion of the ultimate conditions of human existence. The world as experienced, the world of the relative, may be interpreted in the light of categories of the ultimate. The vision of social science, limited to the experienced world, rises but a hair's breadth above experience by means of its general concepts. These refer to classes of experience or, more precisely, classes of attributes of the experiences. Social norms, directives for behavior, and social values, standards for judging the norms or the behaviors, are the terms in which social policy is expressed and are the objects of social scientific theory and research.

By logical implication one can derive "ideal" norms from theological and philosophical statements. These work themselves out in engagement with a structure of social relations producing "real" norms, the actual rules of social behavior. The verbal interpretations themselves, and the attitudes they represent, are conditioned by the social situations in which they are authored. Such a "sociology of knowledge" set forth in Marx's *The German Ideology*, Karl Mannheim's *Ideology and Utopia*, and numerous other works identify the genesis of attitudes, describe how they give meaning to the social situations that spawned them. Max Weber, in his polemic with Marx, agreed that ideas are shaped by social structures, but, once shaped, they have an independent social effect. Ideas become a foundation of action. This essay concentrates on this latter phase in the relation of ideas and actions.

What are the attitudes or understandings of the Holocaust offered by contemporary thinkers? What kinds of action, social policies, seem to be justified by various theological and philosophical interpretations of the Holocaust? Traditional Jewish interpretations of catastrophe are a principal offering. The Holocaust forces its interpreters to struggle with the problem of meaning in itself. Those who cannot then pursue traditional conceptions, which assume the problem of meaning to have been solved, propose innovative interpretations for an unprecedented event.

Two types of actions are proposed. They need not follow the traditional/innovative distinction of the interpretations. One is modeled on Weber's idea of exemplary prophecy. Energy is directed internally. The Jewish people are called upon to be a witness to the world. A second type of action parallels Weber's ethical prophecy. Jewry is called upon to change its social environment, the society and culture of the criminal, and so actively assure the "never again." Memories of dead victims, of martyrs, and of survivors, as well as scientific historians provide the data, the experience, which the theologians interpret and propose acting upon.

Memory: An Obligation

The very theological and philosophical writing itself is a social act in response to principle. The neglect of Holocaust theology and remembering for over a decade after the event is a failure to observe the positive commandment of *zakhor!* remember! Memory is not passively acquired but becomes an obligation, a religious obligation, an obligation to the victims, an obligation to the future generations of Jews. The obligation is to recover the event, to detail it, to document it, to suffer it as a martyrology, or even a martyrdom, and use it judicially, for inquiry, for vengeance, for compensation or as a didactic. Even the last is not passive. The didactic is propaedeutic, a teaching in preparation for study or action. The lessons of the Eichmann trial echo to and fro.

For the historian, Yerushalmi (1982), the historian of Jewry, the formal and professional memorializer is the servant of the people carrying out the Biblical injunction "to remember" as in "Remember Amalek!" Memory is constructive. Yerushalmi says that if Herodotus was the father of history, the fathers of meaning in history were the Jews. Of course, Herodotus's memory also constructed the data of heroism and villainy, and drew the morals for each.

The early resistance to remembering the Holocaust has been puzzling. Brenner (1980), who studied Holocaust survivors, discovered a "need to witness" that was only expressed years after the event. The permission to release the memory may have been related to the Eichmann trial which legitimated public talking, giving testimony.

This repression of memory evokes a charge. Emil Fackenheim, an early theological interpreter of the event, insists that we retrace "again and again, the *via dolorosa* . . ." that led to the destruction of one-third of the Jewish people. This goes beyond the traditional liturgical martyrologies to the creation of contemporary martyrologies which take, as their model, the *via dolorosa* image. Testimony has been voluminous. The dedicated repositories such as Yad Vashem and the YIVO archives are bulging even though only a small minority of the survivors has engaged in this exercise. While Yad Vashem has become a pilgrimage shrine, the audience for the literature of testimony has hardly been overwhelming. The calls for memory are also a censure of contemporary assimilating Jewry.

Sometimes the move from meaning to construction of social policy requires the censoring of memory, the elimination of evidence that would threaten redemption. David Roskies (1984), in his review of the literature of catastrophe, takes it as a principle that the Holocaust yields meaning only when certain of its specifics are censored. He offers the example of the underground ghetto leader, Abba Kovner, who upon entering besieged Vilna in 1944 destroyed the Gestapo files on Jewish collaborators. Also, the ghetto poet, Sutzkever, eliminated from his poems that which might offend the memory of the dead. The more the gray was eliminated, writes Roskies, the more the Holocaust as archetype could take on its specific contours.

The Traditional Understanding

The traditionalist does not doubt the understandableness of the Holocaust. The number slaughtered does not lift it from the history of Jewish catastrophe, the destructions of the Temples, the exiles, the crusader massacres of 1096, the Berber Almohade persecutions of Morocco, the expulsion from Spain, the pogroms led by Bogdan Khmelnitzky, the pogroms remembered under the synecdoche Kishenev or the associated mass conversions of Jews to Christianity.

Berkovits (cited in Katz, 1983), writing as a traditionalist rejects the notion that the magnitude of the horror implies that the Holocaust poses a new problem for Jewish faith. The concept of *hester panim*, the occultation of God, is invoked as an aid to his understanding. Such occultation allows space for freedom, a requirement for man to be a moral creature. Here is the kabbalistic *tsimtsum*, Divine contraction, creating a space for creation. Occultation during the Holocaust opened a space for the Satanic in man.

A classic statement of the traditional position is that of Rabbi Yoel Teitelbaum (cited in Katz, 1983), the leader of the Satmar Hasidim: the Holocaust is punishment for sin, the sins of Zionism and the Reform movement, in particular. That non-Zionists and Torah-true Jews perished does not contradict this position since all Israelites are responsible for one another. The people is responsible for the sins of a minority.

The response to each is enveloped by the responses to the others. The early medieval *eleh ezkerah*, the elegiac martyrdom of sages, is repeated in the Day of Atonement liturgy or the later medieval *kinnot*, laments and penitentials preserved in the Tish'ah b'Av liturgy. Each builds on Lamentations. The earlier events are a metaphor for the current catastrophe. The plot is set. Sin is searched out to account for the divine punishment. The punishment, the fundamental integrative frame, is meted out by Gentiles selected as instruments of God's will. The *piyyut*, liturgical poem, offers a penitential opening to a hope of Israel's return to Torah, a redemptive action, God's renewal of the covenant. The drama interprets the catastrophe and the social prescription for redemption.

Catastrophes become real, Roskies (1984) says, when identified with an earlier one. In his literary record of apocalypse he relates a tale of S. Ansky, Yiddish folklorist and author of *The Dybbuk*. Ansky, visiting a destroyed synagogue in Galicia, observed an icon which had been placed on the holy ark. He associated it with *tzelem bahekhal* (an idol in the Temple), the symbol of desecration preceding the destruction of the Second Temple. This literary tradition of combining tragic events of different periods on the same date is well founded in rabbinic practice. The tradition is that both Temples were destroyed on the Ninth of Av, and that was the historic date specified in the edict of expulsion from Spain for Spain to be free of Jews. Even the calendar holds substantive power, ominous dates and holy dates, all under *mazalot,* the signs of the zodiac.

Roskies (1984) points to the use of parody in reconstructing earlier catastrophes. The *'akedah,* the binding of Isaac, is evoked as an image for mass martyrdom, though no sacrificial death marked the original Jewish traditions. The medieval charge that Jews poisoned wells appears in a poem masked as part of the prayer for rain. Doing violence to the sacred text by means of parody both maintains continuity of meaning and argues for change. It does the latter because the current catastrophe is never a perfect replica of the paradigmatic one.

Tradition and its paradigms encounter difficulty incorporating the Holocaust or, at least, some theologians encounter difficulty. No parody accompanies the telling of the Holocaust. It does not assimilate any earlier experience. After the pogroms at the turn of the century Chagall could paint *White Crucifixion* and Uri Zvi Greenberg could write of the "Kingdom of the Cross." Nothing like this seems to emerge from the Holocaust, except, perhaps, the Maybaum image of the Jewish vicarious sacrifice, recapitulating Christ's Passion, of which more later. Roskies concludes that the reappropriation of Jesus by Chagall and Greenberg was a part of the rebellion against tradition which lost its usefulness once it became clear that the world's idea of redemption was redeeming the world of its Jews. The great *imitatio dei* of the modern period has not been the Jews' endless capacity to suffer, to die for the sanctification of the Name, but to know and mourn and transcend the apocalypse. The fashioning of catastrophe into a new set of tablets is the primal act of creation carried out in the image of God. Roskies does not tell us what might be written on those tablets and so we are left anticipating the social policy lesson.

Innovative Understanding and Conservative Policy

Nontraditional theological literature argues for the uniqueness of the Holocaust. An assertion of uniqueness justifies, even requires, religious innovation. Uniqueness argues that Jewish suffering cannot be assimilated to the general idea of genocide as it applies to the Armenian massacres or Cambodia under the Khmer Rouge. Uniqueness is not simply that the Holocaust is a one-time historical anomaly. It could then be assimilated to traditional understandings as a negative miracle. It is unique because it is not an event in history, not even a divine intervention in history. The cataclysm is metaphysical. So unique and incomparable to any previous catastrophe is it that Yom Hasho'ah, says Fackenheim, "cannot now, or ever after, be assimilated to the Ninth of Av." The event defies any attempt to discern its meaning.

Richard Rubenstein in his early work, *After Auschwitz*, used the metaphor of the "death of God." This is neither divine contraction nor divine occultation. It asserts that the Holocaust had demonstrated the meaninglessness of existence. Rubenstein says that men must create meaning in face of the objective fact that human life has no purpose. This is, fundamentally, what is to be done, not at the policy level but at the theological or philosophical level. All meaning, whether the symbolic interpreting of human relations or the deciphering of the natural world, is created. A traditional theologian seeks to discover a natural order, perhaps hinted in revelation. The nontraditional theologian is an existentialist, rejecting transcendent meaning in favor of meaning inferred from events.

The issue here is how to discover an adequate meaning from the event. The existentialist begins with man acting within the event. How can the observer experience what the subject experienced? Adequacy refers to adequate for a purpose. That purpose may be theoretical, a prediction or recognition of a patterned recurrence of events. The purpose may be to discover action to produce or obstruct a recurrence.

Arthur Cohen (1981) writes that struggling to understand the Holocaust is a matter of understanding the *tremendum*, a term borrowed from Rudolf Otto's *Idea of the Holy*, the human experience of spiritual awe. Was Auschwitz an encounter with the Holy and, for that reason, not comprehensible in the terms ordinarily used to grasp nature? "The death camps are a reality which, by their nature, obliterate thought and the human program of thinking . . . something which, whenever addressed, collapses into tears, passion, rage." Words, he says, no longer command us because they no longer reflect concepts and convictions which directly govern and thereby agitate conscience. If abstract cognitive thought is inadequate, the extremities of subjectivity and passion are to be engaged in evoking the *tremendum*. Passion, as we experience it, is rooted in early human relationships. Why should a reexperiencing of infantile affect be any better than mature cognitive thought for understanding the *tremendum*?

Cohen offers an exercise for approaching and understanding the *tremendum*. It begins with separating the *tremendum* from all things, then descending into the abyss, and then rejoining the *tremendum* to the whole experience of mankind. The referents of these terms are elusive and, indeed, a procedure, or even spiritual exercise, following the prescribed regimen is elusive.

One difficulty in grasping the *tremendum*, according to Cohen, is our custom of thinking of evil in negative terms, as a lack of good, a lack of God. Encountering the holiness of Auschwitz, evil needs to be regarded as substantive, as ontologically affirmative, as a real presence. One might now expect a theology incorporating a mephistophelian element or a Zoroastrian dualism. But, no, Cohen returns to human freedom where God's role is as a filament within historical events. Man can obscure, eclipse, burn out the divine filament. This human act opposes a chthonic counterpoint to transcendence. Evil is in man. Psychologically, we are offered the Freudian image of ego restraining id. Psychohistorically, this is an appeal for a social authority preventing dangerous chthonic impulses, those arising from the subconscious depths, from breaking loose.

The human freedom at issue is not that of the Jews but of their tormentors. A policy chastising Christians might follow from this. Cohen resists this conclusion, choosing to keep the action within Judaism. The Jew who leaves Judaism is his archetype of the one to be chastised. From Paul of Tarsus to Boris Pasternak such a Jew argues that the old Jew is dead, that Judaism has no more life. The living Jew must become the dead Jew in order than the non-Jew be saved.

The mass death becomes, for innovative theology, a caesura, a point of discontinuity. The uniqueness idea circumscribes the caesura within Judaism. The attention is fastened on the victims, not on the perpetrators of the crime. The Holocaust is unique because of the particularity of the slaughter, a visitation upon Jews. The deaths of other people, Cohen says, are *tremenda* in their languages. Every genocidal *tremendum* is unique to the victims. The uniqueness of the Holocaust would only affect Jewish theology, following this argument.

The emerging position is socially conservative and psychologically progressive. The command is not to change the environment but to change oneself. It echoes the conservative Christian struggle against the social gospel as diverting people from the salvation of their own souls. Ayatollah Khomeini, when he was in exile in Karbala, wrote that the primary or "great" *jihad* is the *jihad alnafs*, the struggle with one's own soul. The conservative Christian eventually turned to political engagement and Khomeini to revolution.

Cohen calls for a withdrawal from the world of liberalism and nineteenth-century optimism of progress, of good to come from social assimilation and cultural accommodation. "The Holocaust's configuration of evil drains of credibility every notion of an ongoing teleology of the good that was required by the rational optimism and social Darwinism of the nineteenth century." Social Darwinism, as used by the historian Richard Hofstadter, is an ideology justifying the position of the ruling classes as selected by nature to rule. Cohen invokes the term to undermine the idea of progress or morality in human society. In both events, the lesson is socially conservative because it questions the efficiency of action for social change.

The implication for social practice or conduct, meaning for living, of a descriptive interpretation of events must make the leap from the cold abstractness of the description to the warmth of value content, values to be realized. Such content is evanescent in Cohen's innovative theology. For him, the normative command is to maintain the internal durability of Jewish community and practice against a background of an environment of enmity. The means is to forge a community of shared gesture, a language that opens each human being to the other. Cohen, like Buber, speaks of relationship. Cohen's approach suffers the same weakness. The opening to relationship is a potential for something to happen. The content of what might happen, for

Cohen and for Buber, is left to the spontaneity of the encounter. Such undirected existentialism antedated the Holocaust. In this sense, we have neither an innovative theology nor an innovative social policy.

Literary responses have also attempted to be innovative. Mintz (1984) studying the reactions to catastrophe in Hebrew literature defines catastrophe as an event with the power to shatter existing paradigms of meaning, especially as regards the bonds between Israel and God. The crusader massacres and the pogroms of 1881 were not paradigm shattering. The victims of the first incorporated themselves in the imagery of sacrificial offerings at the Temple. The victims of the second became new exiles. Yet, there is a uniqueness. Hebrew literature has been silent about the Holocaust. As Mintz observes, it placed Holocaust literature in a ghetto. The work of Aharon Appelfeld and Uri Zvi Greenberg are exceptions. The former, a survivor, grounded his poetry in the great mythic structures of Judaism, and so made it not entirely exceptional. The latter, as an outsider to traditional religion, took the experience as a new call to Zion. This latter, a major current of Jewish social policy, is not a response to the uniqueness of the Holocaust. For Zionism, the Holocaust validated an already formed policy. Its aftermath gave a significant thrust to the realization of the Zionist program without a theological reevaluation—unless the decline in Jewish anti-Zionism qualifies as a theological reassessment.

Innovative Understandings and Progressive Policy

A second type of understanding points to the social environment. Emil Fackenheim, philosopher, writes that the event may have been unique but it was not an "accidental relapse into tribalism." Its meaning is found in the intent or motive of the perpetrators. The enemy and the crime, rather than the Jewish victims, holds the interpreter's attention. The slaughter was designed by human beings and it is their crime. The unique in Auschwitz, says Fackenheim, is that it is evil for evil's sake. The crime was not instrumental, intended, for instance, to eliminate a political opposition. The crime was an end in itself. Jews were murdered for being what they were rather than for what they did. The murderers cloaked the act in an ideology of Jewish misdeeds and of their sanctified role as avenging angels. The perpetrators were idealists, ordinary people doing ordinary jobs. They did not "use" torture but "worshipped" it. Jews must refuse to dissolve Auschwitz into suffering-in-general, not allow the Germans to link it with Dresden or American liberals with Hiroshima. These others were instrumental acts, as barbarous as they might have been, aiming at the defeat of, the submission of, the enemy, not his annihilation.

The enemy is not simply the Nazi or the complicitous German or the silent European or American. The animating motive is derived from Christianity, Christian civilization, which has for two millennia cast the Jews as demonic. "Without Jew-hatred in Christianity itself, Auschwitz in the heart of Christian Europe would have been impossible." Fackenheim rejects a doctrine of German exceptionalism. Germany may have organized and led the slaughter but found willing allies in other Christian peoples, in Poland, the Ukraine, and the Baltic Countries, implicating Protestant, Roman, and Orthodox Christianity.

Conceiving the Holocaust as inspired by Christian theology suggests other Christian societies as potential perpetrators. It could have happened in France, Great Britain or the United States. It need not have required the active support of all Christians. A minority of activists who operate in a sympathetic environment is sufficient. That it was resisted in Denmark and even in Hungary before the full occupation, countries no less Christian, suggests that the theological tradition may be a necessary but not sufficient cause. Why, at a given time and place, do certain social elements draw on the tradition? This is more a social science than a theological question.

Fackenheim tells Christians what the necessary redemptive attitude must be. "The post-Holocaust Christian must repent of the sin of supersessionism and Zionism must become a Christian commitment." Conservative Christians may provide the latter but not for the reasons Fackenheim seeks, while some mainline Protestants and some Roman Catholics today revise the role of supersessionism and recognize the continuing validity of Judaism. It is not likely that either of Fackenheim's conditions, rejection of supersessionism and support of Zionism, will be met by a large number of Christians. Nevertheless, his social policy defines a Jewish attitude towards, even a demand upon, Christians.

The Holocaust and Zionism intertwine in many ways. The Holocaust deprived the Zionist movement of its manpower and intellectual resources in eastern Europe and, in postwar years, turned it into a refugee movement with Palestine as the haven. Some contacts existed between Jabotinsky and Polish anti-Semites and between the *yishuv* authorities and the Nazis regarding the transfer of German Jewish property to Palestine. During the war years, anti-British forces in the Arab world could make common cause with the Axis powers and translate some of this political alliance into ammunition for the conflict between Arab and Jewish nationalism in Palestine. This symbolism continued to serve the Arab cause after 1948.

Fackenheim interprets the Arab attack on Israel in 1948, and thereafter, as a continuation of the Holocaust, "a politicide attempt inspired by the genocide." He is misled by the Arab use of Nazi anti-Jewish symbols to merge Muslim with Christian theologies. True, the Arab/Jewish conflict draws on traditional Muslim attitudes toward the Jews but these are a matter of social power. The *dhimmi* suffer political disabilities. This is not a devil theory of Jews, a moral judgement. Fackenheim, in extending the enemy beyond Germany, and even beyond Christendom, sees the devil theory as a disease spreading to the Eastern world. The medical contagion image is not a good metaphor for cultural diffusion. While later Arab propagandists have profited from *Der Stürmer*, the Middle East conflict has its own dynamic which antedated the Holocaust and which, paradoxically, links Jews to Christians, two edges of the European phalanx besetting Islam.

While Cohen concentrates on Jews, a part of his analysis spills over to the Christian tormentors. Cohen writes, "I cannot believe that any Christian theology of a God who has already saved can make much sense after the *tremendum*." He, here, summons Christians to innovate theologically just as he expects Jews to do. More immediately, it permits Jews to ask for Christian revisionism. The Holocaust has put all traditional religion in doubt. The philosopher-theologian now has an awesome task of putting, not only the Jews but, the whole world, at least the Christian and Islamic world, back together. *Tikkun 'olam* is writ very large.

It is a revision of Sinai writ large. The Holocaust is a new revelation. The breaking forth of the spirit of the Holy Ghost, a mystical experience, may be devoid of content. Its meaning would be in the experience itself, its infusion of faith, leaving the question of the object and foundation of faith open. But, a revelation is a revelation of something. Fackenheim takes the Holocaust as the revelation of Satan. His commandment of Jewish survival is set against that revelation.

The destroyer, in Jewish tradition, is not always Satan. As Mintz points out, in Lamentations it is God himself, the nations being his instrument. With this view it is difficult to hate an historical enemy when that enemy was selected as a divine chastiser. Internal remorse and reconstruction is the traditional response. The current secular response is to blame the nations and hold them to account. The nations may be abstractions like the Weimar economy or the Treaty of Versailles. Social policy considers their role, the role of the designers of these arrangements, in the Nazi accession to power.

Historians of the Holocaust have been particularly insistent on fixing blame but, unlike the theologians, are less likely to point to Christianity as a whole and more to the Germans and the secular social arrangements. Raul Hilberg's historical work maintains the tie of the Holocaust to the Christian anti-Judaism tradition.

For Jewish historians, the image of uniqueness remains. Dawidowicz (1981), reviewing the treatment of the Holocaust in contemporary European historiography, finds it contained a metaphor for the "ecumenical nature" of evil. The German dictatorship, she retorts, specifically intended to murder Jews. The first German euthanasia programs were social experiments. Once the dedicated killing facilities were installed, she argues, it became convenient to use them to murder non-Jews who had become expendable such as Russian prisoners of war, Gypsies and various German opponents of the regime.

Historians of the Holocaust have eschewed broad social theories. Dawidowicz writes that "Despite the outpouring of popular and scholarly books on Hitler, no work has yet been produced that satisfactorily explains Hitler's obsessive ideas about the Jews, the readiness of the German people to accept those ideas and Hitler's ability to harness an enormous apparatus of men, institutions, and facilities just in order to murder the Jews." Discovering a "satisfactory" explanation is a refractory methodological problem in the social sciences. Such explanations, though, would not support the uniqueness argument since, by their nature, they tie the event to regular social and historical and psychological processes. The evil becomes "banal," to use Hannah Arendt's term.

In maintaining the uniqueness argument, Dawidowicz sides, for a moment, with German historians such as Meinecke. His *The German Catastrophe* takes National Socialism as an intrusion, destructive of the continuity in German history. This "intrusion" theory, though consistent with uniqueness, shocks Dawidowicz. In the first place, it requires an almost theological assertion that Hitler seduced the German people with his demonic personality. She points out that, though written during the Nuremberg Tribunals, a reader of Meinecke would not know about slave labor, concentration camps, mass shootings, and death factories. Dawidowicz wants it both ways, to see Hitler as continuous with German history and, yet, to hold that genocide and the enslavement of entire nations is an exclusive domain of Nazi Germany. This is technically possible. The guilt need not be equally distributed. The devil can still be identified with trigger men and their supporters.

Soviet histories of the period, which absorb the Jewish tragedy within the larger tragedy of the Russian people, are another version of the "ecumenical notion" of evil. Dawidowicz is particularly riled by the role of Russian Jews in erasing the Holocaust from the records of Soviet history. A 1946 article in *Eynikayt*, the Moscow-published Yiddish serial, complained against those Soviet historians who did not integrate the killing of Soviet Jews with the killing of Soviet people in general. The Russian polity, for its part, certainly did what it could to erase any Jewish particularism in suffering.

What Is to Be Done? Exemplary and Ethical Prophets

We turn from understanding to action. Borrowing the title of Lenin's 1902 essay, we ask *What is to be Done?* Does the type of understanding achieved suggest the action to take? Who should act and with or against whom? We have mentioned a variety of actions implicit in the meanings which theologians have given to the Holocaust. Some involved turning inward on the Jewish world. Others involved a critique of Christianity. We turn to more explicit proposals. Broadly speaking, as mentioned above, proposed action may be modeled on the exemplary prophet or on the ethical prophet, pursuing a goal, calling others to action.

Fackenheim's Auschwitz commandment of survival illustrates the exemplary. The Holocaust was not punishment for our sins or even to be likened to the redemptive suffering of Christ. The policy meaning in the new commandment is that it is forbidden to grant posthumous victories to Hitler. The Jews are commanded to survive. The response is a dramatic act of biological reproduction, in effect a return to the first Biblical commandment, "be fruitful and multiply," but with nothing said about replenishing the earth. This is a nonrational, wordless, planless, dramatic response, a mystic response in the same biological terms that the enemy used for the attack, a dramatic symmetry, a homeopathic magic which undoes the poison by using the same chemical in its healing incarnation. Understood as a command against assimilation it remains a negation, a prohibition on becoming Christian. Nothing is said about what the survivors are to do. Simply, their being there is the response to Hitler, a testament to the defeat of the Nazi program.

One reason for the lack of content is doubt about the efficacy of action and, ultimately, doubt about the reality of a social order. The current survival of Jews, according to Fackenheim, as described in his work *To Mend the World* (cited in Katz), is a historical accident. We are ". . . not a Holy Remnant. We are an accidental remnant." This gives short shrift to the Allied war effort, to the action of "righteous gentiles," to the Jews who succeeded in sequestering themselves in various ways in Nazi occupied Europe, to the partisans, especially to the Jewish partisans, and to the refugee programs, as weak as they were. All of these saved some Jews, too few, doubtless. But the notion of "accidental" not only undercuts planned social action but is a door to anarchism. Social order becomes an elusive mystery. Human responsibility dissolves in doubt. This is not the basis for exemplarism offered by the apostles of Satyagraha, who see witnessing as a potent political weapon. Perhaps it shares something of the Buddhist seeking to detach himself from the world, even from his desires for the world.

Attitude change without an action program is exemplarism. Thus, the Rubenstein call for Jews to renounce their self-image as a "chosen people" as a way for Jews to fulfill a Christian soteriology in order to escape the role of sacrificial victims. Ignaz Maybaum's assertion (cited in Katz, 1983) that the Jews had to die at Auschwitz so that others may live, making of Auschwitz a twentieth-century Calvary, would not bring, but would announce, the utopian age. For Maybaum, utopia is the westernization of all, the end of both the Christian and the Jewish Middle Ages. Both Rubenstein and Maybaum would open the boundary between Jews and non-Jews with Jews becoming like all of the nations. What a contrast to Fackenheim's commandment to survive! Calvary, though, called for action, spreading the Good News and a "follow me."

Eliezer Berkovits reaches the same conclusion pointing to the *adversus Judaeos* theology of medieval times, its roots in the eighth chapter of John, "You are of your father, the devil . . ." and expressed even in modern times in the Passion play. Berkovits, though, recommends Zionist activity. Jewish existence stands as a prophetic disclosure against the moral degeneracy of men and nations. To act is to model. Berkovits's critique of Maybaum is in terms of the ill-fittingness of the Calvary metaphor, not for its failure to call for action. The Holocaust contained no Easter for the crucified ones and the victims did not go willingly to the sacrifice. They are not martyrs in the classic sense but victims and so there is no Calvary.

Jacob Neusner (1979) interpreting the meaning of the Holocaust in American Jewish public life notes how Israel and the Holocaust, two mythic symbols, are joined in a redemption myth. This myth became credible in 1967 when Israel seemed faced with another Holocaust. Neusner recalls other contemporaneous tragedies such as the assassination of Kennedy and Vietnam. Auschwitz has become the Jewish code word for the common malaise of the contemporary Western world. The uniqueness of the Holocaust is that it separates or distinguishes Jews in America from others, from being otherwise wholly "assimilated." Mintz, studying the *piyyutim* following the 1096 massacres identifies this period with the beginning of the cult of death in Judaism, with Kaddish and Yizkor. These rituals become part of witness, exemplary witness, vicarious symbolic witness for the deceased. As in the *av harahamim* prayer of the Sabbath morning services, the recitation of martyrologies is an expression of continuing witness.

In a halakhic responsum by Rabbi Katriel Tchorsh of Tel Aviv (cited in Kirschner, 1985), the act of mourning is offered as an exemplary expression. "All the house of Israel is required to mourn for our six million brethren." The result is otherworldly. As Rabbi Tchorsh argues, "The Kaddish is needed to help the dead ascend from one level to the next."

A direct argument against political action for the sake of Jews is given by Marc Ellis, a teacher of Judaism at Maryknoll school, in his *Toward a Jewish Theology of Liberation* (1987). He warns of the dangers of empowerment saying, "The desire to remain a victim is a disease; yet, to become a conqueror after having been a victim is a recipe for moral suicide." Jewish empowerment confronts, even threatens, Blacks, Hispanics, Native Americans, women, and displaced Palestinian people.

The exemplary prophet acts on himself. The ethical prophet, while preparing himself for the act, acts on the environment. As Katz observes in his discussion of Maybaum, the meaning of Jewish history as disclosed through the State of Israel is the antithesis of the Crucifixion mentality. Katz's critique of Berkovits is that he resorts to the crutch of an afterlife. There he seeks a dimension beyond history in which God redeems all suffering. Since Berkovits is a Zionist, this otherworldly reference ultimately supports action in this world.

The fact is that we are not left with much ethical prophecy. The *tremendum*, the satanic, of the theologians leaves but a paltry social policy of here exemplary living and there a call to Christians for a change they cannot really absorb and survive as Christians. Can theological and philosophical interpretation persist when they are not telling us "how to live" or "what is to be done?"

A concluding thought about a uniqueness of the Jewish response to catastrophe. Other tormented nations have responded viciously to oppression. An Armenian underground exacts a price from Turkey for its role in the 1915 massacres. Revenge is a sentiment quite absent from the Holocaust literature. Anger is against Nazis who no longer exist or against pathetic fugitives from those ranks. Why should there not be a thousand Simon Wiesenthals in the post-Holocaust era? Roskies takes the very literary and liturgical memory of the massacres of 1096 as vicarious aggression. The cry for revenge entered the liturgical calendar in *av harahamim* and remains from an earlier time in the Haggadah in *shfokh hamatkha*. The anger against the gentile authority is muted. Roskies recalls the nineteenth-century Russian Jews facing the cantonist system and the role of Jewish *khappers*. Both the folk and the *maskilim*, for different reasons, turned their energy inward and absolved the higher authorities of responsibility. The tsar would intervene if he knew.

Minorities in the ghettos took action against the enemy. Jewish partisans formed the brigade with the significant name of Nekome, revenge—a response in extremis.

Early Zionists such as Bialik rebelled against the passivity, and Mintz cites how in "The City of Slaughter," written after Bialik's visit to Kishenev, Bialik uses a secularized form of covenantal drama in which the sin is not failure to be faithful to Torah but the failure to undertake political action, even to rebel against God.

Why is the activist response so minor a theme? Why has no Jewish jihad philosophy emerged? Traditional Zionism explains this by the social position of Jews and by the social structure of the Jewish community, a community led by a business elite and jurisconsults. In this view, the active ethical response requires a polity or a sense of potential polity. All over the world, theology and politics reinforce one another. In Jewish society, theology is not constrained to contemplate action, and politics takes its own path unencumbered by a deeper philosophy.

REFERENCES

BRENNER, Reeve Robert. *The Faith and Doubt of Holocaust Survivors.* New York: The Free Press, 1980.

COHEN, Arthur A. *The Tremendum: A Theological Interpretation of the Holocaust*. New York: Crossroad, 1981.

DAWIDOWICZ, Lucy S. *The Holocaust and the Historians*. Cambridge: Harvard University Press, 1981.

ELLIS, Marc H. *Toward a Jewish Theology of Liberation*. Maryknoll: Orbis Books, 1987.

FACKENHEIM, Emil. *The Jewish Thought of Emil Fackenheim: A Reader*. Edited by Michael Morgan. Detroit: Wayne State University Press, 1987.

KATZ, Steven T. *Post-Holocaust Dialogues: Critical Studies in Modern Jewish Thought*. New York: New York University Press, 1983.

KIRSCHNER, Robert, ed. *Rabbinic Responsa of the Holocaust Era*. New York: Schocken Books, 1985.

MINTZ, Alan. *Hurban: Response to Catastrophe in Hebrew Literature*. New York: Columbia University Press, 1984.

NEHER, Andre. *The Exile of the Word: From the Silence of the Bible to the Silence of Auschwitz*. Philadelphia: The Jewish Publication Society, 1981.

NEUSNER, Jacob. *Stranger at Home*. Chicago: University of Chicago Press, 1979.

ROSKIES, David. *Against the Apocalypse: Responses to Catastrophe in Modern Jewish Culture*. Cambridge: Harvard University Press, 1984.

YERUSHALMI, Yosef Hayim. *Zakhor: Jewish History and Jewish Memory*. Seattle: The University of Washington Press, 1982.

3. Demographic Transitions, Modernization and the Transformation of Judaism

Calvin Goldscheider

In the last century a series of revolutions has reshaped the nature of Jewish communities in the United States and in the Land of Israel. Judaism, including the religious ideologies, institutions, and orientations of the Jews, has been transformed as part of, and in response to, the revolutionary changes in the social contexts of the Jewish communities. Hence, to study Judaism in diverse communities requires an analysis of context, of which demographic transitions, modernization, and nationalism have been critical over the last several generations.

The objectives of this paper are first, to identify and review the major demographic transformations that have characterized Jewish communities over the last 150 years. Next, to outline how social scientists study the religion of the Jew and identify and describe the major changes in Judaism in the last century and a half. Third, we link these changes in Judaism to the major social, economic, political, and cultural shifts associated with modernization and nationalism, and specify how the demographic transitions that Jews have experienced are connected to the processes of modernization and nationalism, on the one hand, and to changes in Judaism, on the other. Our examples will be drawn from Judaism as expressed in the United States and in the State of Israel, since these communities represent alternative paradigms of Jewish community life in the late twentieth century.[1] We raise many methodological, theoretical, and research questions in this review, reflecting the preliminary nature of social scientific studies of Judaism.

Demographic Transitions

What have been the demographic revolutions that have affected (and been affected by) religious changes among Jews? Demographic changes are involved in the key transformations that have occurred in the transition to modern society. In the broadest perspective, as Durkheim postulated,[2] population growth generates greater complexities in the division of labor. To the extent that increasing societal complexity and specialization are necessary prerequisites for the development of modern society, population growth is of key importance in modernization. Without positing the centrality of changes in population size as a determinant of the shift from traditional to modern society, we shall argue more cautiously for the importance of demographic factors as integral to the transformations in Judaism.

The demographic system has a convenient system character that is analytically attractive: there are a known and limited number of processes that operate within the system. Combined, these processes are always present in a community or a society and always affect (positively or negatively) population size and structure (age and sex composition). These include the "entering" population processes of fertility and in-migration and the "exiting" process of mortality and out-migration. For population size to change positively (i.e., for there to be population growth) entering processes need to exceed exiting processes; population decline is always the result of greater exiting than entering. For a minority group, entering and exiting can also take place by changes in the definition of who is a member of the group. Often this occurs at some critical life course passage (e.g., marriage). Persons can marry into (and out of) the group thus increasing or decreasing the size of the minority group. For religious groups, this usually involves some sort of religious conversion; more informal redefinitions by persons and communities affect the entry and exiting in groups that are not solely religion based. The complex ethnic and religious basis of Jewish communal affiliation and particularly the relationship between Jewishness and Judaism in the modern period raises the affiliation or membership issue (in the parlance of the community, the question becomes, "Who is a Jew?"). The combination of entering and exiting processes (fertility, mortality, migration, and group membership through identification and/or conversion) determines directly and always the population size and structure of the community and demographic changes.

What have been the major demographic patterns that have in broad outline characterized the Jewish population in the transition to the modern period? In an oversimplified way, we can identify the following five critical patterns:

1. A major demographic revolution has been the decline of fertility and the transition from the large to the small family. This long-term trend does not imply that there were not fluctuations over time, as the conspicuous increases in the posteconomic depression and baby boom periods reveal among American Jews, and as does the postimmigration experience of European Jews in the State of Israel in the 1960s and 1970s.[3] Yet these variations are minor in the longer-term shift toward the small nuclear family of two to three children per family. Indeed, the last remnants of high fertility among traditional Jewish communities in Asian and African countries occurred subsequent to the migration of these groups to Israel as well as to western countries, the most sustained fertility decline without direct government intervention recorded for any group in recent history.[4] The reduction in family size has drastically changed the role of women, the

structure of families, and the relationships between the generations. These changes profoundly altered the nature of religious expression, the structure of religious institutions, and the emphasis of religious ritual.

2. Along with the shift to lower fertility (and often preceding it) was the general transition from high to low mortality. For Jews these declines generally occurred earlier than their non-Jewish neighbors, but there is little evidence to support the argument that the religion of the Jews or the specific values of the Jewish community were responsible for the exceptional timing of these patterns among Jews. Rather, the social, geographic, and political location of Jews (their educational, occupational, and urban residence as well as their position as a minority) accounts for almost the entire difference in the timing of the fertility and mortality reductions for the Jewish compared to the non-Jewish population. The last vestiges of high mortality among Jewish communities disappeared for Asian and African Jews subsequent to their immigration to the State of Israel.

There were enormous mortality losses associated with the Holocaust and the destruction of large proportions of world Jewry and entire Jewish communities in Europe. In demographic terms, the Holocaust was an exceptional pattern breaking the longer-term mortality reduction characterizing the Jewish population. By ending the demographic dominance of European Jews over world Jewry, the demographic locus of Jewish community life shifted to the United States and the State of Israel.

Both the reduction in fertility and in mortality reflected the increased control by persons over deaths and births. This greater control is linked to the concomitant reduction of population growth associated with the new balance of births and deaths. In traditional societies, there were low rates of population growth because the high rates of fertility were balanced by high rates of mortality; in the transition to modern society, the rates of mortality tended to decline first and more rapidly, thereby bringing about rapid population growth through the imbalance of fertility and mortality. In the modern period, a new demographic equilibrium of fertility and mortality emerges, resulting in the stability of population size based on a balance of low rates of natural increase. The increase in life expectancy and in individual control over life and death changed the dependency of individuals on religious ideology and institutions that were God- and otherworld-centered.

3. A third set of processes is associated with the transfer of Jews from country to country and the redistribution of world Jewish population. High levels of immigration to the United States from areas of rapid Jewish population growth in eastern Europe in the late nineteenth and early twentieth centuries occurred as well as continuing immigration from a large variety of countries to the State of Israel. This redistribution of Jewish population resulted in the exposure of Jews to new societies that were developing rapidly, economically and socially. This new contact transformed the Jewish immigrants into new citizens of emerging states and societies. But immigration meant uprooting as well and breaking the traditional hold of families over the lives of individuals that characterized places of origin. Both the exposure to new environments and the uprooting effects of migration resulted in the receptivity of Jews to the opportunities and challenges of modernity. Moreover, immigration also brought Jews into contact with other Jews from other places and Jewish communities became larger, more complex, and more diverse. These new places differed from the communities of origin, and therefore the Judaisms that emerged were also transformed. It should be noted that the immigration of east European Jews to the United States and to other Western countries did not deplete the Jewish community demographically, since the Jewish populations in eastern Europe continued to grow in size despite the emigration of large numbers of Jews. It was the Holocaust, not migration, that destroyed the demographic centrality of Jews in Europe.

4. Migration redistributed the Jewish population within countries as well. Internal migration resulted in the heavy concentration of Jews in urban places and their transition to a fully urban community. There was a greater population dispersal among Jews in the 1980s than at earlier times but they continued to be characterized by high levels of voluntary residential concentration. In the United States, the dispersal has been to new communities and to new regions, requiring

attention not only to the attrition of Jewish population in areas of Jewish out-migration but also to the increase in Jewish population size in new places where Jews settle. The redistribution of population alters the effects of Jewish density on Jewishness and Judaism; by facilitating the development of new and diverse Jewish communities, population redistribution has been critical in providing new opportunities for creative Jewish expressions in new contexts. In Israel, the overlap of ethnicity and residential segregation has emerged in development towns as well as within large cities; throughout the country there was an almost complete residential segregation between Jews and Arabs. In turn, these residential patterns have reinforced forms of religious and cultural expressions that were social class and ethnically based.

5. Finally, there has been an increase over the last century in the rate of marriage between persons born Jewish and those born of non-Jewish parents in the United States. This increase is an inevitable by-product of living in an open pluralistic society with opportunities for contacts between religious groups, along with the absence of political anti-Semitism. Only in the segregated residential areas of modern societies, among isolated Jewish sects, are levels of intermarriage insignificant as they were in the segregated areas of traditional Jewish communities in Europe, and as they are in the Jewish State of Israel.

When the rates of intermarriage began to increase in the United States in the 1960s, there was an increase in formal religious conversions to Judaism as the traditional response to intermarriages. In the last decade or so in various American Jewish communities there has been an increase in the level of intermarriages but not a continuation of comparable rates of conversions of a religious and formal nature. There are indications, however, of strong identification among significant proportions of non-Jewish-born persons (married to Jewish-born persons) with the American Jewish community, even without formal religious conversions. There is also evidence of increasing acceptance by the Jewish community of the informally identified as well as the religiously converted.[5] Thus, unlike in the past, high rates of intermarriage do not necessarily result in the demographic erosion of the Jewish community. Intermarriage may be a net demographic gain to the American Jewish community, through the identification of non-Jewish partners with the Jewish community and through the continuous identification of significant proportions of the children of the intermarried with the Jewish community. Whether there is a qualitative gain to the Jewish community through the next generation remains an open question.

In general, the demographic changes—reductions of fertility and mortality levels, increases in immigration, urbanization, and intermarriage—are not particular to Jews but characterize all groups as they are exposed to the pressures and opportunities of modernization. Only those Jews who basically reject modernity have retained larger family size, greater insulation from the potential of intermarriage, and higher levels of Jewish segregation and Jewish density.

How do these demographic processes translate into the critical ways that Jews express their religion and their Judaism? There are two ways to conceptualize the relationship between demographic and religious changes. The first treats religious change as the determinant and asks, what has been the impact of changes in religious institutions and religious ideologies on the demographic transitions experienced by the Jewish population? The second view reverses the question and treats religious changes as the outcome of demographic change asking, what is the significance of demographic transitions for the transformation of Judaism? In general, specific religious changes have played a minor role as determinants of demographic change; in contrast, demographic changes have played a major role as determinants of religious changes. To understand how these linkages work, we need to clarify how Judaism has changed over this period of time and connect these religious changes to modernization processes.

Social Scientists Study Judaism

It is important to start with basics and ask, what do social scientists study about the religion of the Jew? For the nature of Judaism that social scientists study affects directly how they know what they know, how they test propositions, and what evidence they examine to establish relationships between religion and other dimensions of social life. So we begin with what social scientists study when examining the religion of the Jew.

Four major dimensions of religion[6] are encompassed within the social scientific investigation of Judaism: (1) the religious behavior, beliefs, and values of Jews; (2) the religious institutions of the Jews; (3) the linkages between Judaism and other aspects of social life—family, economy, polity, and culture; and (4) the development of particular religious ideologies and religious social movements. Social scientists emphasize historical and cross-national comparisons, as well as comparisons between Jews and others, to analyze each of these dimensions of Judaism and to examine the variety of indicators of factors within each dimension. Multiple comparisons allow for the identification of those aspects of religion that are unique to Jews and those that Jews share with others. Comparisons over time allow us to determine which special features of Judaism emerge in particular historical contexts, and whether the forms of Judaism within the modern context and within particular communities are unique. We treat the extent of change in Jewish religious values as part of those processes that require explanation, investigating their role in shaping Judaism and Jewish life without assuming the centrality of religious values on theoretical grounds. The social scientific study of Judaism, therefore, treats the religious expression, ideals, and ideologies of Jews as a complex set of variables, changing and varying with different contexts.

In the area of behavior, beliefs, and values, social scientists focus on changes in the patterns of religious observances and religious ritual—variations in what Jews do religiously and what they believe; their attitudes toward Judaism and toward ritual observance; and the importance of religious activities for them and their communities. Changes and variations in religious values, ideologies, and ideals expressed by an elite are also important elements to be examined in the context of whether and how these ideals and values are transmitted to the larger Jewish community.

The social scientific study of Judaism also includes how religious and secular institutions and organizations emerge in different settings as response to, and as shapers of, religious change. Religious movements and religious ideologies that have emerged in the last century reflect new conditions that Jews and their communities have faced in the contexts not only of other Judaic expressions among Jews but also in comparison to other religious movements and ideologies among non-Jews.

A key research issue in the study of Judaism concerns how the changing configurations of religion and religious institutions are related to the changing cohesion of the Jewish community over time and among the societies where Jews live. Do changes in religious observances result in reductions in the extent to which economic and family networks are Jewish? Do shifts in religious ideology lead to changes in the stability of Jewish families? Are changes in religious ideologies associated with increases in occupational concentration, migration, and educational attainment? Do religious values influence the political and cultural expressions of Jews? In what ways is Judaism central or marginal to the lives of Jews and the institutions of their communities? In short, the social scientific study of Judaism attempts to examine systematically the changing determinants and consequences of Judaism (in its multidimensional forms and expressions) for the lives of Jews and the structure of their communities.

This social scientific approach to the study of Judaism moves beyond a description of the internal workings of religious institutions and the expressed ideals of a religious elite for understanding the Judaisms of contemporary societies. Two major limitations characterize an emphasis on studying the internal workings of religious institutions and concentrating on the religious elite: the error of assuming a cross-cultural commonality of one Judaism (i.e., that context does not matter for content), and the error of assuming the disintegrative forces of change (i.e., that newly formed contents are weaker, not only different, than earlier forms).

Studying the internal structure of Jewish institutions and focusing solely on the elite, we center analytic attention solely on Jews and assume that there are cross-cultural religious commonalities among Jews and that Jewish values are monolithic. Religious uniformity and continuity are, however, assertions that require systematic study. The core paradigm of Judaism (which some have argued focuses on exile and return)[7] does not assume that the ways in which the paradigm of Judaism is worked out is identical for all Judaisms. Indeed, each Judaism works out its paradigm of the core content of Judaism in its context and in its mode, moving the content of Judaism into the context of each Judaism.

The focus on the internal structure of the institutions of Judaism and on the values expressed by the religious elite often results in the interpretation of change in the context of religious decline. It is assumed that the forces of modernization have had a negative impact on Judaism and on "traditional" Judaic values. It has always been the case that the values of the religious elite have changed and that the religious institutions of one context have been altered to fit into a new context. It would be untenable in the social science mode to assume that change was unusual or that variation was exceptional. Since changes and variations in Judaism have been integral parts of the variety of the communities, societies, and cultures of the Jewish experience, Judaisms have emerged to interpret and reinterpret the Judaic core paradigm in the multiplicity of forms generated by the experiences of the Jewish context. In this sense, it is a limiting assumption to treat change as disintegration and crisis without allowing for the possibility that change might also represent opportunity and challenge.

Thus, for example, a classic work in the social history of the Jews begins by describing "traditional society" as one "based upon a common body of knowledge and values handed down from the past." It is further asserted that the traditional society "accurately describes the whole of world Jewry, at least from the talmudic era (200 C.E.) up to the age of European Emancipation (during the first half of the nineteenth century), and it applies to some part of Jewish society even in more recent times." The analysis further assumes that there is an "underlying national unity of the Jewish people in the lands of their dispersion." "This unity," it is asserted, "is an indisputable fact."[8] It is not surprising that the focus of that social history is on Judaic values and ideals, assuming that they will reveal the reality of Judaism and Jewish life; the internal structure of the community and its religious institutions are examined, trusting that they will convey the religiosity of the community. There are no systematic comparisons among Jewish communities given the "fact" of underlying unity. It follows from these premises that change is described as "crisis" and transformation as "disintegration."

In contrast, the thrust of our argument is that the social scientific study of Judaism focuses comparative and historical contexts on the analysis of Jews and their communities. The sociology of Judaism focuses on contexts to study how each Judaism is shaped and re-shaped as a Judaism. Each form of Judaism requires analysis; each needs to be identified and studied systematically. Each new Judaism responds to context and shapes it. Thus, we study not only the dimensions of Judaisms but the interrelationships between a particular Judaism and social processes. We expect that forms of Judaism emerge in new contexts and that specific relationships between religion and other social, economic, cultural, and political processes vary with context.

Comparisons of Jews and Others

The methodological argument that we need to study non-Jews in the analysis of the Judaism of Jews requires some comment. It is clearly not appropriate analytically to compare Jews with non-Jews without taking into account and disentangling differential structural and cultural patterns. Thus, for example, comparing the development of religious institutions and religious ideologies among Jews in Germany in the nineteenth century with all Germans, without taking into account the specific jobs, urban location, and education of the Jews, would be misleading. Such a crude comparison would reveal differences between Jews and non-Jews, reflecting in large part social class and rural/urban residential differences but not necessarily specific factors associated with Jewishness or Judaism, the place of Jews in German society, or their "culture." To know that differences between Jews and non-Jews in nineteenth-century Germany are primarily the consequence of socioeconomic and demographic differences, shapes a series of specific analytic questions regarding the determinants and consequences of the particular socioeconomic and demographic characteristics of German Jewry. To simply attribute crude differences between Jews and non-Jews to "culture" and "values" particular to Jews without studying non-Jews directly and without taking into account the social, political, demographic, and economic contexts of our comparisons, results in a series of distortions in our understanding of social change among Jews over the last century. Only through systematic comparison do we begin to understand how and why the core themes of Judaism are translated into the particular forms of Judaic expressions.

In the analysis of religious reform in nineteenth-century western Europe, in the comparisons between the religious transformations of Judaism and other religions in Europe during the nineteenth century and America in the twentieth century, and in the comparisons of religious and political transformations in various countries including the State of Israel, analysis has yielded new insights derived from a comparative perspective.[9] For example, comparative analysis allows us to interpret why some aspects of Reform Judaism emerged in Germany and not in France and points to the underlying similarity of diffusion processes of political ideologies in Russia and religious ideologies in Germany in the nineteenth century. Furthermore, we are able to disentangle the relative importance of changes in religious ideology and economic, demographic, and political factors to account for the differential spread of religious reform throughout Germany. The comparative similarities in the levels of synagogue attendance, to take another example, among Jews in the State of Israel and in the United States suggest general processes of secularization in two very different Jewish communities in distinct sociocultural contexts. These and related analytic findings emerge when multiple comparisons— historical, cross-community and with non-Jews—are the bases for the systematic social scientific analysis of Judaism. Without comparisons, we are left with description and no basis for testing theories and hypotheses.

We analyze the relative cohesion of communities under different conditions; we should not infer the *implications* of change from the changing characteristics of the Jewish community. Thus, for example, the increasing secularization of Judaism, in terms of the reduction in traditional religious ritual observances and ritual practices, has been documented in every study of modern Jewish communities in the United States and in Israel.[10] Often, the inference has been made that patterns of secularization have negative consequences for the cohesion of the Jewish community; from the point of view of the community, therefore, secularization is treated as one indicator of the decline of the Jewish community in modern society. That is the case only when we confuse Judaism with Jewishness and equate the religion of the Jews with the strength of the Jewish community. These dimensions were more interchangeable in the past, when religion was more central in the lives of Jews and connected in integral ways to social, economic, family, cultural, and political aspects of Jewish communities.

In modern pluralistic societies, the two questions have to be untangled: (1) How are changes in religion linked to other processes of transformation? and (2) What are the implications of the new emerging Judaisms for the cohesion of the community? Only if the cohesion of the Jewish community is defined by the religiosity of the Jewish community, then, by definition, would a change in religiosity imply a decrease in Jewish cohesion. The more profound question is phrased differently: How do the new forms of Judaism in modern society link to the nature of Jewish cohesion? And, in turn, how have the new Judaisms translated the Judaism of exile and return in the new contexts of modernity?

Emphasis on the religious behavior and on the characteristics of Jews and their communities needs to be separated from an analysis of values and attitudes, if only to see how behavior and values are related. The study of elites, norms, ideologies, and ideas is important but should not be viewed as substitutes for analyzing the behavior of the masses and the characteristics of communities. Norms, values, and ideas are not synonymous with behavior. Values, ideologies, and culture are phenomena to be explained no less than as sources of explanation. Elite ideas are but one of many determinants of mass behavior; they are rarely the only determinants of the behavior even of elites.

The Transformation of Judaism in Modern Times

A central sociological theme in the social scientific study of contemporary Judaisms is the impact of the transformation or "modernization" of society on the religion of the Jews. We have noted the multidimensionality of Judaism and discussed the various elements involved in studying Judaism in behavioral, institutional, and communal terms. Here we need to clarify issues associated with transformation and modernization as master contexts translating Judaism into Judaisms. We focus on transformation in the social scientific, not the historical, sense. Thus, our question of transformation and Judaism is not addressed to when "modern" society begins, a question of the periodization of history,[11] but rather, how do the processes of modernization, secularization, and transformation unfold, and in turn, how are these processes related to changes in the lives of people, in the institutions of society, in the structure of social relations, and the generational transmission of Jewish values and culture? How do these transformations alter Judaism to form new systems of Judaisms?

Modernization implies that all the systems of society are transformed. The major elements are well known and recognized: industrialization (the shift from agriculture to industry); urbanization (the transition from rural areas and small towns to urban metropolises); political mobilization and centralization (the incorporation of individuals into a broader polity or nation-state); the reformation of the stratification system toward greater social class diversity and, in particular, the emergence of a larger middle class (and, in general, increased levels of education, occupational specialization, and affluence); cultural diffusion and technological change; along with a general shift away from family-community-centered relationships toward individual and personal relationships to bureaucracies, organizations, and the state. The key processes underlying these long-term changes involve structural differentiation and the expansion of the system of political and economic opportunities.[12] Structural differentiation involves the increasing complexity of the division of labor, whereby two or more units of social structure deal separately with problems which at some previous time were dealt with in combination by one unit. A common illustration is the separation of economic from family spheres of activities, where kin no longer dominate and control economic resources or access to them. The breakdown of the whole into separate parts is then followed by their reintegration into new patterns.

In the case of religion the process of structural differentiation involves the shift from the centrality of religion, wherein religion was the center axis of political, social, and cultural control in the lives of individuals and in the structure of community relationships, to the specialization of function by religious institutions. Whereas religion in traditional society was central to the family, economy, polity, and culture, in modern society the role of religion (as with other arenas of social life) becomes separated and specialized. The "decline" of traditional Judaism is, therefore, the decline in the centrality of Judaism in the lives of persons and communities and a shift in the relationship between religion and other spheres of social and cultural activities. While increases in the division of labor involve differentiation of structures, they also involve new forms of integration. New structures and values, new institutions, new ways of behaving and thinking, new jobs, residences, political movements, cultures, and ideologies, as well as new sources of conflict, competition, and inequality, have emerged in the modern era. Structural differentiation is a crucial process in the development of modern society and is critical in our understanding of the processes underlying the changes in Judaism in the last century.

Our master question then becomes: What has been the impact of these transformations on the Jews, generally, and on their religious systems, specifically? How has the modernization of the societies in which Jews lived affected their Judaism? Are the consequences of modernization for the transformation of the Jewish community and Judaism similar to the consequences for others in terms of direction, extent, and pace of change? How have Jews, their leaders and elites (religious and secular), their organizations and institutions, responded to the sweep of modernization? With the dissolution of the older bases of cohesion centered on religion, what new types of communal bonds, associational ties, and cultural forms link Jews to one another? What are the new symbols of the sacred in modern society? In turn, what are the relationships of new forms of communal cohesion and religious transformations? What are the bases of solidarity, in the Durkheimian sense, among Jews and their communities as they are transformed by modernization? And, in turn, how does Judaism transformed relate to these changes? Since it is not tenable to assume that Judaism will not respond to the dramatic changes transforming traditional to modern society, the question becomes, how have the Judaisms of modern society shaped and reshaped the core themes (of exile and return) of Judaism?

It is clearly inadequate to associate the "decline" in Judaism with the development of modernization. "Secularization" does not specify which processes change or with what intensity. By focusing only on what is no longer characteristic of the religious expression of the community, the analysis of secularization ignores what substitutes for the old, and how new forms develop.

One of the features associated with modernization has been nationalism. Where Jews lived as a minority, the processes of modernization resulted in the question of the place of Jews in the new society: Were Jews part of a "people" that transcended national boundaries and, hence, called into question the relationship of Jews to the newly emerging national state and their potential for citizenship? Were Jews solely a "religious" group whose loyalty was to the state on political and social grounds and whose Jewishness was limited to religion per se? The "Jewish question" was asked in all modernizing societies about Jews in particular and about ethnic and religious minorities in general. And the answers to the question varied but everywhere had a profound impact on the Judaism that developed. Most important, the religion of the Jew living in a religiously pluralistic society as a minority subpopulation is unlikely to characterize the religion of the Jews where they are a majority in their own country. Israeli-based Judaisms are significantly different from American-based Judaisms; religious movements in the State of Israel are unlikely to have parallels among Jews living in the United States, and vice versa.[13]

The breakdown of religious centrality in the context of modernization moves the study of religious observances toward the arena of voluntary individual choices, rather than the formal and informal controls exercised by religious authorities over the lives of persons. In the past, religious authorities controlled deviants by constraining their participation in religious activities and, more importantly, by attempting to control the broader social, personal, economic, and political activities of the deviant. These powers of the religious authorities in arenas beyond the specifically religious illustrate dramatically their all-encompassing power, if not actually, then in terms of the accepted norms and the dominance of religious authority in some traditional Jewish communities.[14]

The decline in the centrality of religion, changes in the dominance of religious authorities, the shift away from all-encompassing religious norms, and the emergence of greater personal individual choices in the adherence to religious behavior, and ritual practices and observances, were predicated on the process of structural differentiation, the separation of religion from community membership. In the past, the links between the elements of social structure were so tightly knit that rejecting religious norms implied by necessity the rejection of community. One simply could not be a member of the Jewish community once one rejected the norms and practices of Judaism. In modern societies, the structural separation of Judaism from affiliation with the community facilitated the voluntariness of religious activity and the development of alternative forms of affiliation with the Jewish community that were legitimate. In short, Jewishness and Judaism were separated, and new linkages between the two were formed.

One feature of the new voluntarism associated with structural differentiation occurred at the institutional level. In traditional society, only one form of Judaism was legitimate for the community, and it was that form that the community decided was appropriate. (Again, what was religiously appropriate for one community was not necessarily appropriate for another, and, hence, the Judaism of one was not identical with the other even in traditional society.) In contrast, as modern societies expanded both in their social and demographic complexity, the number of legitimate forms of Judaism within the same community expanded as well. Since it became legitimate to reject all Judaism and still remain part of the Jewish community, it became increasingly legitimate to reformulate Judaism along new lines. The emergence of new religious movements in the process of modernization—Reform, Conservative, and even the Orthodox— became new forms of Judaism competing for ideas and for adherents in the marketplace of the voluntaristic community. These and related nonreligious-based movements emerged over time as expressions of Judaic culture in response to the challenges of modernity and to the transformations associated with them.

Most of these religious reformations attempted to redefine the nature of Judaism in terms that were consistent with, and reflected adaptations to, the position of the Jew within modern societies. They accepted the value of integration and reshaped Judaism in response to context. Other movements were reactionary, in that they rejected the values of modernization and integration, and therefore re-sponded by religious and communal insulation. Their reactions also transformed their Judaism by emphasizing segregation and by estab-lishing new barriers of social control. Whether through adaptation or rejection, all religious institutions and religious movements were transformed in the process of modernization. A third ideal-typical response to modernity was the rejection of Judaism as the basis of Jewish life and the substitution of new forms of identification. In the United States, these new forms became associational networks and secular organizational activities in communal institutions. These forms of identification rejected Judaism in one form, creating a new "civil" religion. Secular Zionism in America (a sense of peoplehood or "ethnic" identification) and in Israel (national-ethnic identity) substituted for Judaism, or redefined Judaism, reinterpreting the sacred symbols of exile and return, of the core paradigm of Judaism, in new ways.[15]

Clearly, there were new combinations of nationalism and religion. Some religious movements excluded the national ethnic component from the religious ideology of Judaism by emphasizing only the reli-gious nature of Judaism and its personal component. In our scheme that meant the religious component became functionally specific in the process of structural differentiation. One definition of Judaism focused, therefore, solely on religion, not on the group as a community or people. Thus, Reform Judaism focused on some aspects of the Judaic system and developed them within the narrower confines of religion per se, and rejected (at least at an early stage) the peoplehood dimension.

An alternative response to the place of the Jew in the new political regime, as Jewishness and Judaism became more separable, was the development of a secular nationalist response. Zionism, or at least some forms of Zionism, developed in response to the new structural conditions by focusing on the national-ethnic component, as a basis for legitimacy as a community and in part by rejecting the applicability of Judaism to modern sociopolitical conditions. So nationalism shaped an alternative to religion, redefining the nature of the Jewish people in nonreligious terms even as it reaffirmed some of the core Judaic paradigm of exile and return. Thus, some posit that Zionism became not only a new Judaic system in the sense of a new definition of the relationship of Jews to peoplehood, but became a new Judaism.[16]

While the initial emphasis of some forms of Zionism was to redefine the condition of Jews in the modern world, it was also clear that a new integration with religion was to be forged, so that religious Zionism emerged as did a Zionist religion. These combinations establish new forms of relationships between Jewish nationalism and Judaism as new integration occurs after structural differentiation.

What emerges most clearly then is that the decline in the centrality of religion changes the nature of religious authority, increases the legitimacy of competing and alternative nonreligious forms of Jewishness, and moves the major forms of the religious rituals of Judaism into the family, emphasizing those that have broader community-based connections and away from daily rituals and dietary and Sabbath restrictions that interfere with the broader integration of Jews in the modern community. Religion simply becomes less central in the wide range of complex decision making that engages modern Jews. People in modern society make their choices in consultation with secular specialists, experts in their fields, based on a reasonable calculus of costs and benefits. Religious authorities play little role in the decisions that are the dominant ones people make throughout the life course.

Demographic Transitions and Judaism

In the most general sense, demographic transitions in fertility, mortality, and migration have been part of the major processes of modernization and nationalism, and have been a key source of structural differentiation. To the extent that population growth and increases in the complexity of the division of labor are integral to one another, population changes have been a major part of the separation of Judaism from Jewishness. The reformations of Judaism in the United States and in the State of Israel could not have occurred without the modernization of Jewish communities in these societies and without the concomitant demographic transformations. Thus, indirectly, demographic transitions and the transformation of Judaism are linked through modernization processes.

But there are more direct linkages between demographic processes and Judaism. First, there is the obvious role of immigration to the United States and to the State of Israel in the reshaping of Judaism in both places. These movements brought about the exposure of almost all Jews in the world to modern and Western societies. These immigrations resulted in the break between families and kin at origin, reductions in the control of the family over access to the resources of the society, and the shift of responsibility to the individual and to the state. Thus, migration, between and within areas, resulted in greater structural differentiation and, in turn, in the specialized, rather than the all-encompassing, role of Judaism. Through uprooting and dislocations, exposure to modern ideas, and other Jewish traditions, migration reshaped the Judaism and Jewishness of those who were formally resident of the small towns of eastern Europe, Yemen, Iraq, Morocco, and other Asian and African communities. Through the transplantation of Hasidic communities to Israeli society and to the United States, migration processes reshaped the nature of Orthodox

Judaism, its religious educational institutions and communal activities. Contacts between different types of Judaic expressions in the cities of modern societies generated responses and reactions, adaptations and, at times, rejection, and competition among Jews with different orientations to Judaism in establishing their "legitimate" expression of Judaism. The dispersal of Jews away from areas of high Jewish density changed the relationship of Jews to their religious institutions as it changed the structure and culture of these institutions.

The decline of mortality reflects a host of technological, socio-economic, and public health changes and is appropriately considered an integral feature of modernization. The decline in mortality levels implies further a drastic change from the ever-presence of death in traditional societies, a shift from the great uncertainties about length of life and away from the mystery surrounding death, particularly in the early years of life. In modern societies, death rarely interrupts the daily activity of the community, occurring largely to older persons in institutions who suffer from degenerative diseases. Probabilities define the risks of death, not mystery and uncertainty.

When life is precarious, when death is frequent and mysterious, social institutions and ideologies are needed to explain and account for the "unknown." The pressing need for such explanations in times of bereavement is considerably reduced when death is removed from daily concerns. The decline of fate and God's will as explanatory concepts in the modern world is related to the extension of life and to the changes in the timing of death. The shift from otherworldly to this-worldly matters accompanies the decline in mortality. Rewards for religious adherence are no longer placed in the other world but in the quality of life in this world. In traditional society, Jews lived in the present but were otherworldly oriented; in modern societies, Jews plan for the future and are this-worldly oriented. Both fit the facts of mortality and its meaning for different societies. An emphasis on cities of God is too far removed from the long span of time that people spend in the cities that they construct. So the substantive content of religion is profoundly influenced by changing mortality conditions.[17]

Another direct linkage between demographic change and Judaism relates to fertility decline and the concomitant changes in the centrality of the family and the role of women. Several critical changes in the nature of Judaism flow from the revolution toward the small family and to the increased role of women outside the household. With increased levels of education and higher rates of participation in career-oriented occupations, Jewish women have moved toward a redefinition of their status as persons, not only as daughters, wives, or mothers. The planning of small family size, after education is completed and after several years of career activities, has reshaped the religious context for Jewish women. In the past, the transition was from daughter to wife status; in modern society there is an increasing time gap between these roles. A similar situation characterizes women who live alone after divorce and widowhood. These changed statuses challenge Judaism in modern societies to develop religious roles for nonmarried women.

Changes away from family-oriented roles to autonomy and egalitarianism have clearly altered the household roles of men and women. These changes impact on Judaism to move toward greater concern for the redefinition of women as part of the community of religious Jews. In part, the redefinitions of Judaism to include women in more egalitarian roles remains in process, since Judaism was for centuries male-oriented and male-dominated. Yet there are clear indications that new definitions are emerging, and indeed, new forms of Judaism are being developed. Women have joined the religious elite that in the past was the sole province of males; religious education has incorporated women at almost an equal level; religious rituals have developed to accommodate these new roles (consider, for example, the Bat Mitzvah); and a feminist Jewish theology has emerged. The Judaism that was family-based has had to adapt to these new patterns, either by incorporating changes and developing new religious expressions or by rejecting the need for adaptation and reinforcing traditional gender-based religious barriers. No more conspicuous illustration of the conflicts generated by new gender roles and some forms of Judaism can be found than the continuing controversy over the rights of women to their own prayer service at the Western Wall in Jerusalem.

A final clear effect of demographic change has been the impact of intermarriage levels on Judaism. The increasing rates of intermarriage in the United States has redefined the membership affiliation of the community. Religious institutions have had to deal with the question of whom to incorporate within the community, who has authority to decide about group membership, and what are the processes of inclusion. Judaism has again attempted to deal with this new demographic reality. Ideological developments and organizational conflicts have emerged around this issue, with some Judaisms redefining the nature of attachments to the community in new ways and other Judaisms closing the options to inclusion. Perhaps no other issues have polarized the religious community of Jews in the United States, as well as in Israel, as have the questions of intermarriage, conversions, and the legitimacy of the variety of Judaisms to define the criteria of who is a Jew.

In Israel, religion has become politicized, and religious observance has declined. In the United States, there is a separation of religion and politics, and religious observance has declined. In America, there is religious pluralism and diversity and creative responses to the challenges among Jews. Because Judaism in Israel is politicized, there has not developed the creative, tolerant religious diversity that characterizes the secular American Jewish community. It is ironic that Judaism can flourish and religious diversity can be encouraged in secular societies like the United States, while in the Jewish State of Israel, religion is divisive and mired in coalition and patronage politics.

In general, there is little impact of Judaism on Jews in a secular society like the United States, except as one of several anchors of identity, personal and communal. The major factors that have influenced the religion of Jews in the United States are the demographic and modernization processes that we have outlined, the Holocaust, and the emergence of the State of Israel. Judaism is affected by broad processes in secular America but it has little impact on the life-styles and life-course choices made by Jews. In contrast, there is an enormous effect of religion and religious institutions and politics on the lives of Israeli Jews, secular and religious, and these also influence Jewish communities outside of the State of Israel. In large part, the difference between these relationships in the United States and in Israeli society reflects the different contexts of the two societies, the key to which is the politicization of religion in the Israeli context and the separation of politics and religion in the United States.

The State of Israel is a major anchor of identity for American Jews, and Israeli society is dependent on the American Jewish community for political and economic support. The establishment of the State and the survival of the society of Israel have become a major part of the "redemption" and "return" component of Judaism. There is a need to reconsider the entire linkage and relationship between American Judaism and Israeli Judaism, to reinforce the Israeli-related anchor of American Jewish identity, and to inject some of the tolerance, diversity, and creativity of American Judaism into Israeli society. There is a need to reinforce the core paradigm of Judaism in the Judaisms of both societies, as each society confronts its own social and demographic reality, and as each searches for new ways to establish the interdependence among Jewish communities.

NOTES

1. See the discussion in C. Goldscheider and A. Zuckerman, *The Transformation of the Jews* (Chicago: University of Chicago Press, 1984).
2. E. Durkheim, *The Division of Labor in Society* (New York: The Free Press, 1933), 256–282.
3. C. Goldscheider, *American Jewish Fertility* (New York: Scholars Press, 1986); D. Friedlander and C. Goldscheider, "Israel: The Challenge of Pluralism," in *Population Reference Bureau*, 1984.
4. Friedlander and Goldscheider, "Israel: The Challenge of Pluralism." *Population Reference Bureau*, 1984.
5. C. Goldscheider, *Jewish Continuity and Change* (Bloomington: Indiana University Press, 1986).
6. There are of course a variety of typologies that social scientists use to describe the content of what they study about religion. The four dimensions listed seem to me to be the ones that can be studied empirically within the social sciences, and are illustrative rather than exhaustive.
7. The development of this core paradigm and the relationship of it to the contexts of Judaism are discussed in C. Goldscheider and J. Neusner, "The Social Foundations of Judaism in Classical and Modern Times," in

C. Goldscheider and J. Neusner, eds. *Social Foundations of Judaism* (Englewood Cliffs: Prentice-Hall, 1989).

8. J. Katz, *Tradition and Crisis: Jewish Society at the End of the Middle Ages* (New York: Schocken Books, 1961), 7.

9. For examples see the discussion in Goldscheider and Zuckerman, *Transformation of the Jews*.

10. See S. Cohen, *American Modernity and Jewish Identity* (London: Tavistock, 1983); Goldscheider, *Jewish Continuity and Change*; C. Goldscheider and D. Friedlander, "Religiosity Patterns in Israel," in *American Jewish Year Book* (Philadelphia: Jewish Publication Society, 1983).

11. L. Kochan, "The Methodology of Modern Jewish History," *Journal of Jewish Studies* 36 (1985): 185–194.

12. See among others, D. Reuschemeyer, "Reflections on Structural Differentiation," *Zeitschrift für Soziologie* 3 (June, 1974): 279–94; Goldscheider and Zuckerman, *Transformation of the Jews*; C. Goldscheider, "Societal Change and Demographic Transitions," in *Population et Structures Sociales* (Chaire Quetelet, 1981), 83–106.

13. Thus, for example, Conservative and Reform Judaism, as well as modern Orthodoxy, in the United States cannot be simply duplicated in Israeli society. Similarly, Israeli Judaisms, either of the "Oriental" variety or Gush Emunim, do not find analogies in American Judaisms, although they may be analogous to other religious movements elsewhere. See the discussion of Israeli Judaism by Deshen and by Aran in Goldscheider and Neusner, eds., *Social Foundations of Judaism*.

14. For some revealing illustrations of the details of these controls, see Goldscheider and Zuckerman, *Transformation of the Jews*, chap. 2.

15. See articles by Woocher and Deshen in Goldscheider and Neusner, eds., *Social Foundations of Judaism*.

16. See for example Deshen on Israeli Judaisms and Aran on Zionist religion in Goldscheider and Neusner, eds., *Social Foundations of Judaism*, and J. Neusner, *Death and Birth of Judaism* (New York: Basic Books, 1987).

17. See for example, C. Goldscheider, *Population, Modernization and Social Structure* (Little, Brown, Boston: 1971), chap. 3.

4. The Challenges of Modernization

Joseph R. Rosenbloom

The Jewish people has lived in numerous social and political situations during its four-thousand-year history. It has survived as an identifiable group as a result of modernizing itself and, at times, others. Its hallmark has been adaptability and innovation. It learned from others and often rationalized its place in society as teacher.

While identified as a religious group, the Jews have been in the past, and are increasingly today, primarily a people, with a special history and culture. A central element of this intertwined historical culture has been its religion, Judaism. Religion is usually seen as central to the Jewish people since it allows Jews to be more easily categorized where the largest Jewish populations have lived, in Christian and Islamic societies.

Modernization is used in this paper as the process of adjusting to whatever situation in which Jews found themselves throughout their history. The single constant has been the specialness of the group and its drive to maintain its identity. This has been carried out through ideological and institutional modification and innovation. At times, this has been dramatic, but has always been related to its past to maintain historical continuity.

Academic studies of modernization proliferated among social scientists in the 1960s and 1970s. Typically, the concept was time-bound, seen as beginning about 1500, and territorial, originating and developing most fully in western Europe and North America.[1] It was also tied to technological development. Marion L. Levy, Jr. measured modernization by the utilization of energy sources: the higher the ratio of inanimate to animate sources of power, the higher the degree of modernization.[2] Richard L. Rubenstein concludes similarly: "By modernization I mean the growth and diffusion of a distinctive set of institutions and values rooted in the technological transformation of the economy and the organization of the state."[3]

This process affected religion in many ways. These include secularization, rationalization, disenchantment of the world, and an emphasis on the material world in contrast to spiritual concerns. Marion L. Levy, Jr. holds that otherworldly religions which stress ultimate ends, devotional behavior, and the attainment of immortality are "incompatible with any considerable level of modernization."[4] Rubenstein agrees: "There is much irony in the fact that the culture of science and technology, which has enhanced the physical culture of large sectors of mankind, has done so at the price of rendering infirm the beliefs, values and institutions that have in the past alleviated humanity's anxiety before its terminal necessity."[5] Levy reinforces this observation when he notes the irresistible force of the material gains resulting from modernization: "There are no peoples, there never have been any peoples, and there never will be any peoples who fail to prefer to some extent being relatively better off to being relatively worse off materially."[6] A somewhat contrary view is offered by C. E. Black: "Anthropologists and historians (in contrast to sociologists and economists and many political scientists) are by training and experience more impressed by the staying power of tradition . . ."[7]

Judaism, from its earliest days, was in a sense already "modern" in that it was to a great extent devoid of magic or reliance on mysterious forces. It may be seen as "disenchanted" in the Creation story of Genesis 1 as "creation was seen as devoid of independent divine or magical forces which man had to appease."[8] The same tendency with a secular orientation is seen in Nathan's denunciation of David in the affair with Bathsheba. The king is viewed as totally human, albeit subject to God's law.[9]

The central thesis of this paper is that modernization as a process as applied to Jewish history began in historical times, in the period of the beginning of the Hebrew Monarchy, circa 1050 B.C.E. While Black acknowledges that modernization may be seen as an "age-old process of innovation," he "modernizes" its contemporary usage "to the explosive proliferation in recent centuries . . . (which) may be defined as the process by which historically evolved institutions are adapted to the rapidly changing functions that reflect the unprecedented increase in man's knowledge . . ."[10] While knowledge and change developed much more slowly in antiquity, the general process was the same.

Our definition of modernization, then, would include those developments brought about in a society as it responds to political, economic, and social changes. These developments may be the result of "modeling," bringing into one's society institutions and enterprises from another society which has led to the resolution of similar problems, and the inventing of entirely new institutions and ideologies. Jews have survived as an identifiable group over a three-thousand-year period through their ability to modernize, adapt, and innovate. Because of their interaction with other peoples and cultures, both as a national entity and as dispersed communities, they became adept, expert modernizers.

Because the Jewish people lived both in its own land and in the Diaspora in ancient times, it developed patterns which could be "brought out of the file" when similar conditions reoccurred. For this reason, the broadest definition of modernization is appropriate for an understanding of the historical experience of Jews, as well as dealing with the entirety of their existence.

Ancient Times

While much of the historical material in the Bible is problematic, it seems to accurately reflect general conditions and tendencies. The period of the Judges, 1200–1000 B.C.E., was a time when the tribes of

Israel were independent and loosely tied together and were confronted with Canaanite culture which seemed to influence the invading/returning Israelites. The code word for the threat of cultural absorption was idolatry. One might hypothesize that the development of a national (sole?) deity would serve to provide greater unity and serve as a barrier to a blending into the cultures of Canaan.

While the invading Israelites were ostensibly all descended from Abraham, Isaac, and Jacob, a "mixed multitude"[11] is said to have joined them during the Exodus. Those with common ancestry, joined by blood ties, as well as those who allied themselves, could be further unified through the same deity, Yahweh. Ties with an earthly father were reinforced by those with a heavenly Father.

This bond with Yahweh was formalized with the *brit*, the covenant or treaty, made by Abraham and his descendants with God. This special relationship could also serve as a barrier to full participation in the Canaanite cults. Having a single God with a formalized "treaty" may be seen as a modernizing movement, one which would be subsequently refined.

The next great threat to the survival of the Israelites came from the Philistines. This Greek island people defeated and displaced the tribe of Dan and challenged the Israelite tribes as they moved east and north from their enclaves on the Mediterranean coast. Their power rested apparently on their political confederation and advanced technology. "No blacksmith was to be found in the whole of Israel, for the Philistines were determined to prevent the Hebrews from making swords and spears . . . So when war broke out none of the followers of Saul and Jonathan had either sword or spear . . ."[12]

Politically, the Israelite tribes were governed by tribal elders, on occasion; in a crisis, by a Judge, with some political and military authority resting with the priestly families of Eli and Samuel. On one level, the Book of Judges points to the need for a change: "In those days there was no king in Israel and every man did what was right in his own eyes."[13] This occurred after the "outrage at Gibeah" and the attack on Benjamin. The clear implication was that a king would prevent such abuses. Similar words are used in judgment of Micaiah who built a shrine for idols.[14]

However, it was the ineffectiveness in battle of the old leadership and the attendant threat to the physical survival of the Israelites which led to their demand of Samuel: ". . . appoint us a king to govern us, like the (other) nations."[15] Quite naturally, the priests and other traditional leaders opposed this modernization. They would lose power, and old institutions and personal and economic relationships would change. But because of the threat, the emerging and more sensitive among the elite were willing to pay the price.[16] That this process fits contemporary views of modernization is seen in Black's comments: ". . . the models adopted by modernizing leaders except in societies that were the first to modernize are always derived in a considerable degree from outside their own society. The problems they face, however, are domestic and in essential ways unique."[17] And, modernization "must be thought of then as the process that is simultaneously creative and destructive, providing new opportunities and prospects at a high price in human dislocation and suffering.[18]

Modernization also involves ideology, as noted above with the emergence of Yahweh as the national deity and later as the only, universal God. A single dramatic event, the destruction of the Judean state by Babylonia in 586 B.C.E., led to the loss of the major elements of Jewish identity, security, and well-being: the Davidic monarchy, independence, Jerusalem, the Temple, and to the dispersion of most of the population. Two long-term ideological developments were formulated to compensate for this disaster, giving meaning to the continued existence of the Jewish people.

First, Jeremiah provided hope through minimizing the importance of the Temple[19] and elevating the worth of those taken into exile.[20] They were the "good figs." Then he pointed out that they could survive in exile and exhorted them to carry on: to build houses, marry off their children, have grandchildren, and accept and work on behalf of the society of which they were now a part; for "on its welfare your welfare will depend."[21] Also, he proclaimed that God is present wherever they are.[22] Neither God nor the Jewish people were territorially bound! This modern ideology for Diaspora existence has served the Jewish people for 2500 years.

Isaiah of the Exile supplemented these developments by rationalizing the destruction and providing an ideology of exalted worth and purpose to the continued survival of the Jewish people. The cornerstone of his program was Yahweh, now seen as universal, without limits, and as the author of history.[23] He then gave them hope: Israel had paid for her sins and God would provide for a great future.[24] Israel's role was established: chosen to be a light to the nations, God had bestowed on her a glorious mission.[25] The Jewish people, with its special relationship to Yahweh, with its extraordinary human role, now had a firm, glorious raison d'être for its existence throughout history, one which has enabled it to survive until now.

From the fourth century B.C.E. through the first century C.E., the Jewish people had dramatic historical experiences which resulted in one of its most innovative modernizing developments, one which dominated Judaism for over two-thousand years. This was a time of being dominated by imperial powers, of a resurgence of Jewish independence, of the trauma of the destruction of the Temple, and of the development of an enduring expression of Judaism. The imperial control by the Greeks, led by Alexander the Great and his successors, the Ptolemies and Seleucids, and then by the Romans, brought to Judea radically new cultural experiences and an exposure to new economic structures.

Jewish independence under the Hasmoneans was a relatively brief and chaotic interlude, during which there developed what appears to be the middle-class led "liberal" movement of the Pharisees. As Judean society was increasingly called upon to adjust to new economic and social influences, the need arose for an ideology and method to continue as Jews and at the same time adapt to new situations. Biblical law, now hundreds of years old, was not responsive to many of the new realities of international commerce. The choice for those participating in the advanced economy was to drop the encumbrances of the Torah legal system or to find a way to modernize it. The first choice was unacceptable to them.

The resolution was the development of the two-part legal system: the written law and the oral law. Both were held to be a part of the Revelation at Sinai with the latter implicit in the former. Gradually, methods were contrived to extend the Torah in an orderly, effective way. A new, scholarly elite evolved, that of the rabbis. With the destruction of the Temple in 70 C.E., priestly Judaism ended and a new religious-legal leadership took over the stewardship of Judaism. It was this group which canonized the Bible and continued to extend the Torah. The Pharisaic-rabbinic methodology allowed for the infinite extension of Jewish law within the Sinaitic framework. Compilations of these laws are found in the Mishnah and the two Talmuds, with the process continuing even now through the Responsa. This ingenious formulation allowed for perpetual adaptation within Judaism and influenced canon law in Roman Catholicism, the Ḥadīth and Shariʻah in Islam, and in a secular form, constitutional law in Western democracies.

The Middle Ages

From the last century B.C.E. until the twentieth century C.E., the Jewish people lived as minority enclaves, for the most part in Christian and Islamic societies. Its official status was usually problematic. While allowed, in general, to live within the Jewish system, economic and social relationships were circumscribed. The Jews' survival depended on their developing specialized economic and social roles. Once again, and in an ongoing way, they repeatedly modernized these roles.

Political and economic relationships were always intertwined. The status of the Jews was fixed by church councils and subsequent legislation by the church and through the evolving Shariʻah and Ḥadīth of Islam. Essentially, this meant that Jews and others not in the system were accorded lower status, both socially and economically. Land taxes within the Islamic realms converted a predominantly agrarian people into merchants, moneylenders, and artisans. The holding of land was even more difficult in Christian countries because of general insecurity, expulsions, and limitations on hiring gentile farm workers.

Although economic data for this period are sparse, some generalizations are possible. Jews adapted brilliantly to their reality. Some of what they did may be called modernization as they moved from agricultural to urban settings and more technologically and economically demanding enterprises. Their second-class citizenship itself, together with their being a nonthreatening minority, facilitated their success. It may be hypothesized that their actual economic and cultural status was far higher than that of the average Christian and Muslim. Secular leaders typically ignored church law toward Jews when it suited their purposes.

The hostility between Christians and Muslims and their desire for trade with one another provided a special opportunity for Jews. They were a threat to neither and could therefore serve as commercial intermediaries between them. In addition, they found contacts on both sides, sharing with other Jews a common language and mutual trust and interests. Each side benefited from this complicated network of hostility.

Because of their lower official status, Jews had to be satisfied with special niches in the economy and became economic specialists, performing tasks which others either did not value or which were prohibited to them. In Islamic lands, this meant virtual Jewish monopolies in tanning, dyeing, butchering, and gold and silver crafts. In Christian lands, moneylending in particular was important because of the church's position on usury. Jews were also important in the transfer of technology from Islamic lands to Christian lands while the former were advanced, until the High Middle Ages.

There was special pressure on Jews to modernize or innovate in business and crafts as their enterprises were co-opted and they were prohibited from engaging in some crafts. This was the result of guilds, moderating church law on usury, and competition by Italian bankers and traders. The hallmark of Jewish communities was their flexibility within whatever milieu they found themselves and adjustment to the transfer of communities because of expulsion, persecution, or declining social-economic conditions.[26]

A development which in a sense may be seen as modernizing was the neutralizing and downgrading of messianic expectations in the seventeenth century following the disastrous Shabbatai Zevi movement. The messianic idea may be viewed as one developed to give hope in extremely despairing situations. It may also be seen as an antimodernizing idea, depending as it does on supernatural intervention and an undoing of the historical process. So upsetting was the

Shabbatean movement that speculation about messianism was thereafter rigorously discouraged. Jewish thought was centered on legal issues, continuing the talmudic process of developing the Torah to contemporary circumstances. The emphasis was on the reasoning process and rationality.

More dramatic changes, modernization and adaptation, occurred in the ancient period than in the Middle Ages because the Jewish people had to respond to greater challenges in kind. They moved from nomadism to settled agrarianism, from autonomous tribal units to nation-state status to developing a mini-empire, from a unified state to a dual monarchy, from independence to vassaldom and domination, and then to Diaspora existence. Each change brought institutional and ideological adjustments, often dramatic. In contrast, the status of Jews during the Middle Ages remained relatively constant: the Jews lived as minority enclaves, physically vulnerable and serving in specialized roles, of value particularly to the ruling elites. Primarily, they served as an intermediate group between relatively small ruling elites and the masses of urban and rural working classes. Modernization was essentially the process of refining their economic roles—developing new techniques and forms as conditions changed and their functions were taken over by those of the majority population. Ideology and institutional changes were minimal, having already been established in antiquity. Mysticism, the Kabbalah, and various legal formulations, including those of Maimonides, may be viewed as antimodern. Mysticism was essentially antirational and reactive to a harsh environment. Maimonides sought to redirect, in part, the dynamic development of rabbinic law, the hallmark of the new Judaism of the Pharisees, toward philosophical speculation.

The Modern Period

From the time of the Arab-Muslim conquests until the collapse of the Shabbatean movement one thousand years later, Jewish communities shared a relative unity of the dominant trends and institutions noted above. These occurred within specific social situations and persisted even as they were buffeted by the flow of events and changing sensibilities. Jews were characterized by a distinctive national and cultural unity unlike that shared by other groups, particularly those they would increasingly live among, Arabs, Germans, and Slavs.

As Jewish history moved into the modern period, earlier patterns were severely tested, particularly the Jewish proclivity for adapting, modernizing, and innovating. The status of the Jews as a religious community and a closed social corporate entity was challenged by the greater direct control of centralized states with absolute power over all their subjects. Furthermore, new economic networks and growing technology brought profound changes in living habits and in the social order. Modern culture and national languages led to the suppression of dialects and other languages within a state. The principle of legal and social equality with participation in educational, political, and social decisions, challenged Jewish particularity and survival.

Discussion of these trends and patterns is difficult in regard to the Jewish people since they lived in so many places and at different levels of development at the same time. The emphasis here will be primarily on those in the most advanced areas which today include the vast majority of Jews.

Early movements of Jews were primarily from west to east (after the thirteenth century), from developed to less developed societies. Beginning with the eighteenth century, the prevailing movement was from east to west, to the major economic and cultural centers of Europe and the United States. While in the earlier period the Jews had much to teach, now they learned much. In a sense, the Jewish people became "Western Europeanized" or modernized. External and internal compulsion in Jewish communal life, as was the case in the medieval world, was gradually replaced by more open, individualistically oriented societies. While earlier Jews were the modernizers, now they were, at least initially, the group to be modernized.

Jews brought many qualities and characteristics which aided them in this process. They had a firm sense of identity and specialness, reinforced by an ideological heritage that had developed over a three-thousand-year period. For most of this period, they lived in a variety of circumstances and survived as an identifiable group through techniques developed during this period. Among their qualities were: intellectualism, a deep respect for learning, and analytical ability, which were invaluable in coping with new and complex situations. With most Jews forced out of agriculture and into towns and cities, they were better suited to the norms of urban existence than most others who moved from rural areas. They had a long history of adapting and of being discontented eventually with every situation they were in. Finally, Jewish mutual support and self-help were long a part of their relationships with one another.

During this three-hundred-year period, every aspect of Jewish life was dramatically impacted. While there had always been a variety of Judaisms from the biblical period on, the increase in variety surged in the modern period. One Judaism prevailed from the first century on: Rabbinic Judaism, based on the Revelation on Sinai and the oral law found in the Talmud(s). This process is still adhered to by a sizable minority of Jews. Beginning with the end of the eighteenth century and accelerating by the middle of the nineteenth, significant numbers of Jews began following a Judaism which denied the historicity and binding nature of the Sinaitic revelation.

What became Reform, Conservative, Progressive, or Liberal Judaism held that while the laws of the Torah, the Talmuds, and later collections contained much of value, they were not divinely sanctioned commandments and could be evaluated by their followers. Their observance, particularly by Reform Jews, was voluntary. This process of delegalizing Judaism was a radical break from the major pattern of Jewish behavior. It was the result of the growing secularization of general society and the full legal acceptance of Jews as citizens of the nations where they lived.

In the sense that Judaism developed in response to social and political situations which were unique for Jews, they modernized their religious expressions. The process of development in western Europe was carried on through a series of movements beginning with Otto I (late tenth century) and culminated with the Enlightenment and revolutions of the United States and France. The Protestant Reformation also served to break life-pattern control from institutional religion with its emphasis on the antinomianism of Paul and salvation through faith rather than works.

Where these developments were more advanced, so was the growth of delegalized Judaisms. This is particularly apparent in the United States where the successor to Rabbinic Judaism, Orthodoxy, even in its current triumphalist mode, represents a small minority of Jews. Furthermore, there are now Orthodox Judaisms which are in contention with one another. The delegalized Judaisms were modernizations of Judaisms which were appropriate responses to their milieus. The new Judaisms served similarly in societies characterized by the need fully to integrate into systems, educationally and socially. The values of the general society were taken on for the most part as Jews participated fully in it. Jews developed Judaisms in which they could be intellectually and socially comfortable. An extreme expression of this pattern is Humanistic Judaism founded by Rabbi Sherwin Wine. While calling its religion Judaism, it has eliminated elements held essential by all other religious Jews: the belief in God, the presence of an ark and Torah scrolls in sanctuaries, and all other references to supernaturalism. This Judaism was developed by people who wanted the symbol "Jew" attached to them in a "religious" sense, but were otherwise fully committed to a secular expression of their Jewish identity. There are many Jewish bodies which base their Jewishness on elements other than religion, specifically Jewish socialist, philanthropic, cultural, and social organizations.

The rise of nationalism in central, eastern and southern Europe culminated with the end of the Ottoman and Austro-Hungarian Empires. Ethnic groups found expression in the nation-states of Albania, Yugoslavia, Greece, Austria, Czechoslovakia, Rumania, and Bulgaria. Jews, influenced by these and other national movements and growing overt anti-Semitism, especially in France and Russia, increasingly concerned themselves with the reestablishment of a Jewish state. While this may be seen as a reassertion of the millennial hope for a homeland in Palestine, modern Zionism may also be viewed as modernization following the model developed throughout Europe.

If, however, Zionism is seen as reversion to an earlier status and counter to the ongoing process of integration into other nation-states

as fully participating citizens, it may be judged as an antimoderniza-
tion movement. In any event, the State of Israel was established in
1948, the result of the Holocaust and strategic concerns of Russia and
the United States. The surviving Jews of Europe required a place to
go. Russia and the United States, replacing England and France as
the dominant powers in the Middle East, sought a special relationship
with Israel.

The Holocaust, while comparable in some ways to other Jewish
national disasters, was of such immensity that it has been considered
unique. Ideological responses to the Holocaust by Jews and others
may be judged at this point to be tentative. Some have concluded that
God does not act in history, certainly not in the manner testified to by
traditional Judaism. Others see in the establishment of the State of
Israel a redemptive element in sequel to the Holocaust. A fully
accepted, "modern" ideological interpretation, if one is to come, will
be in the future.

Increasingly, for ever more Jews, the basic definition of "Jew" is a
person who identifies with the Jewish people culturally, socially, and
in its destiny. The religious component, essential until the eighteenth
century, is no longer universally held. This may be viewed as a modernizing development, as increasing numbers of people live fully
committed to secularism. Jewish loyalties in such diverse places as the
United States, Israel, and Russia remain deep, but as part of a people
rather than as a religious community. These patterns are always in
process and are never complete, but the general direction is clear.

This tendency was clearly articulated by Mordecai M. Kaplan in his
seminal work, *Judaism as a Civilization*: "Judaism as otherness is thus
something far more comprehensive than Jewish religion. It includes
the nexus of a history, literature, language, social organization, folk
sanctions, standards of conduct, social and spiritual ideals, esthetic
values, which in their totality form a civilization."[27] Kaplan's movement, Reconstructionism, while not attracting large numbers institu-
tionally, has been the most influential Jewish religious movement in
America during the last fifty years. All other Jewish religious denominations operate to a great extent in the Reconstructionist mode. The
Jewish Center movement was also profoundly influenced by it.

In Western societies, Jews are increasingly found in ever widening economic enterprises. Traditional roles, determined by exclusion and social and political status, no longer are in place. At the same time, informal prejudice and discrimination reinforce earlier patterns. Excluded from some professions and businesses, Jews specialized in other professions and developed their own niches. In industry, education, and commerce, they innovated and concentrated on areas undesired by others. However, in a general sense, they were fully integrated into the economic systems of which they were a part.

Conclusion

Judaism is commonly held to be the religious system of the Jewish people. It provided its raison d'être. Depending on one's point of view, Judaism came into being from the call of Yahweh to Abram, the revealing of the Torah to Moses on Mt. Sinai and the unfolding of the law by the rabbis, or as the unconscious and conscious development of Jews as they lived in various places, influenced by diverse cultures. Regardless of which orientation is accepted, Judaism as a religious system was seen as inseparable from the Jewish people. They comprised a religious community. While it may be argued that Jewish society was essentially secular at times, during the Davidic monarchy, for instance, subsequently Jews saw themselves and were seen as a religious community. While this remains generally true for non-Jews, from the nineteenth century on increasingly Jews redefined themselves as a "people." Simon Dubnow described this process in historical terms.

Throughout their history, Jews have seen themselves as special. Because of their minority status in their non-national phases, which in a temporal sense predominates, they were also perceived as special by Gentiles, though not in the same way as they saw themselves. As a result, their identity was reinforced even as external forces often led a considerable number of Jews to merge into their host societies. Jewishness, seen as special, became itself an essential element, leading Jews to strive to maintain this identity. Their Jewishness also brought economic and social benefits as they served their hosts in essential ways but also led to persecution and expulsion because of their vulnerability.

Through the millennial history of the Jews the one single constant has been the drive to survive, with no commitment to any particular form, ideology or pattern of behavior. None of these, developed early or late, were ever totally discarded. They were stored in the folk memory and recorded in literature, to be recalled and utilized once again when needed.

The process making this survival possible may be called adaptation and innovation, or as we choose to call it here, modernization. This modernization has two essential modes. In the earliest and latest periods, Jews, following the models of the people of the territory they conquered or migrated to, were modernized or modernized themselves. For the most part, in the middle period, they were the modernizers as they moved from more modern (technologically and politically advanced societies) to less modern societies.

Because ideology typically adjusts to the material realities of a people, the ideologies and patterns of behavior of Jews were modernized as they moved from one place to another or when they lived long enough in one place to experience profound social change. The Jews of the Western world share little with Jews of antiquity or the Middle Ages other than the name Jew, some folk memories, and ideological elements, the content of which has been profoundly altered. What may be seen as the most modern element of the Jewish people is its lack of commitment to anything sacred, that is eternally true, while it sacralized its own existence.[28]

NOTES

1. C.E. Black, *The Dynamics of Modernization* (New York: Harper and Row, 1966), 6, 11.

2. Marion L. Levy, Jr., *Modernization: Latecomers and Survivors* (New York: 1972), 3.

3. Richard L. Rubenstein, ed., *Modernization: The Humanist Response to its Promise and Problems* (Washington, D.C.: 1982).

4. Marion L. Levy, Jr., *Modernization and the Structure of Society: A Setting for International Affairs* (Princeton: Princeton University Press, 1966), vol. 2, 607, 614.

5. Rubenstein, *Humanist Response*, 13.

6. Levy, *Modernization: Latecomers and Survivors*, 9.

7. Black, *Dynamics of Modernization*, 195.

8. Richard L. Rubenstein, *The Cunning of History* (New York: Harper, 1975), 28.

9. Ibid.

10. Black, *Dynamics of Modernization*, 7.

11. Exod. 12:38.

12. I Sam. 13:19, 22.

13. Judg. 21:25.

14. Judg. 17:6.

15. I Sam. 8:5.

16. Joseph R. Rosenbloom, "Social Science Concepts of Modernization and Biblical History: the Development of the Israelite Monarchy," *Journal of the American Academy of Religion* 40 (1972): 438.

17. Black, *Dynamics of Modernization*, 50.

18. Ibid., 27.

19. Jer. 7:3, 4.

20. Ibid., 24:5.

21. Ibid., 29:4, 7.

22. Ibid., 29:12, 14.

23. Isa. 40:15, 31.

24. Ibid., 40:1, 5; 43:14, 15.

25. Ibid., 42:1, 7; 61:1, 5–7.

26. There is a paucity of specialized studies on economic endeavor of Jews in the ancient and medieval periods. Two very good summaries of available research have been utilized: Marcus Arkin, *Aspects of Jewish Economic History* (Philadelphia: Jewish Publication Society, 1975), and Nachum Gross, ed., *Economic History of the Jews* (New York: Schocken, 1975).

27. Mordecai M. Kaplan, *Judaism as a Civilization* (Philadelphia: Jewish Publication Society, 1981), 178.

28. Norman Roth in a recent article holds that in its earliest period Jews saw themselves as a people. The term "Judaism" itself was an innovation of the Hellenistic period. He suggests that Jews were made into a religion

to deal with those Jews in Spain who converted to Christianity. Since these Jews joined Christianity, a religion, they must have come from another religion. Similarly, as the Jews integrated into democratic societies, they were seen and saw themselves as members of a religion rather than of a people. He reversed the process suggested in this paper, namely, that Jewish civilization gradually and inevitably became a *religious* way of life. See Norman Roth, "Jews or Judaism," *Judaism* 37 (1988): 200–205.

5. Modern Jewish Studies and Bible Research

Benjamin Uffenheimer

The aim of this paper is to describe the present state of Jewish studies in general and that of Jewish Bible research in particular, and their impact on modern Jewish existence and thinking. For this end we should keep in mind that the historical setting of contemporary Jewish Bible studies is the rise of the Jewish renaissance movement and that of the critical study of Judaism, called *Wissenschaft des Judentums*. Both movements flourished simultaneously by the end of the nineteenth century and the first decades of the twentieth century. They reflect the radical changes that Jewish life, mentality, and self-understanding have undergone during modern times.

The first movement was initiated by outstanding Jewish scholars who lived in the German-speaking part of central Europe, where great German historians like Ranke, Mommsen, Willamowitz, Edward Meyer, etc., and the representatives of the Neo-Hegelian school had forged the spiritual atmosphere. Jewish scholars like Zunz, Geiger, and Zecharia Frankel then managed to lay the foundations of Jewish studies in terms of the historical philological method.[1] These studies included the critical approach to Talmud and Midrash, to medieval Hebrew literature, poetry, and philosophy, etc. It was the bibliographer M. Steinschneider, who forged the bibliographical backbone to all these branches.

The most impressive achievement, however, is doubtlessly H. Graetz's magnum opus, *History of the Jews from Ancient Times until the Present Day*,[2] comprising eleven volumes, these being the most brilliant contribution to Jewish historiography. From the philosophical and theological point of view, it is Hermann Cohen's work: *Religion der Vernunft aus den Quellen des Judentums* (Leipzig, 1919) (Religion of Reason According to the Sources of Judaism), which reflects the spiritualizing and rationalistic tendencies inherent in this movement.

Two were the major concerns of the *Wissenschaft des Judentums*: First, to correct the distorted image of Judaism, resulting from deeply ingrained prejudices stemming from nearly two thousand years of virulent enmity of the *ecclesia militans*. In this respect they have done outstanding work, even if their apologetical zeal sometimes overshot the mark. Here, too, Graetz is a typical representative of the trend. To mention only one instance, his disquisitions on the origins of Christianity with their strong sentimental coloring are entirely a reflection of his national-religious convictions, while when he treats of other chapters of Jewish history he is guided by his boundless admiration of and veneration for the great rationalists of Jewish thought and by his vivid hatred of all irrational currents.

Like contemporary scholars of Judaism, Graetz rejected the irrational trends in Judaism as offshoots of primitive vulgar superstitions—a distorted view of history which persisted until our times and was rectified only by the monumental works of Buber,[3] Scholem,[4] and Yitzhak Baer.

The second concern of the *Wissenschaft* was of political character, i.e., a confessionalizing tendency. By reducing historical Judaism to a mere faith, the universal mission of which they claimed to be the proclamation of moral monotheism, they wanted to enable their coreligionists to take their place in the German nation as citizens holding the "Mosaic faith." One of these scholars spoke of "preparing an honorable burial to Judaism," which was tantamount to paving the way toward emancipation and assimilation.

In such an atmosphere no place was left for the rise of modern Bible studies. For what the Bible so clearly stresses is the national character, the peoplehood of Israel and its bond with Eretz Israel, in contrast to the spiritualizing and confessionalizing tendencies of this trend. Additionally, the Bible was the only spiritual basis of the so-called Mosaic confession; it seems that instinctively they were afraid of any attempt to destroy this last link by scientific dissection. This is why, strangely enough, the first Jewish reaction to Wellhausen's work came from the Orthodox camp. I am referring to a little booklet, *Die wichtigsten Instanzen gegen die Graf-Wellhausensche Hypothese*, written in 1902–3 by the Orthodox scholar David Hoffman of Berlin, whose main field was Talmud and Bible exegesis.

As a matter of fact, the rise of modern Bible research coincided with the Jewish renaissance movement, most of whose exponents were from eastern Europe, where Hebrew and Yiddish literature flourished around the turn of this century. The men who created this literature were engaged in a conscious search for expressions of Jewish popular culture. In their work, Jewish religion is usually envisaged as a function of national culture or an expression of folk spirit. The stories of Yitzhak Leibush Peretz and the collection of Jewish legends of Micha Josef Berdyczewski (Bin Gorion; also published in a German translation as *Die Sagen der Juden*, 5 vols., 1912–27, and *Der Born Judas*, 6 vols., 1916–23) depict this folk element with great love. The same stress on the organic link between nation, land, culture, and religion, with its markedly romantic overtones, is reflected also in Berdyczewski's theoretical essays, in the historical works of Simon Dubnow, and in the early writings of Buber. We should also bear in mind that a romanticist of modern Hebrew literature, Abraham Mapu, who preceded the above-mentioned scholars and writers, wrote two novels (*Ahavat Tzion* and *Ashmat Shomron*), set in Eretz Israel during the biblical period, whose Hebrew style was an imitation of biblical Hebrew.

It is this trend which gave the first impetus to the study of all those movements and creations of Jewish popular culture that had been put aside by the *Wissenschaft des Judentums*. The spiritualizing and moralizing interpretations of Judaism were rejected, and thus, for the first time, the road was free for a nontheological interpretation of the

Bible, which produced a man like Arnold Ehrlich (1848–1919), author of the famous *Randglossen zur Hebraeischen Bibel* (6 vols., 1908–14) and its somewhat shorter predecessor *Mikra ki-Peshuto* (3 vols., 1899). Ehrlich uses the entire scholarly equipment of his generation to explain the Bible text critically according to strictly philological principles. Other outstanding representatives of this trend were Abraham Kahana (1878–1946), H.P. Chajes, S. Krauss, M.Z. Segal, Simon Bernfeld,[5] and Zalman Rubashov, who later became known as President Shazar of Israel.

The turning point for Jewish and biblical studies was the establishment of the Hebrew University in 1925, its first department being the Institute of Jewish Studies. These studies developed quickly during the thirties and forties, in particular after the establishment of the State of Israel, when additional Israeli universities intensified the interest in Jewish studies.

Since then, already two generations of scholars have made their contributions to Jewish inclusive biblical studies.

What are the common features of these researches?

What is their contribution to the study and understanding of Judaism and the Bible?

What is their impact on modern Jewish self-understanding and on the new Jewish culture which is in the making?

Jewish Studies and Apology

As to the first question, two major features differentiate between the classical *Wissenschaft des Judentums* and modern Israeli Jewish research:

First, the Israeli research is emancipated from any apologetic constraint whatsoever. It is a dialogue between our present generation and our heritage. We ask ourselves about the meaning and relevance of our tradition without concerning ourselves with the reaction of the outside world. This dialogue, which only *starts* at the academic level, has its powerful impact on our educational scheme and is of major importance for our future spiritual image.

The second trait of present Jewish learning is the deep interest in all phenomena of Jewish history and culture, rational and irrational alike: Kabbalah, Hasidism, Messianic movements, etc., including all expressions of folk culture. The interest in mysticism, Kabbalah, Hasidism is due to men like Buber, Scholem, Y. Baer, and others, who devoted a lifetime to the research of these phenomena, thereby balancing and rectifying the shortcomings of the *Wissenschaft des Judentums*.

Myth and Judaism

The problem of myth and Judaism, which arises from the study of later Jewish sources, has its bearings on biblical studies as well. In order to make myself understood, I shall have to describe the present situation of Bible studies in Israel. It is a commonplace that the first generation of Bible scholars in Israel, M.D. Cassuto, M.Z. Segal, and N.H. Tur-Sinai in particular,[6] devoted their energy mainly to linguistic and literary problems of the Bible. Biblical theology was mainly the field of Kaufmann,[7] while Buber, Benno Jacob,[8] and Franz Rosenzweig[9] (who never reached Eretz Israel) added significant contributions to the research of the artistic structure of biblical prose and poetry.

Cassuto's first comprehensive work on biblical problems, written in Italian, *La Questione de la Genesi* (1933), was a thoroughgoing discussion with German Protestant scholarship. In his commentaries on the first eleven chapters of Genesis,[10] he developed the antithesis based on the assumption that the story of the Torah is the prosaic repetition of an ancient epic written in ancient Hebrew poetry like the epic of Ugarit or the Homeric epic in Greece. In these works, in particular in his comprehensive essays,[11] he tackled the problem of biblical monotheism and Canaanite pagan myth, i.e., the ways and methods of the Bible which aimed at neutralizing Canaanite myth.

The historical and phenomenological analysis of monotheism was the major topic of Kaufmann's magnum opus: *Toldoth haEmunah haYisr'elit* (The Religion of Israel).[12] In it he seeks to invalidate the three-phase theory of the origin of monotheism, which he ascribed to Wellhausen. His purpose was to show that the Torah sources—or the

Torah literature, as he calls it—entirely reflect Jewish popular culture. Monotheism is not, as modern Protestant Old Testament studies would have it, an artifact produced by the classical prophets from the eighth to the sixth century B.C.E. On the contrary, in his view, it is the original creation of the ancient Israelite folk mind; not the result of a long and complicated evolution, but something born together with the nation and brought into existence by Moses. It is the intuitive creation of the a-mythical "folk spirit" or mentality of Israel, whose writers and prophets were completely alienated from pagan mythology. The gap between the monotheistic and the pagan mythological consciousness cannot be bridged by any evolutionary theory, whatever its nature may be. Monotheism, being the result of a sudden outburst of popular intuition, is the formative element which shaped Israel's ancient culture.

Kaufmann's conception of monotheism as resulting from an a-mythological mentality, and his identification of myth with paganism, are indeed the heritage of Hermann Cohen's rationalistic philosophy.

This rationalism is the critical point of departure of Buber's approach. Even in his younger days, Buber sought the monotheistic myth—one of his famous addresses, given at the beginning of this century, was "The Myth of the Jews"—a title which Kaufmann would call self-contradictory, since myth is for him by definition pagan. In his Koenigtum Gottes, Buber describes the monotheistic myth of ancient Israel with a masterly hand. In his late philosophical writings Buber made untiring efforts to develop his ideas on the subject of myth even further, for he felt constrained to defend them against neorationalistic tendencies prevalent in modern Protestant theology under the impact of Bultmann and his school.[13]

But despite his great interest in the affinity of biblical monotheism to myth, Buber did not point at the structural differences between monotheistic and pagan myth. This question, which is of crucial importance for a nonrationalistic understanding of biblical monotheism and the spiritual atmosphere of midrashic and talmudic Judaism, is still open to philosophical, phenomenological, and exegetical discussion.[14] As Rosenzweig's Star of Redemption shows, it is of deep concern to a modern Jewish theology, myth belonging to the basic needs of the human soul.

Another trend which has been dominating Israeli Bible studies since the first decades of this century refers to the tangible problems of the Bible and the ancient history of Israel. During the present generation, the interest in militant polemics against Protestant Old Testament studies à la Kaufmann has waned, largely because there is no longer any daily contact with the Christian world. The major interest of this generation shifted from theological to historical, geographical, and archaeological problems. The *Encyclopedia Miqra'it*, initiated by scholars of the preceding generation, but mainly written and edited by the present generation, gives witness to this trend. The enthusiasm of this generation for the above-mentioned problems, far from being the result of antiquarianizing tendencies, rather expresses the deep experience of the first generation to grow up in the country which is the concrete setting of the Bible. We should keep in mind that modern Zionism arose from the age-long yearning of the Jewish soul for Eretz Israel; this generation which had to fight five wars for its very existence has developed a new bond with its ancient homeland— a bond which is deepened and strengthened by the study of the Bible, Jewish history and literature. The most moving moments of this struggle, which has been going on since the beginning of this century, occurred when we managed to return to historic Jerusalem and to Judaea, Benjamin, and Samaria, the cradle of the First and the Second Commonwealths. The enthusiastic archaeological and historical research of these parts of Eretz Israel is not only a matter of academic interest. It is part and parcel of our historic consciousness.

NOTES

1. Cf. H. Liebeschuetz, *Wissenschaft des Judentums und Historismus bei Abraham Geiger: Essays Presented to Leo Baeck* (London:, 1954).

   G. Scholem, "Wissenschaft des Judentums einst und jetzt," *Judaica* (1963).

   Nahum N. Glatzer, "The Beginnings of Modern Jewish Studies," in *Studies in Nineteenth Century Jewish Intellectual History*, ed. A. Altmann (Cambridge, Ma.:, Harvard University Press, 1964), 27–30.

A. Altmann, *Jewish Studies: Their Scope and Meaning Today* (London:, 1958).

K. Wilhelm, "Zur Einfuehrung in die Wissenschaft des Judentums," in *Wissenschaft des Judentums im deutschen Sprachbereich*, ed. K. Wilhelm (Tuebingen:, 1967), vol. 1, 3–58.

2. H. Graetz, *Geschichte der Juden*, (Leipzig: 1876–1891).

3. M. Buber, *Reden ueber das Judentum* (Gesamtausgabe, Frankfurt a/M), 1923.

4. G.G. Scholem, *Major Trends in Jewish Mysticism* (Jerusalem: Schocken, 1941).

5. S. Bernfeld, *Literary-Historical Introduction to the Holy Scriptures* (Berlin:, 1904) (Hebrew).

6. For bibliography on these scholars, see my paper, "Some Features of Modern Jewish Bible Research," *Immanuel* 1 (1972): 3–14.

7. Y. Kaufmann, *Toldot Ha'emunah Hayisr'elith*, 4 vols. (Tel Aviv:, 1937–1956).

8. B. Jacob, *Das erste Buch der Tora, Genesis* (Berlin: Schocken Verlag, 1934).

9. F. Rosenzweig, *Kleine Schriften* (Berlin: Schocken Verlag, 1937).

10. M.D. Cassuto, *From Adam to Noah* (Jerusalem: The Magnes Press, 1953). (Hebrew).

   M.D. Cassuto, *From Noah to Abraham* (Jerusalem: The Magnes Press, 1949). (Hebrew).

11. M.D. Cassuto, *Biblical and Canaanite Literature*, 2 vols. (Jerusalem: Magnes Press, 1972, 1979). (Hebrew).

12. See note 7; on Kaufmann as Bible scholar see my essay, "Yecheskel Kaufmann—der Bibelwissenschaftler der juedischen Renaissance," *Freiburger Rundbrief*, 27 (1975): 159–167.

13. See B. Uffenheimer, "Buber and Modern Biblical Scholarship," in *Martin Buber, A Centenary Volume*, eds. H. Gordon and Y. Bloch (Ben-Gurion University of the Negev: KTAV Publishing House, 1982), 163–211.

14. On this problem, see B. Uffenheimer, "Myth and Reality in Ancient Israel," in *The Origins and Diversity of Axial Age Civilizations*, ed. S.N. Eisenstadt (Albany: State University of New York Press, 1986), 135–168, 505–10.

6. The Holy and the Orthodox

Samuel C. Heilman

Before they are able to reason and make sense out of the condition of their existence, human beings inhabit the realm of feeling. At the beginning, we have little more than bodily sensations which are initially quite inchoate, vague, and undifferentiated. Only later, in the context of reasoned and growing bodily experience, do these sensations become more differentiated and distinct. Later still, but nevertheless early in the process of human development, come emotions and feelings: bafflement, happiness, sadness, anxiety, fear, determination, and courage. At first these also remain rather blurred and hazy so that we are not certain exactly what emotions we feel, simply *that* we feel. Only at a relatively late stage of our development do we begin to put these sensations and feelings into some sort of syntax and make rational sense out of our condition and situation.[1]

Although Emile Durkheim was undoubtedly right when he noted that "there was no given moment when religion began to exist," one might suppose the development of religion to replicate this pattern of human maturation.[2] That is, before the emergence of a syntaxic religion, the development of its rational and ordered elements, feelings and mysterious sensations were dominant. Or, to put it differently, the nonrational aspects of religions precede the rational. We begin with inchoate sensations which only later emerge as full-blown and intellectualized religion. Accordingly, a consideration of religion might properly begin with those aspects of it that cannot be easily grasped by the intellect. Let us begin with mystery.

To fathom the mystery of religion, one cannot simply examine texts, even those considered to be sacred scriptures which form the basis of many, if not most, organized religions. This is very simply because "expositions of religious truth in language inevitably tend to stress the 'rational' attributes of God."[3] The assertions of the Gospel according to Saint John notwithstanding, in the beginning was not the Word but rather the feeling of mystery, a sense of the ineffable. Indeed, the rational Word may be considered only a subsequent representation of the mystery. And what is most mysterious is something utterly different.

In fact, the holy—what Rudolf Otto calls "the real innermost core" of religion—is the epitome of the utterly different.[4] As *kadosh* in Hebrew, *āgios* in Greek, and *sanctum* in Latin—all translations of what we call "holy"—denote, the holy is set apart, wholly other. Moreover, as something wholly other, the holy cannot be wholly known or understood or described in words, for otherwise it would not be perceived to be overwhelming or so absolutely set apart from one's being. It must be always mysterious and awe-inspiring, a *mysterium tremendum*.

The essential aspect of otherness that pervades the holy, Otto has called, "the numinous."[5] To experience the numinous, he tells us, a person first must experience the "emotion of a creature, submerged and overwhelmed by its own nothingness in contrast to that which is supreme above all creatures."[6] This is precisely the attitude that is inherent in the beginnings of human consciousness, as Freud tells us: "The origin of the religious attitude, can be traced back in clear outlines as far as the feeling of infantile helplessness."[7]

To the newborn, life is filled with mystery and awe. Everything is potentially startling and anxiety-provoking. While we strive throughout life to resolve many of these mysteries, particularly those which make us anxious, mystery in general remains with us—always surprising us from a variety of sources: the world, our bodies and self, and others.[8]

Similarly, in their beginnings, and ever after, human beings who gave birth to the religious disposition were undoubtedly likewise struck by "that which is beyond conception or understanding, extraordinary and unfamiliar."[9] One can see the parallels between the experience of the child confronting the anxiety-provoking and dreadful unknown, and the adult before the ineffable. For both, God, the holy, emerges out of these.

This *mysterium tremendum*, the objective aspect of the numinous, has thus always remained a part of religion. It contains within it—as does all of the unknown—an element of dread. We are, if not afraid, awed by what is completely different from all we know and understand. It must leave us perplexed in the extreme. Otto has portrayed the *mysterium tremendum* as surrounded by "absolute unapproachability" and "absolute overpoweringness," two attributes that he represents by the term "majesty."[10] Yet while the majestic seems at times inapproachable, it is at the same time fascinating and attractive. Indeed, precisely that which is forbidding is also what is most alluring. Once approached, however, the majestic reveals its awe-provoking powers and becomes overpowering, awakening in us the feelings of helplessness and dependence, while persuading us of the transcendence and potency of the Other. And then we are once again thrown back—but even more powerfully than before—to the feeling of being submerged and overwhelmed by our own nothingness. The witness to God's majesty is precisely the one who proclaims most fervently: "I am naught, Thou art all."[11]

To be sure, much of what as children seemed to us the incarnation of the holy turns out to be quite mundane as we grow. The same could be said for civilization in general, that it has moved from awe to understanding and therefore gradually diminished the realm of the holy in favor of the mundane. We today often treat the unknown as the not-yet-known rather than the unknowable. As such we tend to be less awed by mysteries which are treated by us as essentially temporary. However, as a result we have far fewer encounters with the numinous.

The Wrath and Rules of the Gods

The numinous was in the history of religion often encountered in tandem with the ominous wrath of the gods. As Otto suggests: "There is something very baffling in the way in which it 'is kindled' and manifested. It is . . . 'like a hidden force of nature,' like stored up electricity, discharging itself upon anyone who comes too near."[12] Through wrath, the god has inspired awe in others. Only when people try to make sense of that wrath does it yield something more specific than awe. To discover precisely what kindled God's wrath is to find a way of controlling or at least avoiding it.

One way to handle God's wrath is to discover a set of rules, laws, commandments according to which he has enjoined us to live. These rules are revealed to us—usually in the course of history. And along with that revelation comes a code which warns the believers that if they but do what the gods have commanded them, they shall be able to know the gods, ward off their wrath, and somehow share in their ineffable power. Hence, many—if not most—religions in their development find themselves supported by a series of laws, rituals, commandments that are meant to make life possible according to God's will. These rules of the religion can be learned. What cannot be taught, however, is a feeling of awe and a sense of the numinous. That "must be 'awakened' from the spirit."[13]

To be sure, the organization of the religion is meant to be such that by following the rules, holding the beliefs, and enacting the rituals, a person will be brought to a feeling of holiness and an appreciation of the numinous. But, in part because religion, like other institutionalizations, tends to become routinized, a sense of the numinous cannot always be assumed to be a product of organized religion. What may have engendered awe and a feeling of the numinous at one point in the history of a religion, may fail to do so at another. One generation's spirituality may become another's dead ritual or lifeless ceremonial. The words of a prayer which, when it was first articulated, stimulated a feeling of holiness, may not continue to do so when that prayer has become a formalized incantation.

Indeed, much prayer or ritual is aimed at once at arousing the numinous as well as mitigating the sense of dread that accompanies it. By praying, for example, the worshipper touches or at least approaches the ineffable but also demystifies it at the same time. He makes what is transcendent into something immanent. He makes the god into the one he can name, address, expiate, cajole, and influence in some way or another. Hence all the concern in the Bible about God's names, character, and the manner in which he should be addressed. Yet, just as the religious person seeks to understand the god whom he addresses, he realizes that for that god to remain divine there ought to remain limits on what the worshipper can comprehend. As Plato put it: "We ought not to ask what God is altogether; for it can neither be discovered by any nor stated in words. . . . [God] whom the human mind has no power to appraise. . . . For He is too sublime and too great to be grasped in the thought or speech of man."

Identification

Sometimes we deal with the feelings that emerge out of the numinous not so much with rational laws as with identification. We identify the gods, giving them form and reality. In some cases, they are discerned in plants, animals, celestial bodies, or imaginary creatures, and in other cases they inhabit the living or the dead. This is, as Richard Gilman has argued, because of "our inability ever truly to grasp the spiritual except as somehow incarnate, clothed."[14]

Then, when we have identified the gods, we associate or identify ourselves with them. It is this process which Freud describes when he writes of man: "Long ago he formed an ideal conception of omnipotence and omniscience which he embodied in his gods. To these gods he attributed everything that seemed unattainable to his wishes, or that was forbidden to him. One may say, therefore, that these gods were cultural ideals."[15] To be sure, this often—and some would argue, ultimately and inevitably—requires a loss of self, a willingness to be absorbed in the Creator. And that once again leads back to the numinous which yields a feeling of absolute nothingness.

And why? Why do those who could be called religious do this? Some have put fear or at least anxiety at the root of the process. "For what doth the Lord ask of you but that thou shouldst fear him." "That thou mightest fear the Lord thy God. . . ."[16] Awe and dread lead inexorably to a sense of the ominous and numinous which in turn lead to a feeling of nothingness and the religious inclination along with an attendant willingness to live by whatever rules and regulations will mitigate the feeling of dread. I do what I believe God has commanded me because I fear him and because I am nothing compared to him and therefore cannot presume to challenge him.

Others argue that neither identification nor dread or fear lead to religion. They point instead to the twin tendencies toward fascination and possession. The religious life begins in the desire "to remain in these strange and bizarre states of numinous possession [which] becomes a good in itself, even a way of salvation. . . ."[17] In its purest form, this fascination and possession is what we call "spirituality," and what has also sometimes been referred to as "the love of God."

These two possibilities—to be religious out of fear or out of love—could be described respectively as the negative and positive aspects of the religious inclination, the former emerging out of a desire to avoid the suffering and the latter more a constructive wish to be caught up in and establish a relationship with something greater than oneself.

But whether one approaches the numinous out of a negative or positive inclination, out of fear or love, one comes away with a sense that only through contact with the holy does a person become holy. This means that carrying out the gods' will (either out of fear or love, a sense of dread or spirituality)—or being one with those gods—is a way of sanctifying oneself. Once thus consecrated, the religious are freed from their profane being and their existence is lifted above the mundane. This, for example, is what is involved in atonement.[18] Once accomplished, atonement—whatever form it takes—yields a feeling of bliss, a sense that, because the gods have forgiven and accepted us, we are in a higher or more improved state of being.

Faith and Ritual: The Limits of Meaning

If religion—as was suggested at the outset—bridges the space between what the human can comprehend and what is beyond understanding, it nonetheless limits the meaning it provides in order to retain the numinous and the blessings that a sense of holiness provides. What fills that gap in meaning is faith. Faith goes beyond rules and identifications and settles upon mystery. As Martin Luther proposes, "all things that are believed must be hidden away."[19]

Religion allows for the permeation of the nonrational with the rational; the overwhelming is circumscribed by moral order. The holy then is more than simply the numinous. Rather, as Otto argues, "we must no longer understand by 'the holy' or 'sacred' the merely numinous in general . . . ; we must always understand by it the numinous completely permeated and saturated with elements signifying rationality, purpose, personality, morality."[20]

As part of organized religion, the numinous becomes attached to justice, goodness, rules of behavior, and all else that is part of what we understand by full-blown religion. This is a process of rationalization and institutionalization. But, in the process, the numinous becomes stripped of much of its original power and mystery.

Still, when one examines religious doctrine or ritual, within them can still be found reverberations of the numinous. Thus, for example, rules of what is clean and unclean, relations with the dead, founding myths which are dearly held, and a variety of obscure rituals whose meaning remains shrouded in mystery—all point toward a time in the development of that religion when the numinous was at full strength. And, strangely enough, these elements tend to continue to fascinate the religious. Indeed, precisely those aspects of religion, which are beyond the routine and reason and which recall a time when the *mysterium tremendum* still reigned, are among the universals in all religions which have survived in the contemporary world.

People still try to infuse these elements of the earlier religion with power. And when they work in arousing in worshippers the feeling of awe and holiness, there is a sense of having awakened to the feelings that were always within one but simply submerged. That is, the numinous, when it returns to its original potency, seems to have always been there, a part of life. When Otto speaks of holy as an a priori category, he seems to mean this. This is probably what American Christians mean when they speak of being "born again" and what Jews mean when they say they "have returned to faith." What is born again and returned to is the sense of the numinous. The believer is returned to a feeling of being a creature, of being helpless and dependent, fearing and loving God. Once again, he has experienced the numinous and is in the presence of the holy.

It waketh the power of feelings obscure
That in the heart wondrously slumbered.[21]

The Holy and the Ultra—Orthodox

There is a tendency to assume that the ultra-Orthodox in particular and indeed the Orthodox in general are Jews for whom holiness of the sort I have described in the preceding pages is a fact of life, the essential emblem of their being. The assumption is that in their everyday existence they are able to call forth the numinous and arouse the feelings of sanctity easily. To be sure, there are genuine feelings of such sanctity that make their way into the lives of the Orthodox, but if they do they do so in spite of the pattern of Orthodox existence rather than necessarily because of it. The reasons for this are rather simple.

Orthodoxy with its punctiliousness and attention to the detail—often the most stringent interpretations of the detail—of religious ritual often finds itself caught up on the one hand with the technicalities of ritual—something that tends to diminish the awesome and numinous—and on the other with the constancy of ritual. The latter forces both the rationalization and institutionalization of religion. It turns what was once volitional and even spontaneous—the result of a profound feeling of spirituality and the numinous—into something inertial, quotidian. The inertial, albeit the mortar of religious life, tends to diminish the volition and the numinous.

Specifically, this has made most Orthodox Jews stress the need to provide properly kosher food, continuing prayer (although the emphasis is often on gathering the quorum or making certain the right words are said in the right order and tune rather than on the spiritual experience), or the institutionalization of education rather than on the numinous.

This is not to say that the Orthodox are not "born again." Paradoxically, those who are so renewed and spiritually invigorated are the newly Orthodox, the returnees to the faith of their forebears, the *baale teshuvah*. These are Jews who can breathe the life of volition into their faith—but often this is precisely because they have not institutionalized it. For them, the extraordinary and the unfamiliar, the *mysterium tremendum*, is precisely what makes their faith fresh. But because they know little about what they have possessed, because it is largely a mystery to them, it can be a Great Mystery.

The challenge, of course, is to keep it fresh and new as they become more familiar with it. This is the difficulty of the institutionalization of the newly Orthodox; and it presents a great test for the newly faithful.

There is yet someone else for whom religion can remain spiritual, numinous, mysterious. The child. The Orthodox—who intuitively realize the spiritual difficulty inherent in their Orthodoxy—therefore stress the importance of the children. The entire focus of their energies is on the religious education of the young (although the education ironically often lacks the spiritual element). As Orthodoxy in general and ultra-Orthodoxy in particular has become more assured of itself and has grown in size and stability in the face of modern society, so it has emphasized education more. Thus, at present, there are more Orthodox young people in yeshivot and day schools than ever in Jewish history. And women, once relegated to a minor or nearly negligible Jewish education, now are expected to get a significant Jewish education. Among the modern Orthodox this means an education equal to the boys' and among the ultra-Orthodox it means something far more developed than ever before in a network of special girls' schools.

For the Orthodox then, spirituality, ecstasies, passion, numinousity is the province of the newly religious: the penitents and the young. Here is the spiritual heart of Jewish life. But it is a heart that beats fast and often to another rhythm from that of the rest. Whether its beat will be the dominant one or whether the old beat will have the day is a question which only time will answer.

One last point. The problem of maintaining holiness and the spirit of the numinous in the quotidian existence of Orthodoxy is by no means only a Jewish one. It is at the heart of routinization of all religion. It is the challenge confronting the process of institutionalization through which all religion which seeks to fulfill the quotidian needs of existence must pass. The holy is after all fleeting, evanescent, even as religions seek to be everlasting. The way in which each faith comes to terms with this challenge makes for its spiritual richness. That Jews—particularly the Orthodox—still manage to create moments for themselves when mystery overshadows the mundane concern with punctiliousness and ritual complexity, may account for Judaism's staying power and continuing attraction in a world where religion was supposed to disappear.

NOTES

1. See Harry Stack Sullivan, *The Interpersonal Theory of Psychiatry* (New York: Norton, 1953), esp. 28–30, for a discussion of what he calls prototaxic, parataxic, and syntaxic experience—stages which generally correspond to what I describe here.
2. Emile Durkheim, *The Elementary Forms of the Religious Life* (New York: Macmillan, 1915), 20.
3. Rudolf Otto, The Idea of the Holy (London: Oxford University Press, 1923), 2.
4. Otto, *Idea of the Holy*, 6.
5. Otto, *Idea of the Holy*, 8 *et passim.*
6. Otto, *Idea of the Holy*, 10.
7. Sigmund Freud, *Civilization and Its Discontents* (New York: Norton, 1962), 19.
8. "We are threatened with suffering from three directions: from our body, which is doomed to decay and dissolution and which cannot even do without pain and anxiety as warning signals; from the external world, which may rage against us with overwhelming and merciless forces of destruction; and finally from our relations with other men." Freud, *Civilization and Its Discontents*, 24.
9. Otto, *Idea of the Holy*, 13.
10. Ibid., 19.
11. Ibid., 21.
12. Ibid., 18.

13. Ibid., 60.

14. Richard Gilman, *Faith, Sex, Mystery* (New York: 1986), 118.

15. Freud, *Civilization and Its Discontents*, 38. That Freud could say that today identification has led some to believe that they have almost become gods themselves suggests the success of the attack that reason and science have mounted against the forces of religion, at least in some quarters.

16. Deut. 6:2.

17. Otto, *Idea of the Holy*, 33.

18. Ibid., 55.

19. Ibid., 101.

20. Ibid., 109.

21. F. Schiller, *Der Graf von Habsburg.*

7. Pluralism and Orthodoxy

Michael G. Berenbaum

In the three decades since I received my high school diploma from Ramaz—then considered the most liberal of all Orthodox yeshivot in America—Orthodox Judaism in America has undergone a renaissance. While it still remains a distinct minority among American Jewry's denominations, four factors distinguish it from other segments of American Jewish life and from its more precarious situation in 1963.

First of all, it has momentum. When I was being raised as an Orthodox Jew, there was a sense of erosion. Seemingly, each passing generation of American Jewry was becoming less observant than its predecessor, less committed to tradition, less reliable in its religious beliefs. Orthodox Jews keenly felt the lure of the world beyond the community. Even for those who remained faithful, the outside world was an option—better yet, a temptation. Everyone knew someone, usually someone quite close, who had left Orthodoxy, abandoned religious observances, and moved either into other denominations of American Jewish life or into a strikingly secular environment.

In contrast, the worldwide reemergence of fundamentalist religious faiths, the recent phenomena of a *baale teshuvah* movement,[1] and the more prevalent example of secular, Reform, and Conservative Jews who have intensified rather than diminished their religious observance have given Orthodox Judaism a special élan. The successes of synagogues such as the Lincoln Square Synagogue in New York and suburban Orthodox synagogues and prayer houses in virtually every large city in the country—many of whose members were not raised in Orthodox homes—have given contemporary Orthodox Jews the sense that time is on their side.[2] They now have reason to believe that Orthodoxy will certainly endure and, perhaps, eventually triumph—if not by convincing others of the veracity of its ways, then by the power of endurance. Over time, non-Orthodox forms of Jewish life in the Diaspora will wither. The way to get ahead is to stay the same.

Second, Orthodox Jews seem confident that their children will remain Jewish. Conservative, Reform, Reconstructionist and secular Jews appear a lot less certain that their grandchildren will be Jewish.

High intermarriage rates and the wide array of other options available to contemporary American Jews require that Judaism compete in the open marketplace of ideas and be chosen as a personal option for those American Jews who chose to remain Jews.[3] Since the outside world no longer imposes Jewish identity on the American Jew, that identity must be self-chosen, the free act of an independent individual, and for significant numbers of non-Orthodox Jews, Jewish identity wanes.

Rabbi Joseph B. Soloveitchik has described the double covenant of the Jewish people as *brit goral*, the covenant of fate, and *brit ye'ud*, the covenant of meaning.[4] For the first time, many American Jews no longer sense that fate has imposed their Jewishness upon them. It must be inner-determined because it will no longer be outer-determined; if, in Sartre's terms, it takes the anti-Semite to make the Jew, then with anti-Semitism on the decline, it is more difficult for Jews to remain Jews.[5] As a result, contemporary Jewish parents feel that the Jewish identity of their children is uncertain. What steps have been taken to protect that fragile identity follow the prescriptions of Orthodox Jewry a generation ago. The Jewish day school, now in its

Conservative, Reform and community varieties, is regarded as the first line of defense against the secular assault on Jewish identity.

Third, in Orthodox Judaism there is little gap between the paid professionals and the laity. A generation ago, many more Jews identified with Orthodox Judaism though they were not Orthodox in praxis. Jews affiliated with Orthodox congregations wanted their rabbi to be Orthodox and synagogue practice to remain traditional, but they did not regard synagogue affiliation as personally binding on their behavior. Such is largely the case within Conservative Judaism, where often the only Conservative Jew whose practice reflects the movement's ideology is the rabbi. As a result of the success of the yeshivah movement, Orthodoxy has succeeded in creating an involved, educated laity, whose practice reflects the tenets of the movement. In fact, some Orthodox rabbis have complained that, as a result, the pressure from their laity is for greater observance, less compromise, less openness to the world, and greater fidelity to the perceived teachings of tradition.

Finally, Orthodox Judaism now has a sense of its own power. In Israel, Orthodox religious parties have achieved a virtual monopoly on the religious life of the people. Until recently, only Orthodox synagogues were funded, and the Orthodox infrastructure received funds disproportionate to its numbers from both the State of Israel and the Jewish Agency. Two separate government-sponsored school systems are in place to train young Orthodox Jews. From family law to *kashrut*, Orthodox Jews set the standard, administer the law, supervise the bureaucracy, and exercise virtually complete power.[6]

II

The power of Israeli Orthodoxy is matched by its insulation. Structurally, Orthodox Jews live in an increasingly segregated environment including separate schools, youth movements, neighborhoods, and social institutions. Even for those Orthodox Jews who serve in the army, national service is often in special units composed of like-minded adherents to the tradition. Similarly, university training can be undertaken in an Orthodox environment. Separated from their fellow Jews, Orthodox leaders are under less pressure to accommodate to the modern world. At home in Israel among Jews, they are protected by nationalist sentiments from the struggle with the non-Jewish world. The result has been a growing fanaticism and intolerance that has led to the expression of religious and political sentiments (that in an earlier age would have been restrained in a self-imposed silence) and violations of the norms of civility that characterize the behavior of American Jews, at least in the English language.

For example, Israel's chief rabbi has forbidden Jews to sell flats to Gentiles.[7] Former Sephardi Chief Rabbi Ovadia Yosef ruled that if copies of the Hebrew Bible and Christian Scriptures are bound together, the latter should be ripped apart from the former and burned.[8] Similarly, Christians are increasingly referred to as "'ovde 'avodah zarah (pagans) whose institutions are to be destroyed according to Halakhah.[9] Similarly, there have been savage verbal assaults on the diplomatic appointment of an Israeli Druze as Consul General in Atlanta, Georgia, because, according to Maimonides, "a non-Jew may not hold office in a Jewish state."[10]

Yehoshafat Harkabi has argued that the two clauses that previously provided dispensation "for the sake of peace" and "in order not to arouse hostility" seem less applicable in an Israeli context. Furthermore, they avoid the core of the problem—the nature of these religious teachings themselves—and grapple only with the issue of timing.[11]

Lest we believe that incivility is restricted to non-Jews alone, advertisements publicizing a rabbinic ruling that it is better for Jews to stay home and not go to synagogue on the High Holidays than to hear shofar blowing in non-Orthodox congregations, appeared throughout Jerusalem. This sentiment may be shared by some Orthodox rabbinical authorities in the Diaspora, but they are far more reticent to publicize their views.

This empowerment of Orthodoxy in Israel has spread to the Diaspora, where the issue is seldom state-endorsed power, but legitimacy. Precisely because it is most resistant to change, Orthodoxy is regarded as the voice of tradition, as the authoritative interpreter of Judaism, by many Jews who are not themselves Orthodox, but who look for its imprimatur to confer legitimacy. However much Conservative and Reform rabbis may complain, however often scholarly works are written that challenge the authority of Orthodoxy, many American Jews still turn to Orthodoxy as authoritative even while they are unprepared to bow to its teachings.

John Cuddihy has written extensively about the rule of civility in the interreligious life of America. In his work, *No Offense*, Cuddihy demonstrates that pluralism and civility have led to a major transformation in American religious life.[12] Roman Catholics ceased to argue that there is no salvation outside the Church. Protestants were quiet about their views that the only way to the Father is through the Son, and Jews did not proclaim their chosenness outside of the prayers recited in synagogues and homes. In fact, the Roman Catholic position first advanced by John Courtney Murray became the dominant voice of the entire Church with the pronouncements of Vatican II.

Whenever extremists offer uncivil opinions, there is an immediate effort to moderate the views and hence to preserve the civility of interreligious life. Consider, for example, the response to Reverend Bailey Smith who proclaimed that "God does not hear the prayers of the unredeemed," i.e., the Jews. His statement surely was not uncommon in Protestant thought, but the swiftness of the public response had little to do with the correctness of his theology. More to the point, he transgressed the unwritten laws of American religious life.

American Jews have overwhelmingly embraced the religion of civility. Leonard Fein and Charles Silberman have written persuasively of the role of pluralism in the inner life of American Jews.[13] The acceptance of diverse practices and teachings, the separation of Church and State, and the openness of America to a wide variety of points of view have created a climate that has allowed American Jews to flourish as Jews in a manner unprecedented in the Diaspora. They have shaped a form of Judaism that is distinctively American, the core of which includes a deep, passionate commitment to pluralism. Only Orthodox Jews dissent from the American Jews' "religion of pluralism." Their dissent is theological and is reinforced by political and social structures.

III

For the past one hundred years in America and for the better part of half a century before that in Europe, Orthodox Jews were forced to make peace with the reality of non-Orthodox forms of Judaism but not with their legitimacy. No one could deny the presence, the power, and the pervasiveness of Conservative and Reform Judaism in America, of liberal Judaism in western Europe, and none could ignore the dynamism of Zionism in Israel—but there is an enormous gap between recognizing a sociopolitical religious reality and granting theological recognition to that reality.

Let us examine the case of the late revered Rav Kook, the former chief rabbi of prestate Palestine. Rav Kook was a passionate mystic and a compassionate rabbi. More than any other figure of his time, he bridged the abyss that separated the Zionist *yishuv* from the pietistic Jewish communities living in the Holy Land. He is fondly remembered as a religious leader who reached out to the secular community and who understood the potential of Zionism. With time, as the distance grows and as tensions mount between religious and secular Jews in Israel, Rav Kook's tenure as chief rabbi is regarded as the "golden era" of mutual tolerance.[14]

And yet, theologically Kook denied the legitimacy and the durability of the Zionist revolution even as he described it as the dawn of redemption. He offered a now famous analogy between the secular Zionist enterprise and the building of the Holy of Holies. When the holy Temple was being built, Kook taught, every simple worker could traverse the Temple mount and walk into the Holy of Holies. No special state of purity was required, no estrangement from defilement and no special rituals were to be observed to enter the most sacred of Jewish sites, the place that in the consecrated Temple, only the High Priest could enter once a year, on the Day of Atonement, after following an exacting ritual of purification. So too, Kook told doubting pietists, secular Jews are building our Holy of Holies, and once their efforts are consecrated, we will recognize that the current situation is but temporary. In short, Kook viewed secular Zionism as a temporary ally in the sacred vocation of the Jewish people. He never envisioned it as a permanent reality nor was he prepared to accept secular Zionism on its own terms. Kook's views did pave the way for Orthodox Jews to cooperate with the Zionist movement and to actively participate in it. Yet in the back of their minds, this was a short-term strategy rather than a partnership for the duration.

In America, cooperation between Orthodox and non-Orthodox Jews was essential. Rabbi Joseph Soloveitchik provided such cooperative efforts with an overriding legitimacy. His distinction between the covenant of fate and the covenant of meaning provided the framework. The former is the covenant of Egypt and the latter is the covenant of Sinai. Fate has imposed upon all Jews a shared history and quite often a common enemy, and to grapple with that shared fate cooperation—loving and wholehearted cooperation—is not only permitted but mandated. Yet the covenant of meaning, the Event of Sinai—which according to Orthodox teaching, yielded both the written and oral Torahs—divides rather than unites Jews, some of whom are prepared "to do and to hear" and others are not, yet all are equally bound by the revelation and the response at Sinai.

As chairman and sole member of the Orthodox Rabbinical Council of America's Halakhah Committee, Soloveitchik played a critical historical role in permitting intra-Jewish cooperation. His precise role is currently being rewritten as some of Soloveitchik's more strident followers find his apparent openness embarrassing. Because of poor health and advancing age, Soloveitchik withdrew from public life and teaching in 1986 and none of his would-be successors are likely to replicate—or even endorse—his decisions.[15]

It was on his authority that Orthodox rabbis joined the Synagogue Council of America, the national rabbinic group that includes Conservative and Reform as well as Orthodox rabbis. His decision is cited time and again by those Orthodox rabbis who want to resist periodic pressures to withdraw Orthodox participation. So too, in the 1950s, Soloveitchik worked with Professor Saul Lieberman of the Jewish Theological Seminary toward the creation of a joint *bet din* between Conservative and Orthodox rabbis to handle issues such as marriage, divorce, and conversion. Here too, Soloveitchik's role is repeatedly used to bridge the gulf between these two movements. The fact that such a proposal failed was due to pressures from the rabbis of both denominations and not because of some intrinsic theological objection by Soloveitchik toward the idea.

As chairman of the Rabbinical Council's Halakhic Committee, Soloveitchik also recognized as valid *gets* written under the supervision of Professor Boaz Cohen of the Jewish Theological Seminary. His decision was binding on the Orthodox Rabbinical Council of America. In 1986, this precedent was cited by Norman Lamm, president of Yeshiva University, to indicate that the halakhic competence of a *bet din* and not the institutional affiliation of its members is critical to the acceptance of its decision.[16] Similarly, during the height of the negotiations over the Vatican II statement *Nostra Aetate* in the early sixties, Soloveitchik and Rabbi Abraham Joshua Heschel were in daily contact acting on behalf of the Jewish people in this most sensitive theological document. Rabbi Wolfe Kelman, the Executive Vice-President of the Conservative Rabbinical Assembly of America often acted as the intermediary without regard to his seemingly political position. Later decisions by Soloveitchik seemed less open to other religious movements, but they may have been a symptom of the time.

The towering personality and scholarship of Rabbi Soloveitchik as well as his unique record of cooperation with non-Orthodox Jews has concealed a dimension of his thought that remained impervious to religious pluralism. Until recently, it was difficult for one who was not a student of the Rav (as he was called by his students and disciples) to assess the nature of his thought. By family tradition, he was reticent to publish his writings, and those that found their way into print were often public statements and the notes of his students. The few works that appeared, ranging from Hebrew essays to papers in *Tradition* were cherished as glimpses of the man's greatness. Even today, with the appearance of more than a half dozen works in English and a larger number in Hebrew, there is a sense that the true power of the man, which can be gleaned in his writings, was best revealed orally in the encounter between student and master, the Torah and its Creator.[17]

In his early work, *Halakhic Man*, a free-wheeling manifestation of the inner life of a *mitnaged*, Rav Soloveitchik describes halakhic man as insulated from the world. Halakhic man can share elements of the consciousness of cognitive man, and can even operate in that universe. He too can share the sensitivities and some of the urgency of *homo religiosus*, but he need not fall prey to the spiritual unrootedness nor to the sway of emotionalism and spiritual oscillation that characterizes the religious life of the latter. Soloveitchik depicts the Halakhah as a divinely revealed "a priori system," which is then applied to reality by halakhic man. If the Conservative movement has stressed the historicity of Halakhah and its role as the product of the Jewish people in dialogue with revelation and with the Holy One, Blessed be He, Soloveitchik situates the Halakhah outside of history, independent of history, the system by which adherents to Halakhah orient themselves to the historical events.

As no other Jewish thinker since Franz Rosenzweig, Soloveitchik also positions the Jewish people outside of history, engaged in applying the categories and system of an eternal, a priori system, to transient events of history.

> When halakhic man approaches reality, he comes with his Torah, given to him from Sinai, in hand. He orients himself to the world by means of fixed statutes and firm principles. An entire corpus of precepts and laws guides him along the path leading to existence. Halakhic man, well furnished with rules, judgments and fundamental principles, draws near to the world with an a priori relation. His approach begins with an ideal creation and concludes with a real one.[18]

Ironically, it is because of this structural immunity to history that Soloveitchik can be open to contemporary scientific and philosophic thought and operate in the world of science and technology without feeling either threatened or pulled. Archetypal halakhic man is insulated but not isolated. He is blessed with an inner stability that allows him to overcome the vicissitudes of life—even to confront death. He can handle the turmoil of intellectual struggles and of a turbulent era because his point of orientation is clear. His sense of divine presence is assured. "There is no real phenomenon to which halakhic man does not possess a fixed relationship from the outset and a clear, definitive, a priori orientation,"[19] Soloveitchik writes. Similarly, in his essay "The Lonely Man of Faith," Soloveitchik distinguishes between magisterial man, the man of dignity who knows God as Elohim, and covenantal man who, aware of the personal existential psychological drama of loneliness, encounters the personal God of revelation. Covenantal man is halakhic man, a Jew bound by the covenant. Soloveitchik's would-be successors appear less open to the outside world, perhaps because they are less protected.

IV

The issue of pluralism in contemporary Orthodoxy is most often less theological than it is practical—centering on four aspects of current practice: Orthodox participation in joint rabbinic bodies, marriage and divorce ceremonies, and Orthodox acceptance of individuals converted to Judaism by non-Orthodox rabbis. While Rav Soloveitchik approved Orthodox participation in the Synagogue Council of America, periodic attacks on that very participation continue to surface. The attacks are always from the right. Withdrawal is threatened as any change in the status quo is suggested. For example, after the Reform movement ordained women in the early seventies, there was a move to withdraw from Orthodox participation in the New York Board of Rabbis. Ironically, the movement was squashed with the very argument that delegitimated all non-Orthodox rabbis. The reasoning was simple. Since Orthodox rabbis "know" that Reform (or Conservative) rabbis are not "real rabbis," what difference does it make if they are men or women? While de facto relations are always cordial and often excellent, de jure recognition presents a much greater problem.

If participation in rabbinical organizations is of little consequence to lay people, the issues of marriage, divorce, and conversion are of genuine concern, threatening a communal rift and impacting on the lives of many individuals. Ironically, until divorce became so widespread in the American Jewish community, the recognition of marriage presented the least of the problems. Because Halakhah presents three means of marriage (all of which are combined in the traditional religious wedding service)—a ring, a document (*ketubbah*), and union—and because there is no inherent, permanent stigma to the unmarried, it was of little interest to Orthodox rabbis to challenge the legitimacy of non-Orthodox ceremonies. All this changed with the increase in divorce rates and with the decision of the Reform and Reconstructionist movements not to require a traditional divorce, which raised the problem of *mamzerut* to alarming proportions.

According to the Torah, a child born of the union between a married woman and a man other than her husband is a *mamzer* and may not marry into the community of God for a thousand generations. Thus, a child born in a second marriage to a women whose first marriage was not ended with a *get* would be a *mamzer*, since according to Halakhah she is still bound to her first husband and may not again remarry. Because of the harshness of the penalty, rabbinic authorities have tended to be lenient on the question of *mamzerut*. Thus, as we have seen, Soloveitchik recognized on behalf of the Rabbinical Council the validity of a Conservative *get* and Rabbi Norman Lamm repeated that recognition in his proposal for a joint rabbinic court. Even in Israel, where problems tend to be intensified and where there is little pressure for accommodation, Conservative divorces have been recognized without much fanfare or publicity. Thus, the problem is not between Conservative and Orthodox rabbis, but with Reconstructionist and Reform rabbis who do not insist on religious divorce.

In a decision that was described as lenient—and indeed it was so because it enabled a child who might otherwise have been considered a *mamzer* to marry—the late Rabbi Moshe Feinstein ruled that Reform marriages are not halakhically binding and hence they do not require a religious divorce.[20] Feinstein thus ruled that *mamzerut* did not apply to a child born of the second marriage of a women whose first marriage was conducted by a Reform rabbi. Since the marriage was not valid, divorce was not required, and the circumstances of the child's conception was without stigma. Rabbi Lamm's proposal for a joint *bet din* sought to reinforce this decision by asking Reform and Reconstructionist rabbis in the name of Jewish unity to tell couples approaching them that the marriages they perform are not *k'dat Moshe v'Yisrael*, not according to the time honored traditions of Moses and the people Israel.[21] Thus, according to Lamm, there would be no doubt as to the nonvalidity of the marriage by halakhic standards, and if the marriage ended in divorce and the women remarried without a *get*, no religious stigma would attach to the child born of a subsequent marriage. Needless to say, Lamm's proposal, like Feinstein's halakhic decision—lenient as they may be—did not arouse great enthusiasm on the part of non-Orthodox rabbis.

V

Though the problem of pluralism primarily reflects itself in practical and seemingly unsolvable problems,[22] the issue is also theological. Only two current thinkers, Irving Greenberg and David Hartman, present a case for religious pluralism. Both are publicly identified— though not necessarily accepted—as part of Orthodox Judaism and both seem to define its limits. The fate of either thinker may well determine the boundary of the movement. Because the faith of both men is not without its doubts and its struggles, they recognize the possibility that others may choose another direction.

Greenberg is most closely identified with the issue of pluralism in Jewish life. His widely publicized essay "Will There Be One Jewish People in the Year 2000"[23] catapulted the issue of Jewish unity to the forefront of American Jewish concerns. Although he was not the first to argue of the dangers of a schism, his essay drew significant attention, and he created the organizational apparatus to sustain the issue. It is not our purpose to rehearse Greenberg's argument regarding the possibility of a schism, but rather to consider his theological justification of religious pluralism as put forth in two rather different ways: first as an internal argument within the Orthodox community where his purpose is to persuade within categories acceptable to the community; and second, as a central component of his own religious thought, a basic part of his systematic theology.

Greenberg offers two very different types of arguments for religious pluralism. In his popular work, which has appeared mainly in pamphlet form as organizational publications of CLAL (a center for Jewish leadership training in America), Greenberg offers a most spirited defense of religious pluralism. Playing the politics of the situation carefully, Greenberg walks a narrow ridge between warring camps. He builds upon Soloveitchik's distinction between the two covenants. All Jews, Greenberg argues, are bound by a covenant of fate. There are four elements to the covenant of fate; shared historical events, shared suffering, shared responsibilities (for Israel, Soviet Jewry, etc.), and shared actions (public demonstrations, acts of charity). Greenberg suggests that legitimacy is derived from and applies to all groups that share the covenant of fate. "Once having extended legitimacy, one has every right to criticize and disagree with the actions by groups that violate the covenant of destiny."[24] Thus, while Rav Soloveitchik limited the applicability of his principle to secular Jewish organizations and Zionist groups but not to liberal religious groups, Greenberg extends Rav Soloveitchik's logic to other groups. The requirement to preserve the covenant of fate, Greenberg claims, must moderate not the substance but the tone of our disagreements regarding the covenant of destiny.

Thus, the significance of the Jewish agenda for our common future offers an overriding pragmatic justification for pluralism that transcends denominational differences.

Yet Greenberg is not only a popular theologian. The form of his many publications often masks a more intensive, consistent, and systematic theological endeavor in which he reformulates Jewish thought in the aftermath of the Holocaust and the rise of the State of Israel. With the exception of "Clouds of Smoke, Pillars of Fire," which was first presented at the International Symposium on the Holocaust held at the Cathedral of Saint John the Divine in New York City on June 3, 1974, the bulk of Greenberg's major works have appeared in pamphlets, oral presentations, and newspaper articles, odd but important forums for serious theological discourse.

Greenberg argues that the Holocaust and the rise of the State of Israel have initiated the third great era of Jewish history. The very nature of the divine-human relationship is being transformed before

our eyes. Even though the *content* of that covenant has been altered
and the circumstance and interrelationship between God and the
Jewish people have been changed, continuity is to be found in the
covenant that binds Israel and God and moves history toward redemption. Unlike most of his Orthodox colleagues who speak of the
simultaneity of the biblical and rabbinic teaching, (written and oral
revelation), Greenberg writes of transformations and discontinuities,
of the shifting role between Israel and God, and of the revolutionary
impact of history.

According to Greenberg, in the biblical era God is more active with
Israel. Divine intervention includes commandment and historical
reward. The human role is essentially passive, obedient. The symbol
of the covenant, circumcision, is "sealed into Jewish physical existence, and thus is experienced in part as 'involuntary.' "[25]

In the rabbinic era, Jews were called to a new level of covenantal
existence by God. "God had 'constricted' or imposed self-limitation to
allow the Jews to take on true partnership in the covenant."[26] Direct
revelation ceased, Greenberg argues, "yet even as the Divine Presence becomes more hidden, it becomes more present; the widening
of ritual contact with the Divine goes hand in hand with the increased
hiding."[27] The Divine Presence is to be found in Torah study and in
deeds of kindness and graciousness, God is not only in the Temple but
in a seemingly secular environment.

Greenberg also speaks of the shattering of the covenant in the
Holocaust. Following Elie Wiesel and Jacob Glatstein, Greenberg
recognizes that the Holocaust has altered our perceptions of God and
of humanity. He offers a powerful verification principle, which must
become the test of religious integrity after the Holocaust. "No statement, theological or otherwise, should be made that would not be
credible in the presence of burning children."[28]

Greenberg argues that the authority of the covenant was broken in
the Holocaust, but the Jewish people, released from its obligations,
chose voluntarily to renew it again. "We are in the age of the renewal
of the covenant. God was no longer in a position to command, but the
Jewish people was so in love with the dream of redemption that it
volunteered to carry out the mission."[29] Our choice to remain Jews,

Greenberg argues, is our response to the covenant with God and between generations of Jews, our reutterance of the response to Sinai, "we will do and we will hear." The task of Jewish existence is to recreate the divine image and the human image shattered in the world of the Holocaust, to respond to death by creating life, and to continue the journey of the Jewish people in history; in short, to bring the redemption.

It is not our purpose to delve into the specific responsibilities that Greenberg assigns to contemporary Jews, to the new forms of our institutions that we have created and continue to create, to the role of Israel. Suffice it to say that beyond the pragmatic political arguments offered in defense of pluralism, essential to Greenberg's theological vision is the recognition that history has altered the form, substance, and content of Jewish life, and in the generation after the Holocaust, the nature of Jewish existence must, of necessity, remain pluralistic. His openness to history, his view of the Holocaust, and his evolutionary perspective on Jewish history represent the boundary line—the limits of contemporary Orthodoxy.

VI

While Greenberg's rethinking of the covenant is influenced primarily by the Holocaust and more indirectly by the rise of Israel, the issue for David Hartman is the rebirth of the Jewish State and the opportunity for a full Jewish life that the renascent state provides. Yet he, too, constricts God's role in history in order to minimize God's presence at Auschwitz. Unlike his mentor and teacher Soloveitchik, Hartman is less interested in the questions of self-surrender before God. His challenge is to reshape an understanding of the covenant that speaks of human adequacy and empowerment, of the synthesis between the intellect and faith.

Hartman takes pluralism for granted. Ordained by Yeshiva University's Rabbi Isaac Elhanan Theological Seminary, Hartman was also trained in philosophy at Fordham, a Jesuit University in New York City. Thus, his mentors included Orthodox rabbis and Jesuit priests.

He understood and appreciated—even if he did not accept—the religious integrity of his Roman Catholic teachers. He is not reticent to quote liberal Jewish thinkers such as Martin Buber or Conservative theologian Abraham Joshua Heschel, whose writings he treats with respect.

The streets of New York and the environment of a pluralistic America also shaped Hartman's commitment to pluralism. He disposes of the problem quite simply:

> A result of the American experience with its openness to modern philosophical currents was to show me that people can live a significant human life without making a commitment to a personal God. What I learned in America, in these various ways, can be summed up in my resolution to speak only of the value of Jewish particularity, never to make claims to know a Jewish uniqueness that demonstrates absolute superiority of Judaism to other ways of life.[30]

Thus, Hartman makes no claim that Jews are superior or unique. He merely defends their particularity and the integrity of that specific way. The Jewish way of life Hartman describes has emerged from the ghetto into American freedom, and he has no desire to reghettoize Orthodox Jews. "There are Jewish religious thinkers," Hartman writes, "who had experiences similar to mine, yet their understanding of Judaism was unaffected. They continued to perceive the system as complete; countervailing evidence was set aside . . . [they] did not feel called upon to reshape anything in their received tradition so as to incorporate or respond to them."[31]

John Pawlikowski has indicated that Hartman "calls for a new pluralistic spirituality rooted in a radical, all-embracing abandonment of previous claims to absolute truth on the part of Judaism, Christianity and Islam."[32] Hartman writes:

> We cannot in some way leap to some eschaton and live in two dimensions; to be pluralistic now but to be monistic in our eschatological vision is bad faith. We have to recognize that ultimately spiritual monism is a disease. It leaps to the type of spiritual arrogance that has brought bloodshed to history. Therefore, we have to rethink our

eschatology, and rethink the notion of multiple spiritual communities and their relationship to a monotheistic faith.[33]

While Greenberg wrestles with the question of faith and doubt, no contemporary Orthodox thinker is as willing as Hartman to minimize a truth claim in order to serve the inner truth of his faith.

Hartman also sees no need for Orthodox Jews to constrict their role in contemporary Israel as parochial defenders of specific religious observances without offering a vision of the totality of Israeli society. Independence, stability, and freedom allow for a more complete realization of the divine-human covenant, which can now address the entire gamut of Israeli issues from domestic welfare policy to the appropriate use of military might, and not just ritualistic issues.

Hartman recognizes the subjectivity of his approach and the selectivity of his use of the tradition. Indeed, time and again, he asserts that his view is *a* legitimate reading of Jewish tradition, most specifically of rabbinic Judaism. He never argues that it is the only possible reading.

Though Hartman and Greenberg differ on details and on overall conceptions, they share four fundamental aspects of their thought. The covenant is central to both their philosophies—it builds from history, from Sinai, toward redemption. For Greenberg, as we have seen, Judaism is currently entering its third great era, and the voluntary covenant will be reshaped to accommodate history. For Hartman as well, the covenant is voluntary, based less on coercion as in the biblical model and more on the loving acceptance of *mitzvot*, commandments, which mediate God's presence in the world.

For both, the image of God's relationship to the people of Israel is less on a father-child model and more of a marriage motif, where love, commitment, and reciprocity characterize the relationship. Indeed, both for Hartman and Greenberg, even the marriage motif is quite modern with greater equality between man and woman, greater exchange, and a more intense degree of companionship. And for both, the role of the Jewish community is decisive. Hartman writes:

> I do not wish to divide my world into two separate realms, one which is characterized by autonomous action based on human understanding of the divine norm, and the other by anticipation of a dependence upon

divine interventions. I prefer to see God's will for Jewish history just like God's will for Jewish communal life, as channeled exclusively through the efforts of the Jewish community to achieve the aims of the Torah given at Sinai . . . The sphere of unilateral divine intervention shrinks, whether in the community or in history, shrinks as the range of activities and areas of life subject to *mitzvah* increases. Jews can be encouraged and energized to act when they become conscious of the broad range of activities for which they are autonomously responsible by virtue of the Sinai covenant of *mitzvah*.[34]

Greenberg is wrestling with two tendencies among American Jews: assimilation and the rejection of the tradition on the one hand, and on the other, an Orthodoxy that seeks to divide itself from the great common struggle to secure the fate of the Jewish people. He seeks to keep Orthodoxy from retreating into the ghetto and from writing off the rest of the Jewish community.

For Hartman, the struggle is also two-fold. He seeks to demonstrate to secularist Jews the inner vitality of the living covenant that can speak to the Jewish future and find continuity with the Jewish past. He does so by describing the inner life of a halakhic Jew in the very same categories of adequacy and self-affirmation that characterize the modern ethos. At the same time, he is fighting those aspects of Israeli Orthodoxy that reject modernity and human adequacy and rely upon a form of divine intervention—either the messianic appearance of a redeemer, or a saving God who can rescue an Israel swiftly propelling itself toward an apocalyptic politics. While Hartman seeks to enlarge the contribution of covenantal Jews to the state and the Jewish future, he offers a more modest role for God in history and a more restrained image of the role of the Jew in history.

A generation ago, when I was a student at Ramaz, both Hartman and Greenberg would have received a more receptive audience within an Orthodoxy proud of their synthesis of modernity and tradition. Today, their very acceptance of the categories of modern civilization make them alien to large segments of contemporary Orthodoxy both in Israel and America. For some, their very engagement with modernity makes them outsiders. For others, the attempt at synthesis is alienating—for even if some Orthodox Jews do live within the modern world and not in a self-ghettoized environment, they prefer a bifurcated religious consciousness rather than a synthetic consciousness. They often prefer a modernity untouched by religious consciousness and a religious consciousness untainted by modernity.

Yet the degree to which the thought of David Hartman and Irving Greenberg resonates within the Orthodox community may well determine its ethos, its relationship with other Jews, and its embrace of the modern world.

NOTES

1. See Janet Aviad, *Return to Judaism: Religious Renewal in Israel* (Chicago: University of Chicago Press, 1983), and Adin Steinsaltz, *Teshuvah: A guide for the Newly Observant Jew* (New York: Free Press, 1987), first published in Israel in Hebrew in 1982.

2. Reuven P. Bulka, ed., *Dimensions of Orthodox Judaism* (New York: Ktav Publishing House, Inc., 1983), 5–33.

3. See Charles Silberman, *A Certain People* (New York: Summit Books, 1986); Leonard Fein, *Where We Are* (New York: Harper and Row, 1988); Calvin Goldscheider and Alan Zuckerman, *The Transformation of the Jews* (Chicago: The University of Chicago Press, 1984), 172–88.

4. Joseph Soloveitchik, "Kol Dodi Dofek" in *In Aloneness and Togetherness* [in Hebrew] (Jerusalem: Orot, 1976). Irving Greenberg translates *brit ye'ud* as "the covenant of destiny." I prefer David Hartman's translation, but will use the two interchangeably especially when referring to Greenberg's writing.

5. Jean Paul Sartre, *Anti-Semite and Jew*, trans. George J. Becker (New York: Schocken Books, 1965).

6. See S.Z. Abramov, *Perpetual Dilemma: Jewish Religion in the Jewish State* (Fairleigh: Dickinson University Press, 1976).

7. *HaAretz*, January 17, 1985, based on the injunction of Deut. 7:2 as explained by Maimonides *Hilkhot 'Avodah Zarah VeHuqot HaGoyim* chap. 10:4) cited by Yehoshafat Harkabi, "Judaism: A Call for a Change," unpublished manuscript revised and enlarged version of his presentation to the Council of Reform and Liberal Rabbis at the Liberal Jewish Synagogue in London, May 26, 1987.

8. *HaAretz*, October 23, 1979 cited by Harkabi, "Call for a Change."

9. See Maimonides, op. cit., chap. 7:1, cited by Harkabi in "Call for a Change."

10. Lisa Hostein, "Atlanta Brave: Trying Times for Israel's Arab Counsel," *Washington Jewish Week* 24, no. 5 (February 4, 1988).

11. See Yehoshafat Harkabi, "Call for a Change."

12. John Cuddihy, *No Offense: Civil Religion and Protestant Taste* (New York: Seabury Press, 1978).

13. Charles Silberman, *Certain People*, and Leonard Fein, *Where We Are*.

14. See Zvi Yaron, *The Teaching of Rav Kook* [in Hebrew] (Jerusalem: World Zionist Organization, 1974), and Michael Berenbaum in Richard L. Rubenstein, ed., *Spirit Matters* (New York: Paragon Press, 1987), 187–208.

15. See Larry Yudelson, "Orthodox Rabbis Fume: What Ties With Other Jews?" *Washington Jewish Week* (May 28, 1987).

16. Address to CLAL conference on Jewish Unity, Princeton. See report of the conference and the text of Norman Lamm's address "Unity and Integrity," *Washington Jewish Week* (March 27, 1986), and Michael Berenbaum, "Will There Be One Jewish People in the Year 2000?: Leaders Put Forth Bold Programs," *Washington Jewish Week*.

17. Several works have appeared in English. They include: *Halakhic Man* (Philadelphia: The Jewish Publication Society, 1983); *The Halakhic Mind: An Essay on Jewish Tradition and Modern Thought* (New York: Free Press, 1986); Pinchas Peli Hacohen, *Soloveitchik On Repentance* (New York: Paulist Press, 1984); *In Aloneness and Togetherness* [in Hebrew] (Jerusalem: Orot, 1976), ed. with an introduction by Pinchas Peli; *Five Addresses* trans. S.M. Lehrman and A.H. Rabinowitz, ed. Zvi Faier (Jerusalem: Tal Orot Institute, 1983); *Reflections of the Rav: Lessons in Jewish Thought* (adapted from lecturers by Rabbi Joseph Soloveitchik) by Abraham R. Besdin (Jerusalem: The World Zionist Organization, 1979). His major articles include: "The Lonely Man of Faith," *Tradition* (1965), "Confrontations," "The Community," "Majesty and Humility," "Catharsis," "Redemption, Prayer, Talmud Torah," "A Tribute to the Rebbitzen of Talne" in *Tradition* 17, no. 2 (Spring 1978).

18. Joseph B. Soloveitchik, *Halakhic Man*, 19.

19. Ibid., 19.

20. See Irving Greenberg, "Will There Be One Jewish People by the Year 2000?," *Perspectives* (a CLAL pamphlet) 3.

21. Lamm, "Unity and Integrity."
22. Gary Rosenblatt, "Judaism's Civil War: How Deep is the Rift?" *Baltimore Jewish Times* (January 29, 1988).
23. See Irving Greenberg, "Will There Be One Jewish People in the Year 2000", *The Baltimore Jewish Times* (July 4, 1985).
24. Irving Greenberg, "Toward a Principled Pluralism," *Perspectives* (A CLAL pamphlet) 28.
25. Irving Greenberg, "Voluntary Covenant" (A Pamphlet of the National Jewish Resource Center, 1982) 4.
26. Greenberg, "Voluntary Covenant," 7.
27. Ibid.
28. Irving Greenberg, "Clouds of Smoke, Pillar of Fire: Judaism, Christianity, and Modernity After the Holocaust," in: *Auschwitz: Beginning of a New Era? Reflections on the Holocaust*, ed. Eva Fleischner (New York: Ktav Publishing House, Inc.; The Cathedral Church of St. John the Divine; Anti-Defamation of B'nai B'rith, 1974), 23.
29. Greenberg, "Clouds of Smoke," 17.
30. David Hartman, *The Living Covenant: The Innovative Spirit in Traditional Judaism* (New York: The Free Press, 1985), 12.
31. Ibid., 12–13.
32. John T. Pawlikowski, OSM, "Towards a Theology for Religious Diversity: Perspectives from the Christian-Jewish Dialogue" *The Journal of Ecumenical Studies* (forthcoming).
33. David Hartman, "Jews and Christians in the World of Tomorrow," *Immanuel* (Spring 1976): 79; quoted by Pawlikowski, "Religious Diversity."
34. Ibid., 232–233.

8. Themes in Modern Orthodox Theology

Charles Selengut

From the outside, Orthodox Judaism is viewed as a monolithic religious system emphasizing a fundamentalist and static approach to Jewish law and religious life (Halakhah), a literalist understanding of Torah and revelation, and social isolation from modern culture. There are, indeed, important segments within Orthodox Jewish life today, as in the past, who hold firmly to these beliefs and insist upon separatism and fundamentalism as essential to Jewish piety. Two groups who hold this position are Yeshivah Orthodoxy, centered around the deans of religious seminaries (yeshivot) in the United States and Israel and politically associated with the Agudath Israel party, and Hasidic Jewry centered around the charismatic leadership of a wide variety of *Rebbes*. While there are deep and continuing differences between these groups and even within each of them, they are in agreement that modernity and Judaism are inexorably opposed and that authentic Judaism requires the rejection of contemporary culture and secular learning.[1]

A third category, Centrist Orthodoxy, rejects the social and intellectual separatism of the yeshivah and Hasidic communities and even some of their more stringent religious prescriptions but has, to this point, not challenged their basic theological worldview and halakhic paradigm. Centrist Orthodoxy acknowledges the validity of secular education, and contemporary dress and manners and even advocates a more lenient approach to Jewish religious law, but it has not been able to articulate a theological vision which relates modernity and Orthodoxy. The modernity of Centrism is one of behavior and form— contemporary dress, decorous synagogue services, and education for occupational mobility—but its theology remains anchored in funda- mentalist categories and, with few exceptions, isolated from philo- sophical and cultural developments.[2]

During the past three decades, a small group of rabbis, rabbinic scholars, and Orthodox intellectuals have begun to articulate a Mod- ern Orthodox approach to Judaism. This fledgling movement nomi- nally associated with Centrist Orthodoxy and Yeshiva University— most of Modern Orthodoxy's leading spokespersons have received rabbinic ordination from Yeshiva University—objects to the compart- mentalized modernity of the Centrists, as it is opposed to the isola- tionism of the traditionalists in the right-wing Yeshivah and Hasidic communities.

Modern Orthodox thinkers stress, even insist upon, the compati- bility of Orthodox belief and contemporary culture. They reject an authoritarian and dogmatic approach to Jewish law and behavior and claim that personal autonomy, religious doubt, and religious pluralism are fully consonant with Orthodox Jewish theology and law. They view Halakhah as changing, ever evolving and inherently adaptable to societal and technological change. Moreover, they argue that tradi- tional Jews and Judaism need not be protected from discoveries in the social or physical sciences, nor need they avoid familiarity with devel- opments in philosophy, theology, or religious studies.

There is no formal organization of Modern Orthodox Jews nor can it rightfully be called a movement. Rather, to use Emanuel Rackman's expressions, these thinkers are "mavericks," "rebels," and "critical intellectuals" who want to prod Orthodoxy to a full rendezvous with modernity. Though few in number, their work has been published widely and discussed in all circles of Judaism and even in other faith communities. It is also possible to point out, as did Professor Konvitz of Cornell University, that large numbers of Orthodox Jews are in essential agreement with the moderns but are unable, and sometimes intimidated, to articulate these positions.[3]

The writers and thinkers I want to deal with in this essay include Emanuel Rackman, now Chancellor of Bar Ilan University in Israel and formerly an American rabbi and professor at Yeshiva University; David Hartman, an Israeli philosopher and rabbi; Yitzhak (Irving) Greenberg, also an ordained rabbi and president of CLAL, a center for Jewish leadership training in America; Eliezer Berkovits, an Orthodox writer and philosopher; and Norman Lamm, President of Yeshiva University. These thinkers do not agree on all the issues discussed in the following pages, but taken together as a cluster of working scholars, they represent a significant genre of contemporary Jewish theological reflection.

It is of importance to mention that these "new Orthodox" thinkers insist on their Orthodox identity. They all acknowledge Halakhah, in Norman Lamm's words, as "the authoritative norm for behavior and belief" and, despite their varying liberal positions, view Orthodoxy as the sole legitimate expression of historical and normative Judaism.

An Evolving Halakhah

Modern Orthodox thinkers stress the human component in the formulation and interpretation of Torah and Halakhah. In contrast to those who view the "law" as externally imposed and wholly theocentric, these thinkers articulate a position which demonstrates the crucial role of human agency in the making of Jewish law. While traditional Orthodoxy may to a limited degree acknowledge this approach, the Modern Orthodox are distinguished by their emphasis on the human cocreation of Torah law and on the pluralistic conclusions—legal, behavioral, and theological—drawn from their understanding of rabbinic law. David Hartman in his book, *A Living Covenant*, sees the human-centeredness of Torah law as key to Jewish covenantal responsibility.

Torah . . . should not be understood as a complete, finished system. Belief in the giving of Torah at Sinai does not necessarily imply that the full truth has already been given and that our task is only to unfold what was already present in the fullness of the founding revelation. Sinai gave the community a direction, an arrow pointing to many surprises. Halakhah, which literally means walking, is like a road which has not been fully paved and completed. The Sinai moment of revelation, as mediated by the ongoing discussion in the tradition, invites one and all to acquire the competence to explore the terrain and extend the road. It does not require obedience and submission to the wisdom of the past.[4]

A much quoted aggadic passage in the Talmud makes this point in a particularly revealing way. Rabbi Eliezer declared, on sound talmudic reasoning, a particular item ritually impure. The rabbinical majority remained unconvinced and refused to accept Rabbi Eliezer's ruling. Convinced of the soundness of his position, he invoked a series of supernatural miracles as proof of the correctness of his decision. Still the rabbis refused to accede to his position. Frustrated, he sought the ultimate proof by appealing directly to God to affirm his view. Eliezer proclaimed,

If the law is as I say, let it be proved from heaven! Whereupon a heavenly voice cried out: "Why do you dispute with Rabbi Eliezer seeing that in all matters the law is as he says." But Rabbi Joshua arose and exclaimed: "It is not in heaven" (Deut. 30:12). What did he mean by this? Rabbi Jeremiah said, "Since the Torah had already been given at Mount Sinai, we pay no attention to a heavenly voice, because Thou hast long since written in the Torah at Mount Sinai 'After the majority one must incline' (Exod. 23:2). Rabbi Nathan met Elijah and asked him, 'What did the Holy One do at that moment (of disputation)?' Elijah replied, "He laughed, saying 'My sons have defeated me, my sons have defeated me.' "[5]

The Modern Orthodox view of rabbinic law acknowledges the theocentric character of Jewish law—the revealed Torah—and the sovereignty of tradition and precedent. God revealed Torah to Israel but its precise meanings and directions are the province of faithful but human interpreters.[6] The religious Jew is not just an "obedient servant" but "he participates in the discovery of God's will for every situation."[7] Torah, in this view, is the result of a divine-human interaction.

The Halakhah as the guideline for Jewish law and norms cannot, then, be oblivious of the actual conditions, emotions, and societal realities of the Jewish people. The law, in this understanding, does not exist in a social and moral vacuum. Consequently, there is in most instances no singular right, correct halakhic decision. The Halakhah, in loyalty to itself, will in different times and places and from the perspectives of different rabbi-scholars yield different, sometimes contradictory, Torah law.[8] "It is possible," writes Norman Lamm in an attempt to respond to the traditionalist critique of the lenient halakhic positions taken by Yeshiva University, "to have more than a single valid solution (to a halakhic problem); halakhic truth is not necessarily identical with absolute truth".[9]

The "freedom of interpretation" inherent in Jewish law would explain how different *poskim*, decisors of the law, acknowledging revelation and rabbinic tradition, come to different conclusions. For example, some authorities permit abortion in a case where a fetus is known to have Tay-Sachs disease, while others view it as forbidden. Some Orthodox authorities have permitted the use of automatic microphones on the Sabbath, have considered nonobservant Jews as valid witnesses, or have permitted Orthodox rabbis to serve in mixed seating synagogues, while others have ruled differently. In political and social issues as well, halakhic authorities come to contrasting positions. Some authorities, particularly followers of Rabbi Zvi Yehudah Kook, claim on halakhic grounds that it is forbidden to give up any part of the territories of Judea and Samaria, since "the land is ours given to us by God"—as part of a sacred war. Others, including Rabbi Joseph B. Soloveitchik of Yeshiva University and Rabbi Schach of the traditionalist nonmodern wing, argue that the category "sacred war" does not apply in the current situation and that the danger to Jewish life overrides the desirability of Israeli administration.[10]

The necessity of interpretation, suggests Emanuel Rackman,

extends even to the revealed norms of Torah itself. Human agency is critical not only to the applied case but to the general rule as well.

> The halakhic authority . . . must also veer frequently between antithetical values found in the basic norm, the covenant itself, such as universalism and particularism, freedom and self-control, the needs of society and the needs of the self, this-worldliness and other-worldliness.[11]

Rackman has called for a "teleological approach" to Halakhah which would seek to discover the inner meaning of the revealed norm rather than a fundamentalist approach which he views as mere behavioral execution of the Halakhah. An awareness of "inner meaning," the "telos" of the Halakhah, enables Jewry to continually redefine Jewish life in the spirit of the original revelatory moment. Conversely, a static approach stressing the behaviorism of the text appears faithful to original intent but may well remove itself from its underlying meanings.

The emphasis on freedom of interpretation in the context of divine law enables Modern Orthodox thinkers to respond creatively to the changing social and political situation of Jewry. Rabbinic law, for example, specifies a *get*, a Jewish divorce contract, to be given by the husband to his wife in order to permit remarriage. Some husbands, in attempts at revenge or for reasons of economic extortion, refuse to give a *get*. Traditionalist Orthodoxy has steadfastly maintained that, apart from some social pressure, they were constrained by Halakhah from invalidating the marriage. Modern Orthodox thinkers, particularly Eliezer Berkovits, have shown how new interpretations and creative procedures—i.e., a rabbinic *t'nai* of conditional marriage—could alleviate this problem. From this point of view, there would be room to rethink the conventional rabbinic view of the inequality of women in Jewish law.[12] Irving Greenberg suggests a pluralist approach to Shabbat. For those not comfortable with the classic Shabbat prohibitions and observances, Greenberg encourages alternative modes of Sabbath consciousness. It is not unlikely that Modern Orthodox thinkers would agree with Jacob Katz, the Israeli historian, who is reported to have said that the limits of interpretive freedom "are what the community is in fact prepared to accept as Torah."[13]

Perhaps the most innovative—and troubling to the traditionalists—is Modern Orthodoxy's insistence on the unity of Judaism, on
the oneness of Klal Israel regardless of denominational label. The
freedom of halakhic interpretation is extended to—albeit limited—
theological pluralism. Norman Lamm has referred to non-Orthodox
Jewish religious groups as "valid religious groupings"[14] and has urged
Orthodox rabbis and organizations to remain active in synagogue and
communal umbrella groups with non-Orthodox rabbis and lay leaders.[15] A particularly problematic issue in Jewish unity today is the
nonrecognition by Orthodoxy of the Jewish validity of marriages
consecrated by non-Orthodox rabbis. Rabbi Moses Feinstein, now
deceased but formerly a leading Rosh Yeshivah and rabbinical de-
cisor, declared that such marriages have no Jewish status since they
took place under the aegis of non-Orthodox clergy who are not "valid
witnesses" and therefore unable to officiate. Modern Orthodox
thinkers have attempted to develop halakhic understanding which
would recognize the Jewishness and legality of these various unions.
In the words of Eliezer Berkovits:

> It is our conviction that Halakhah has to be stretched to its limits in
> order to further Jewish unity and to better mutual understanding. In
> the Orthodox camp there are certain psychological impediments that
> have to be overcome. It is time that Orthodox rabbis face without
> dogmatism the issue of their relationship to rabbis of the non-Orthodox
> denominations. Judged in the light of the real situation, it is just not
> true that the latter, because of their Conservative or Reform inter-
> pretation of Judaism, are incapable of *Yir'at Shamayim*. To insist that
> this is so is a prejudice; it is insisting on an untruth that, as such, is a
> violation of important biblical commandments.[16]

A New Era in Jewish History

The Holocaust and the State of Israel are of considerable theological
significance for Modern Orthodox thinkers. Their view is that these
events usher in a new era in Jewish history which should rightfully
transform Jewish theology and society. Unlike the traditionalists of the

Yeshivah and Hasidic world who, to this point, see no theological *novum* in the events of the Holocaust or in the establishment of the State, the new Orthodox thinkers see these twin events as heralding the end of exile, *galut*, the flowering of the messianic age and the reentry of Jews and Judaism into the world community.

Irving Greenberg has offered a most interesting theological midrash in this connection. The events of the Holocaust, Greenberg says, are so shattering, so devastating, and the assault on Jewish life so total that the original covenant at Sinai and even its successive renewals can no longer be binding on the Jewish people. There can be no relationship, especially a covenantal relationship, where death is an integral element of the relationship. For Greenberg the events of the Holocaust shattered forever the original understanding of covenant.

> One cannot order another to step forward to die. One can give an order like this to an enemy but in a moral relationship one cannot demand the giving up of another's life. One can ask such a sacrifice but cannot order it. To use an image of Elie Wiesel's: When God gave us a mission that was alright. But God failed to tell us it was a suicide mission.

Consequently, the biblically based covenant stressing contractual obligations, rewards, and punishment has lost meaning.

> The most horrifying of the curses and punishments threatened in the Torah for failing to live up to the covenant pale by comparison with what was done in the Holocaust . . . No divine punishment can enforce the covenant for there is no risked punishment so terrible that it can match the punishment risked by continuing faithfulness to the covenant.[17]

Still, the Jewish people have, in post-Holocaust years, "voluntarily," in Greenberg's phrase, renewed the shattered covenant. This renewal of the now "voluntary covenant" is seen in the rebuilding of Israel, the commitment to Torah studies, the support of Jewish institutions, and the continuing willingness to identify as Jews, as people of the covenant. The post-Holocaust covenant is, however, radically different;

God can no longer command, God has lost authority, God cannot define the fullness of the relationship with Israel. The people, the 'am, the nation of Israel is now called upon to become the "senior partner" in its encounter with God.

Jewry has, in Greenberg's view, entered a new era in history. Put simply, the biblical covenant based upon "unequivocal command" and "visible reward" is invalid. Pluralism, individualism, and autonomy are now essential elements in the renewed voluntary covenant. Unlike past eras when Torah and Halakhah could rightfully command, the new covenant can but suggest, inspire, encourage. The path to divine human encounter can no longer be drawn with clarity. No one Jewish position is more "right," every type of Jewish response or Jewish commitment, is covenantal. The new reality of "voluntary covenant" is the basis for authentic Jewish pluralism. Pluralism is not, in Greenberg's view, simply prudent, dictated by current sociological realities, but is now based upon the "recognition that all Jews who have chosen to make the fundamental Jewish statement at great personal risk and cost" are covenantal partners. In this sense, suggests Greenberg, all Jewish religious affirmations are legitimate.

Rackman, to the consternation of rightist Orthodoxy, has similarly emphasized the oneness and unity of Jewry even in the absence of a common theological consensus. Following Rabbi Joseph Soloveitchik's discussion of the twin covenants—Sinai and Egypt— Rackman argues that a contemporary Jew who no longer accepts the covenant of Sinai—the covenant of law—is nonetheless to be acknowledged as a covenantal participant by virtue of the covenant of Egypt—the covenant of communal experience, suffering, and faith.

While not all Modern Orthodox thinkers agree with the full implication of Greenberg's view of post-Holocaust Judaism, there is clear agreement that the Holocaust and the emergence of the State of Israel represent the end of *galut* Judaism. Martyrdom as a religious act (*kiddush hashem*), acceptance of political powerlessness, and the retreat of Halakhah from full social and political involvement—all part of *galut* life—have no moral justification in this new era. Judaism as religion, legal system, and social order must now realize itself in the lived life of a functioning society, the State of Israel, and among the community of nations. Israel is not, as for rightist Orthodoxy both in Israel and the Diaspora, a mere place of refuge, but a force for the redefinition of historical identity and a transformation of the Jews' relationship with God. "The normalization of the Jewish people brought about by Zionism," insists David Hartman, "makes possible a new appreciation of *mitzvot*, whereby the social, ethical and political attain their full covenantal place."

The retreat from exercise of power is countermanded in the new context of statehood and post-Holocaust reality. Prayer, study, and *mitzvah* observance alone, once the hallmark of Jewish piety, is now, in Greenberg's words, "an erosion of covenantal responsibility." Continued Jewish existence now requires the exercise of power and with it coming to terms with the moral ambiguities inherent in power. The earlier Jewish retreat from history was based upon actual political powerlessness and buttressed by a theology of miraculous divine intervention and redemption. As a "pariah people" the Jews necessarily and perhaps ethically remained apart from mundane history.

> Under such circumstances, the holy often becomes defined by what separates Israel from the nations. For that reason, Sabbath observance in the home, *kashrut* laws, and similar *mitzvot* that set Jews apart from their environment became the focus of the covenantal passion. However, when Judaism becomes a total way of life of a reborn nation, the covenantal passion cannot be poured only into those *mitzvot* which separate Israel from the rest of humanity. When Jews live in their own environment and are responsible for the unfolding of the spirit of Judaism in a total society, they must also link their covenantal religious identity to the *mitzvot* through which they share in the universal struggle to uphold human dignity.[19]

The events of the Holocaust and the almost limitless power of nation-states for mass destruction have shattered the traditional Jewish psychological and theological framework. In place of passivity and the "suffering servant of Israel" there must now come the people Israel as an active and assertive partner in the encounter with God, and Israel as full participant in this as yet unredeemed world. A post-

Holocaust theology asserts that the taking of power is the will of God. The normalization of Jewish consciousness is "not antithetical to covenantal consciousness but is a necessary condition for its full realization."[20] Normalization represents, so to say, a Jewish "coming of age," a recognition of God's self-limitation and the increased role of Jewish activity in history.

For the Modern Orthodox, the events of history must result in a changed understanding of Torah and Halakhah. *Talmud Torah*, the study of Torah, understood in much Jewish history as the relentless pursuit of *Torah lishmah*, Torah without worldly application, must now give way for a Torah which seeks to serve as a blueprint for a full social order. Eliezer Berkovits, in his interesting book, *Not in Heaven*, refers to the "exile of Halakhah." Berkovits views the Halakhah itself as having been in *galut* because the "abnormal" conditions of Jewish history have kept it from serving as framework for a fully functioning Jewish society. Removed from the realities of life "it was forced into a straight jacket" and rendered unable to develop to meet the challenges of modern society. The emergence of the State of Israel, however, represents the return of Halakhah to its original mandate.

> Halakhah, which in the *Galut* had to be on the defensive, building fences around communal islands, ought to resume now its classical function and originate new forms of relevant Torah realization in the State of Israel. It should concern itself with questions of social justice, of economic honesty and fairness, with problems of labor relations and of the work ethos, with the social gap, with ethics and morality in public life, even with such matters as traffic laws in the cities and on the highways . . . Unfortunately, on all these issues and other related ones, Halakhah is silent today. For the time being, Halakhah is in exile in the land of Israel as it was before in the lands of Jewish dispersion. It is still the Halakhah of the *shtetl*, not that of the State.[21]

The Halakhah, in the view of Modern Orthodoxy, is fully able to function in a modern nation state with its technological requirements as well as its pluralistic culture. It is, they argue, their traditionalist right wing Orthodox adversaries who refuse to recognize the *novum* of the State and the new obligations and opportunities engendered by nationhood who are responsible for current stagnation of Halakhah. Rackman and Berkovits offer detailed analyses of rabbinic response—in the areas of conversion, marriage, work and leisure, medicine—in efforts to demonstrate the viability of Halakhah in a modern state. The possible schism facing Jewry is not a consequence of halakhic intolerance but, in the view of these thinkers, the result of the fundamentalism and *galut* religiosity of right wing Orthodox rabbis.

Faith, Autonomy and Doubt

In key ways, the Orthodoxy of these thinkers is a type of orthopraxis, an emphasis on the normative tradition and behavior rather than on the specifics of doctrine and belief. Unlike traditionalist Orthodoxy which has a literalist supernaturalist—in their words, "mechanical"[22]—understanding of revelation, Modern Orthodox thinkers acknowledge revelation as *Torah min Hashamayim* but are open to varied meanings and even contradictory interpretations.

Torah, particularly Talmud but also the Pentateuch, is the result of the Jewish encounter with God and history. There is no one external event or moment in which the full revelation takes place. Rather Torah is seen as a process recounting the Jews' religious journey. The process has divine elements or moments but these are best left unspecified nor are they issues of dogma and doctrine. The acknowledgement of *Torah min Hashamayim* is sufficient; it is this avowal which is the sign of faith, *Emunah*.[23]

The openness of its understanding of revelation permits Modern Orthodoxy to approach Torah in a less supernaturalist or perhaps mystical way than the traditionalists. Unlike the traditionalists, Modern Orthodox thinkers encourage the study of biblical criticism, archaeology of the Near East, and comparative history as means for the better understanding of Torah. Religion, in this modernist view, need not avoid scientific scrutiny but welcomes it as an aid to self-understanding.

Orthodoxy must train a body of scholars especially in biblical criticism; we should acknowledge a debt to Bible critics. They have shown that the Torah is not toneless, but has elements in common with the experience of the Ancient Near East . . . We need to understand biblical criticism in order to more fully understand our own revelation.[24]

A case in point is Rackman's recent creative study[25] of *Sotah*, the indiscreet wife. Utilizing a comparative historical and textual analysis of Talmud and Pentateuch, Rackman shows how the biblical "ordeal" prescribed for an alleged adulterous woman should be understood as a type of psychodrama designed to assuage the husband's anger and avoid possible violence. Rackman rejects a supernaturalist interpretation and views the ritual of holy water as an attempt to either "evoke a confession or reinvigorate a marriage plagued with doubt."[26] The Torah treatment of *Sotah* is to be seen as a humanistic advance over earlier Middle Eastern treatment as recorded, for example, in the Code of Hammurabi. In that system, the mere accusation of adultery was cause for execution. The ritual of *Sotah*, Rackman explains, "stands in beautiful contrast to the true ordeal mandated by the Hammurabi Code."[27]

The view of Modern Orthodoxy is that Torah and normative Judaism need not be hidden from scientific and rational methods of inquiry. Even so integral a part of Orthodoxy as *Torah min Hashamayim* and the divinity of Pentateuch can be read—as in the case of *Sotah*—differently from the literal text and understood in the context of an evolving religious system. From this point of view, Judaism is a rational religious system which does not preach acceptance of the absurd nor does it demand a faith which manifestly rejects reason and historical fact.

These thinkers do not defend any one view of revelation or religious truth but rather support what they consider to be the radical pluralism of Jewish theology, doctrine and, Halakhah. The "thirteen principles of faith" enumerated by Maimonides and popularly, if naively, viewed as Jewish dogma, is shown to have been itself challenged by other rabbinic scholars. What does tradition mean by Messiah? Is there punishment for sins? Do miracles occur? What is the nature of God's corporeality? These questions and many others of this type are shown by Modern Orthodox thinkers to have been given varied answers by rabbinic tradition, including the authoritative premodern *Rishonim*. The lesson then to be gleaned from these controversies is that, indeed, the Torah tradition is pluralistic—"These and those are the living word of God." Educated, faithful Jews have the right to decide for themselves.

There is, therefore, no Jewish authority that can rightfully define the parameters of Jewish belief—even Orthodox belief. The individual, learned Jew, at home in the rabbinic texts, can make religious choices. The rabbis may offer learned opinions but they have no authority per se to define doctrine. The current emphasis on "*Gedolim*," Roshei Yeshiva, and Hasidic rabbis is bemoaned by these thinkers. "I regard this phenomenon (reliance on *Rebbes*) as unfortunate" writes Rackman. Making personal choices in the context of knowledge of rabbinic tradition is the preferred norm. Undue reliance on "specialists" or even past tradition is to be unfaithful to the special nature of the diversity and variability of Torah. The rabbis rejected systematic theology not because they could not think "in a coherent philosophical way," but because systematic theology could not do justice to the vitality and complexity of experience.[28]

A particular emphasis on personal autonomy and on the openness of traditional Judaism to multiple interpretations is a hallmark of David Hartman's book *A Living Covenant*. Hartman offers a radical normative, behavioristic view of Orthodox Judaism. For Hartman, the key to Jewish covenantal responsibility is performance of *mitzvot* and adherence to Halakhah for motives of "mature love." There need be no other faith affirmation and no need to compromise personal beliefs or deny doubts. The religious Jew need not assume that God will intervene in history nor must one acknowledge the future redemption of Israel. The covenant as the Halakhah remains potent even in the situation of God's absence from history. For Hartman, traditional Judaism does not demand belief in messianic redemption, the immortality of the soul, or the resurrection of the dead. Hartman does not deny the wide acceptability of these beliefs in traditional Judaism but claims that these "eschatological beliefs are not constitutive of the Sinai covenant and that . . . the covenant can retain its vitality even when those beliefs are not adduced in its support or when they are given a demythologizing reinterpretation."[29]

Hartman presents a careful but extreme reading of Maimonides' dictum "the world pursues its normal course," showing that Judaism permits an understanding of the human condition in which "finitude is willed by God." For Hartman "the world functions according to its own morally neutral pattern . . . not everything that occurs in human history and in nature expresses the moral judgement of a personal God."[30] Hartman hopes this way to offer a reading of rabbinic Judaism that makes it consonant with the terrible events of twentieth-century history as well as with the skepticism of supernaturalism which pervades modernity.

The emphasis on human freedom and personal responsibility is an essential element in Modern Orthodoxy's attempt to forge a synthesis between modernity and the rabbinic legalism and eschatological assumptions of Orthodoxy. Hartman puts it this way:

> I therefore do not accept that all of history embodies an inscrutable form of divine justice. The tragic is present in human life because contingency and the possibility of suffering are intrinsic to it. To reiterate Maimonides, it is "foolish" to imagine that one could be human and yet not be vulnerable to death and suffering. Undeserved suffering is a permanent possibility of life in this universe. In "pursuing its normal course," the world functions according to its own morally neutral pattern. It is therefore an error to try to explain such a world *in toto* by means of human ethical categories. Not everything that occurs in human history and in nature expresses the moral judgement of a personal God. Nor does the covenant of *mitzvah* offer a worldview that enables everything that occurs in the world to be placed within a larger, rational moral scheme—not now and equally not in an eschatological future. Rather, it provides a way for living in a universe shot through with the possibility of suffering.[31]

Modern and Traditional Orthodoxy

Modern Orthodox thinkers, though few in number and fighting against a fundamentalist mood in contemporary Orthodoxy, are not without significance for modern Judaism. Modern Orthodoxy seeks to avoid the modernist bias by not surrendering the essentials of the historical and normative tradition—covenant, revelation, and Halakhah—while eschewing fundamentalistic avowals of a unitary doctrine and a largely supernaturalist view of Jewish history, experience, and redemption. Though anchored in halakhic Judaism, the Modern Orthodox express tolerance for other expressions in Judaism and even for spiritual groups outside of Judaism.[32] These thinkers, unlike the bulk of non-Orthodox theologians, are fully competent in classical and Responsa literature and are therefore able to evaluate traditionalist claims in context. Because they are personally observant Jews and talmudic scholars, they represent a potential bridge between the non-Orthodox mainstream and the increasingly sectarian traditionalism of contemporary Orthodoxy.

Nonetheless, the differences between the modern thinkers discussed here and the traditionalist Orthodoxy of the Yeshivah and Hasidic worlds are serious, perhaps thoroughgoing. Despite their scholarship—both talmudic and philosophical—these thinkers do not sufficiently appreciate the weight of historical precedent and accepted practice in Orthodox practice and culture. Modern Orthodox thinkers, as intellectuals everywhere, do not recognize the importance of folk and liturgical religious practice in shaping and defining a religious system. The ritual festival chanting "and for our sins were we exiled," the repeatedly expressed reliance on divine intervention, the explicit or implicit traditionalist view that Jewish suffering is not anthropologically normal but only theologically explainable, cannot be expunged from Orthodox consciousness through theological or philosophical argumentation.

While Modern Orthodox thinkers decry the seemingly unquestioned authority of *roshei yeshivah* and Hasidic rabbis, they forget that this was always the case in Rabbinic Judaism. The rabbinical establishment always shaped the tradition. Though the rabbinic tradition may leave certain ritual or procedural issues open to further discussion and evolution, the contemporary rabbis, as their talmudic forebears, have the power to foreclose discussion and deny the legitimacy of change. Put differently, change in Orthodoxy is not so much dependent upon the text as it is upon the willingness of rabbis and decisors to so interpret.

Ironically, it is the very human quality of the halakhic process which now retards it from the changes the moderns would like to see. For example, much of the basis for gender inequality in Jewish marital law is based upon the talmudic dictum that a woman prefers any type of husband—even a bad one—to none at all. In contemporary society, one could—as have several Modern Orthodox rabbis—rightfully question the correctness of this legal supposition which, if removed, makes Jewish marital law more equitable. Yet, the Orthodox rabbinate, including the moderate Rabbi Soloveitchik, have argued that the talmudic dictum, in this instance, "is a metaphysical pronouncement and not subject to change."[33] In this instance, then, the usual rabbinic procedures to affect change cannot operate. The immutability of the law is not based upon text per se, but upon rabbinical consensus. The rabbis have the power to interpret Jewish law in the direction of change as well as foreclose change in a particular instance.

The traditionalists, it appears, implicitly recognize the centrality of rabbinical consensus and transform the current established norms into "absolute truth." The right-wing rabbis now are not merely discussants or even decisors of Torah law but givers of divine law. Chaim Dov Keller, of the Telsher Yeshivah in Chicago said it directly:

> . . . absolute truth can be ours only and insofar as, and to the degree that, we can lose ourselves in G-d's teachings. The *gadol batorah*, therefore who totally lives Torah is our conduit to G-d's truth.[34]

The controversies between Modern and traditional, finally, is not about the minutiae of Halakhah or the interpretation of text, but over the nature of Judaism, correctly Orthodox Judaism. The traditionalists affirm, as did the great forebear Rabbi Yochanan Ben Zakkai, "Give me Yavneh and her Torah scholars." Judaism, in this view, entails the retreat from history, the culture of scholarship and discipleship, and the faithful but ever determined belief in the final redemption of Israel. The modern emphasis on personal autonomy, pluralism, and the Jewish reentry into history clashes with classical rabbinic Judaism and will, in this view, veritably result in a breakaway non-Orthodox modernism. Are the traditionalists correct? Or is a new Orthodoxy responsive to the unparalleled events of Holocaust and Israel possible?

NOTES

1. Shelomoh Danziger, "Orthodox Modernism," The Jewish Observer (October 1966): 3–9.
2. Earlier exceptions include Rabbi Joseph B. Soloveitchik but recent representatives, for example, Rabbi Hershel Schachter, have followed key rightwing positions.
3. Milton Konvitz, "Emanuel Rackman," paper read at City University, reception in honor of Emanuel Rackman, May 26, 1977.
4. David Hartman, A Living Covenant: The Innovative Spirit in Traditional Judaism (New York: The Free Press, 1985), 8.
5. Baba Metzia, 59b.
6. Emanuel Rackman, "Secular Jurisprudence and Halakhah," The Jewish Law Annual 6, 58.
7. Konvitz, "Emanuel Rackman."
8. Traditionalists generally assert that the Rabbis merely discover or rediscover prior given laws or procedures. In fact traditionalists do proceed as moderns but disavow the novelty of halakhic decisions.
9. Norman Lamm, "Pluralism and Unity in the Orthodox Jewish Community," Jewish Life (fall 1979).
10. Rackman, "Secular Jurisprudence," 59.
11. Ibid., 60.
12. Eliezer Berkovits, Not in Heaven (New York: KTAV Publishing Co., 1983), chap. 1.
13. Hartman, Living Covenant, 8.
14. Norman Lamm, "Centrist Orthodoxy," speech given Avenue Synagogue, March 22, 1989.
15. Participation in umbrella Jewish groups remains an enduring point of contention between the right-wing groups and Centrist or Modern Orthodoxy.
16. Berkovits, Not in Heaven, 107.
17. Irving Greenberg, Perspectives (New York: CLAL-The National Jewish Center For Learning and Leadership), 35.
18. Ibid., 38.

19. Hartman, *Living Covenant*, 290.
20. Ibid., 284.
21. Berkovits, *Not in Heaven*, 91.
22. Danziger, "Orthodox Modernism."
23. Emanuel Rackman, *One Man's Judaism* (Tel Aviv: Greenfield Ltd.), chap. 1.
24. Danziger, "Orthodox Modernism."
25. Emanuel Rackman, "The Case of the Sotah in Jewish Law: Ordeal or Psychodrama," *National Jewish Law Review* 3 (1988): 49–64.
26. Ibid., 64.
27. Ibid., 63, The right-wing Agudath Israel *Jewish Observer* termed Rackman's essay "blatant *kfira*."
28. Hartman, *Living Covenant*, 199.
29. Ibid., 257.
30. Ibid., 268.
31. Ibid., 268.
32. For example, Irving Greenberg has referred to Jesus as a "failed messiah" rather than a "false messiah." Others have called for increased conversation with religious representatives, unusual for Orthodox rabbis.
33. Rackman, "Secular Jurisprudence," 68.
34. Chaim Dov Keller, "Modern Orthodoxy: An Analysis and a Response," *Jewish Observer* 6, no. 8, 13.

9. Progressive Jewish Liturgies in Great Britain

John D. Rayner

To say that there has always been in Judaism a tension between particularism and universalism is both a platitude and a truism: a platitude because it has been said so often, and a truism because if Judaism ceased to be particularistic it would cease to be Jewish, and if it ceased to be universalistic it would cease to be monotheistic.

But it does not follow, as is sometimes implied, that the two tendencies have received equal emphasis. "Tension" does not mean "equilibrium." Not only has the balance shifted from age to age and from author to author, but if I were to venture a generalization, it would be that in Rabbinic Judaism particularism has been decidedly more pronounced than universalism.

If that generalization is true for rabbinic Judaism as a whole, it applies especially to its liturgy, which is perhaps its most characteristic and normative expression, since, more than any other product of Jewish religion, it is a creation of the people, a repository of its thoughts and longings in many lands and ages, and a daily companion and guide of the observant.

Not that universalism is entirely absent from it. On the contrary, the God to whom its worship is addressed is the Sovereign of the universe, and the Creator of the stars. Rosh Hashanah is declared to be "the birthday of the world." The penitential season is conceived as one of divine judgment on humanity as a whole. The feast of Sukkot, in one of its aspects, celebrates the bounty of universal nature. In various places the hope is expressed that one day all humanity will be united in the worship of the One God; for instance, in the medieval hymn, well known from Israel Zangwill's translation, "All the world shall come to serve Thee" (Routledge Machzor, Rosh Hashanah volume, pp. 151 f.); in the "Teach all Your works to stand in awe before You"; and in the *Aleinu*, with its fervent longing for the time when all mankind will call upon God's name, and all who dwell on earth will understand that to him alone every knee must bend and every tongue swear loyalty. There is even, in the daily *Tefillah*, a special commendation to God's mercy of non-Jews who convert to Judaism.

Nevertheless, particularism predominates for two reasons which need to be understood. One is that Jewish worship is, to a large extent, an act of collective rededication to the responsibilities which rest upon the Jewish people in consequence of its covenant relationship with God, in which non-Jews are not participants. The other is that the Jewish people's experience of its non-Jewish environment has been during the greater part of its history and was, particularly during the formative period of its liturgy, a predominantly negative one. Although some medieval Jewish authorities declared Christians and Muslims to be monotheists, that perception of them (since it came too late) exerted little if any influence on the liturgy, so that the non-Jews, insofar as they are mentioned at all, seem to be generally thought of as both idolatrous and hostile.

For both these reasons there is in the liturgy of rabbinic Judaism great emphasis on the uniqueness of the Jewish people: "Who is like Your people Israel, a nation unique on earth?" There is repeated reference to the Jewish people's high status because of its special relationship with God, "who has chosen us from all peoples and exalted us above all tongues." Israel is said to be distinguished from the nations as holy is from profane, and light from darkness. Its enemies are assumed to be God's enemies, whose defeat is to be hoped for. "Pour out Your wrath upon the nations that do not acknowledge You," pleads the Passover Haggadah in a quotation from the book of Psalms (79:6). There is constant reiteration of the hope that ultimately the Jewish people will be gathered from the four corners of the earth and return to their own land, there to reestablish their national independence under a Messiah-King of the Davidic line and to rebuild their national sanctuary on Mount Zion, where a restored priesthood will again offer the Pentateuchally prescribed sacrifices. God has redeemed Israel; God will redeem Israel; God heals the sick of his people Israel; and God will bring peace upon us and upon all Israel.

Non-Jews, as we have seen, feature favorably only in the context of the eschatological scenario of the Messianic Age when they will turn to the worship of the true God, and in the case of proselytes, who, as it were, anticipate that time. Although the Talmud tells us that in the ancient Temple, during the feast of Sukkot, seventy bullocks were sacrificed on behalf of the seventy nations of the world (Sukkah 55b), there is in the liturgy of the synagogue virtually no expression of any concern for the welfare of unconverted Gentiles here and now. The only exception I can think of is the Prayer for the Government, and even that tends to emphasize the hope that the ruler will "deal kindly with all Israel" and to end with the petition that "Judah shall be saved and Israel dwell securely" (Jer. 23:6), and that "a redeemer may come unto Zion" (Isa. 59:20).

Universalizing Tendencies in Modern Jewish Liturgies

For the reasons already stated, the preponderance of particularism over universalism in the liturgy of rabbinic Judaism is perfectly understandable. But whether it is *satisfactory*, especially in modern circumstances, is another question. Orthodox Jews evidently find it so, since they have shown no inclination to alter it. But even among them there is at least one exception to be noted. Joseph H. Hertz, who was Chief Rabbi of the United Hebrew Congregations of the British Empire from 1913 until 1946, made two changes, significant for our purpose, in the liturgy. In the Prayer for the Government, he omitted the Jeremiah verse, "Judah shall be saved, and Israel dwell securely," and substituted the universalistic phrase, "May our Heavenly Father spread the tabernacle of peace over all the dwellers on earth." And in the Hanukah song, Maoz Tzur, he emended the phrase that asks God "to prepare a slaughter of the barking foe" to express the hope that God "will cause slaughter—as well as the barking foe—to cease" (*The Authorized Daily Prayer Book of the United Hebrew Congregations of the British Empire*, Revised Edition, 1947, pp. 506 and 950).

But of course it was chiefly the Reformers who, already a century before Hertz, felt irked by what seemed to them the inordinate particularism of the traditional liturgy and proceeded to modify it. For they welcomed the Emancipation and the new relationship between Jews and Gentiles, as neighbors, fellow citizens, and sharers in a common European civilization, which it brought into existence. They were anxious to identify themselves to the fullest possible extent with the society they were now free to enter, even while maintaining their religious identity and distinctiveness and sense of "mission." To them, therefore, any excessive emphasis on the difference between Jew and Gentile, and especially any suggestion that Jews were a nation-in-exile, only temporarily domiciled in European society, destined ultimately to withdraw from it and reestablish a national existence in a land of their own: all that was an embarrassment. It ran counter to their self-understanding and their understanding of God's purpose for them in the new circumstances.

This struggle to redefine the role of the Jewish people and its relation to humanity within the divine scheme was a major preoccupation of the Reform movement from its inception, and much of it concentrated on the revision of the liturgy. Fortunately, we now possess a definitive history of the Reform movement in general—I am referring to Michael A. Meyer's *Response to Modernity* (Oxford University Press, New York and Oxford, 1988)—as well as a meticulous study of its liturgical revisions in particular—here I am referring to

Jakob J. Petuchowski's *Prayerbook Reform in Europe* (World Union for Progressive Judaism, New York, 1968).

While Professor Petuchowski's study shows a broad consensus, it also reveals a wide range of differences. What some Reformers found objectionable others found acceptable, and the revision took a variety of forms. Sometimes the Hebrew text was left intact but the translation, or paraphrase, given a "twist"; sometimes a Hebrew phrase, or a whole prayer, was deleted or reconstructed; sometimes new prayers were interpolated to supply what was felt to be missing.

But Petuchowski's book has three limitations for our present purpose. First, it does not focus exclusively or even primarily on the issue of particularism versus universalism that concerns us. Second, it deals with Europe only, so that the history of worship reform in America and other non-European countries remains to be written. Third, it was published over twenty years ago, in 1968, when a whole new phase had only just begun.

Progressive Judaism and Its Liturgies in Great Britain

The new phase began in 1967 with the publication, in Great Britain, of *Service of the Heart*, for that turned out to be the first of a whole new generation of Progressive (and Conservative) prayerbooks which have appeared since then in the English-speaking world on both sides of the Atlantic (to some extent also in Israel and France). What, in spite of the wide differences between them, they all have in common may be summed up under three headings. First, they combine tradition and innovation, mostly going further in both directions than the liturgies they replaced. Second, (and this is just one relatively minor aspect of their innovativeness), in their translations as well as their new prayers they have abandoned archaic in favor of modern English, so that, for instance, God is no longer addressed as "Thou" but as "You." Third, they are the first Jewish prayerbooks in which a serious attempt is made to take into account, and to give expression to, the implications of the Holocaust and the establishment of the State of

Israel, as well as other changes in the global situation which have occurred since World War II.

It is the last point that is relevant for our purpose since it raises the question: How, then, have these changes affected the perception, in Progressive Jewish circles, of Jewish-Gentile relations and hence of the issue of particularism versus universalism? Let us examine some of the evidence supplied by the new prayerbooks, chiefly in Great Britain but with an occasional comparative glance across the Atlantic and elsewhere. First, though, a rapid historical survey.

British Jewry is unique in having not one but two Progressive movements, popularly known as "Reform" and "Liberal" respectively. The Reform movement, which has always been the more conservative and is today by far the larger, goes back to 1840 when the West London Synagogue of British Jews was founded by eighteen Sephardi and six Ashkenazi Jews. Its first *Siddur*, edited by the Reverend David Woolf Marks, appeared in 1841 under the title *Forms of Prayer*. It went through several editions, the sixth of which, substantially revised under the guidance of the Reverend Morris Joseph, appeared in 1931 and will be referred to as *FOP*(31).

The Liberal movement derives from a society, established in 1902 under the leadership of Claude Montefiore and Lily Montagu, which called itself the Jewish Religious Union. Later it added to its name "for the Advancement of Liberal Judaism" and in 1910 founded a congregation, the Liberal Jewish Synagogue, which in the following year appointed the radically and independently minded Rabbi Israel I. Mattuck its minister. The Jewish Religious Union produced its own collections of prayers, but these were ultimately superseded by Rabbi Mattuck's *Liberal Jewish Prayer Book* (weekday and Sabbath volume, 1926, revised 1937), which will be referred to as *LJPB*(37).

Both movements grew substantially in the years before and especially after World War II, by which time they had become known respectively as the Reform Synagogues of Great Britain (RSGB) and the Union of Liberal and Progressive Synagogues (ULPS). In the last twenty years or so, the former has made particularly rapid progress, and today they number about thirty-eight and twenty-six congregations respectively. They have long cooperated with each other in various areas, including the World Union for Progressive Judaism, established in 1926, and Leo Baeck College, founded in 1956. But they have remained organizationally separate and ideologically (to some extent) distinct, and a merger attempt in 1985 failed narrowly.

Liturgically, too, each has continued to go its own way. The ULPS replaced its previous liturgy with *Service of the Heart* (for weekdays, Sabbaths, and Festivals) in 1967 and *Gate of Repentance* (for the High Holydays) in 1973, both edited by Rabbis John Rayner and Chaim Stern; the former will be referred to as *SOH*(67). The RSGB produced a new *Siddur* in 1977 and a new *Machzor* for the Days of Awe in 1985, both edited by Rabbis Lionel Blue and Jonathan Magonet, under the previous title, *Forms of Prayer*, Volumes I and III respectively. We shall refer to the former as *FOP*(77)I.

The new prayerbooks of the ULPS served as a stimulus and, to some extent, as a basis for the production of a whole new series of liturgical publications by the Central Conference of American Rabbis (CCAR), edited by Chaim Stern, including *Gates of Prayer* (1975) and *Gates of Repentance* (1978). These replaced the *Union Prayer Book* (UPB), which itself went back to Rabbi David Einhorn's *Olat Tamid* of 1856. The former will be referred to as *GOP*(75).

It should be mentioned that the Rabbinical Assembly (American Conservative) has also come out in recent years with a new liturgy, edited by Rabbi Jules Harlow, viz., a *Mahzor for Rosh Hashanah and Yom Kippur* in 1972 and *Siddur Sim Shalom* in 1985. In France the older Liberal prayerbooks *Des Ailes à la Terre*, 1913, and *Rituel des Prières Journalières*, 1925) were succeeded in 1968 by *La Montagne de Dieu*, edited by Rabbi André Zaoui, and more recently, in the case of the Mouvement Juif Libéral de France, by yet another new liturgy, beginning with a volume for the High Holydays, *Réponds-nous*, edited by Rabbi Daniel Farhi, in 1977. The Progressive Movement of Israel published its current *Siddur, Service of the Heart*, in 5742 (1981–82).

It has been a remarkable burst of liturgical creativity, as the following tabulation will reemphasize.

1967 ULPS: *Service of the Heart*
1968 Union Liberale Israelite: *La Montagne de Dieu*
1972 (Conservative) Rabbinical Assembly: *Machzor*
1973 ULPS: *Gate of Repentance*
1974 CCAR: *A Passover Haggadah* (ed. Herbert Bronstein)1975
1975 CCAR: *Gates of Prayer*
1977 RSGB: *Forms of Prayer I*
1977 MJLF: *Réponds-nous*
1978 CCAR: *Gates of Repentance*
1981 Israel Progressive Movement
1981 ULPS: *Passover Haggadah*
1982 (Conservative) Rabbinical Assembly: *Passover Haggadah*
1985 RSGB: *Forms of Prayer III*
1985 (Conservative) Rabbinical Assembly: *Siddur Sim Shalom*

It should be added that the RSGB is in process of preparing a new *Machzor* for the Pilgrimage Festivals, and the ULPS is working on a new *Siddur* which, it is hoped, will replace *Service of the Heart* and be the first of yet another new generation of prayerbooks.

We shall now select twelve "test-case" or "tell-tale" liturgical passages (with respect to the issue of particularism versus universalism) and examine how they have been treated in the new, compared with the older, prayerbooks, chiefly of the RSGB and ULPS. But before doing so, we should make two general points about these movements. The first is that, in general, while the RSGB has tended to *adjust* Judaism as and when it seemed necessary, while cultivating an image of traditionalism, the ULPS has tended to *reconstruct* Judaism in accordance with conscience-dictated principles. The second is that, in spite of this difference in approach, recent times have seen a growing convergence of attitudes, policies, and practices between them: a convergence particularly noticeable in the area of liturgy, for whereas that of the RSGB formerly tended to be traditional rather than innovative and that of the ULPS innovative rather than traditional, the new prayerbooks, on both sides of the divide, show a remarkably similar desire to do justice *both* to the claims of tradition *and* to those of modernity.

Treatment of Problematic Traditional Liturgical Passages

1. RETURN TO THE LAND

The *Ahavah Rabbah* traditionally includes a messianic petition which, in its Ashkenazi form, reads: "Bring us in peace from the four corners of the earth, and lead us upright to our land." This was retained (in a modified wording) in the earlier editions of *FOP*, but has been omitted since 1931 and has never featured in the liturgies of the ULPS or the CCAR.

2. REDEEMER OR REDEMPTION

The first benediction of the *Tefillah*, known as *Avot*, which refers to the Patriarchs, traditionally expresses the conviction that God "will send a redeemer to their children's children." This allusion to the Messiah was turned by David Einhorn, in his *Olat Tamid* (1856), into a reference to the Messianic Age, by the device of amending "redeemer," to read "redemption," a precedent followed in all the liturgies of the ULPS as well as the CCAR. The RSGB, on the other hand, has always retained the traditional reading but, it would seem, with growing discomfort, for whereas the earlier editions of its liturgy translated the word "Redeemer" (with a capital *R*), the 1931 edition had "redeemer" (with a small *r*), while *FOP*(77) paraphrases: "brings *rescue* to the generations."

3. HOLY JEWS?

The third benediction of the *Tefillah*, known as *Kedushat ha-Shem*, contains the phrase "holy beings praise You daily." This is obviously an allusion to the angels singing God's praise in heaven, and the editors of *SOH*(67), not wishing to affirm the existence of such creatures, amended the Hebrew to read "every day we will praise Your holiness," thus making the worshipping congregation the subject of the verb. But some prayerbook compilers seem to have labored under the illusion that the traditional text was always meant to refer to human beings, specifically Jews, and, not wishing to affirm the proposition that Jews are (*sans phrase*) holy, have disguised what they mistakenly supposed to be the meaning of the Hebrew in their "translations." Thus *GOP*(75) renders "those who strive to be holy"; *FOP*(77) "those who seek holiness"; and *Siddur Sim Shalom* mistranslates: "Holy are those who praise You daily."

4. HEALER OF THE SICK

The eighth benediction of the *Tefillah*, known as *Refu'ah*, traditionally ends with a *hatimah* (concluding eulogy) which praises God as "Healer of the sick of His people Israel." That is the version still found in *FOP*(31) and would have been followed in FOP (77)I but for the fact that, when I happened to be shown the final proofs, I persuaded the editors to adopt the emendation of *SOH*(67) and *GOP*(75), both of which had substituted an equally ancient text which simply reads "Healer of the sick" (Sifre Deut. to Deut. 33:2; J. Ber. 2:4). Oddly, LJPB(37) had the particularistic concluding eulogy in Hebrew but a universalistic one in English (p. 59). The prayerbook of the Israel Progressive Movement (1981) also opted for the particularistic *hatimah*.

5. INGATHERING OF THE EXILES

The tenth benediction of the *Tefillah*, known as *Kibbutz Galuyot*, "The Ingathering of the Exiles," reads (according to Ashkenazi tradition): "Sound the great horn for our freedom: lift up the banner to gather our exiles, and gather us from the four corners of the earth. Blessed are You, O Lord, who gather the dispersed of Your people Israel." As one would expect, this benediction was universalized in practically all prayerbooks of the Progressive movement from its inception (see Petuchowski, op. cit., pp. 216–20), but not in the early editions of *FOP*, which retained the traditional text (in its Sephardi version) until 1931, when it was omitted altogether. *SOH*(67) rephrased it and somewhat freely rendered: "Sound the great horn to proclaim freedom, inspire us to strive for the liberation of the oppressed, and let the song of liberty be heard in the four corners of the earth. We praise You, O Lord, Redeemer of the oppressed." This version was adopted by *GOP*(75). *FOP*(77)I constructed a version which combines universalism with particularism and is translated: "Sound the great horn for our freedom, and speedily may the voice of liberty be heard in the cities of our lands, for You are a God who redeems and rescues. Blessed are You Lord, who redeems His people Israel in mercy." (Why the editors preferred this is not clear. Neither is it obvious why they rejected "the four corners of the earth" in favor of "the cities of our lands"; but it may be safely assumed that the latter was not meant to imply a territorial claim exceeding that of the Greater Israel Movement!)

6. RESTORATION OF AUTONOMY

The eleventh benediction of the *Tefillah*, known as *Birkat Mishpat*, traditionally begins: "Restore our judges as at the first, and our counselors as at the beginning." Again, Progressive prayerbooks have tended to universalize it as well as to avoid the implication that there was once a better time which needs to be restored (Petuchowski, op. cit., pp. 220–23). *SOH*(67) substituted: "Pour Your spirit upon the rulers of all lands; guide them, that they may govern justly." This version was also adopted by *GOP*(75). *FOP*(77)I, with the same intent, but untroubled by the golden-age-in-the-past concept, has: "Restore Your judgment of righteousness in the world."

7. REBUILDING OF JERUSALEM

The fourteenth benediction of the *Tefillah*, known as *Boneh Yerushalayim*, "Rebuilder of Jerusalem," reads (according to Ashkenazi tradition): "And to Jerusalem, Your city, return in mercy, and dwell within it as You have spoken. Rebuild it soon in our days as an everlasting building, and speedily re-establish the throne of David within it. Blessed are You, O Lord, who will rebuild Jerusalem." This has troubled reformers chiefly because of its wish for the restoration of the Davidic monarchy but in some cases also because of its implication that God has been "absent" from Jerusalem and needs to "return." In *SOH*(67) it is recast to read: "And turn in compassion to Jerusalem, Your city. Let there be peace in her gates, and quietness in the hearts of her inhabitants. Let Your Teaching go forth from Zion, and Your word from Jerusalem. We praise You, O Lord, who will set peace in Jerusalem and all the earth." (A still more universalistic version is given in the notes at the back of the book as having been considered but rejected.) The *SOH*(67) version was adopted by *GOP*(75) but with the omission of the universalistic ending "and all the earth." *FOP*(77)I has: "Turn in mercy to Jerusalem and may Your presence dwell within it. Rebuild the city of righteousness soon in our days, and may it be a center of prayer for all people. Blessed are You Lord, who builds Jerusalem." (It will be noticed that the Hebrew word meaning "return" is rendered "turn," and that in the lovely allusion to Isa. 56:7, the word meaning "institute" but translated "center," is preferred to the prophet's "house.")

8. OFFSPRING OF DAVID

The fifteenth benediction of the *Tefillah*, known as *Birkat David*, is traditionally a supplication for the speedy coming of the Messiah, descendant of King David, which begins: "Speedily cause the off-spring of David, Your servant, to flourish, and let his horn be exalted by Your salvation." Progressive prayerbooks have sometimes universalized it by such devices as substituting for "offspring of David," "shoot of righteousness" (Jer. 33:15; see Petuchowski, op. cit., pp. 228–30.) Following that precedent, *SOH*(67) begins the benediction: "Cause the plant of righteousness to spring up soon; let the light of salvation shine forth according to Your word." This version, with a somewhat different translation, was adopted by *GOP*(75). *FOP*(77)I preferred the following: "Fulfill in our time the words of Your servant David, so that men are again ruled in justice and in the fear of God. Let light dawn in the world in our days . . ." Here David is invoked, not as the ancestor of the Messiah, but as the author of a well-known

prophecy about the redemption of all humanity. Since it is not immediately obvious which prophecy is meant, one suspects that the chief
function of the mention of David is to give the text a semblance of
traditionality; but if it is *tiré par les cheveux*, it makes the universaliz-
ing impulse all the more striking.

9. RESTORATION OF THE TEMPLE CULT

The seventeenth benediction of the *Tefillah*, known as *Avodah*, "Worship," was originally, before the Temple was destroyed, a plea for
God's acceptance of the (sacrificial) worship offered to him by Israel
in that place and probably concluded "whom alone we worship," a
version preserved in the Cairo *Genizah*, or "whom alone we worship
in reverence," a version preserved in the Jerusalem Talmud (*Sotah*
7:6) and still recited in Orthodox synagogues during the rite of *du-
chaning*. After 70 C.E. it was reformulated as a petition for the restoration of the sacrificial cult in a rebuilt Temple. The reformers have
generally recast it as a prayer for God's acceptance of Israel's
present—synagogue—worship (see Petuchowski, op. cit., pp. 231–
35). This version was adopted by *SOH*(67), which translated it: "Be
gracious, O Lord our God, to Your people Israel, and in Your love
accept their prayers. May our worship now and always be acceptable
in Your sight. We praise You, O Lord, whom alone we serve in
reverence." Yet its successor, *GOP*(75), has reverted in part to the
traditional text, so that it concludes (and translates with some license):
"Let our eyes behold Your presence in our midst and in the midst of
our people in Zion. Blessed is the Lord, whose presence gives life to
Zion and all Israel." The liturgy of the British Reform movement
originally had a slightly modified version of the traditional Sephardi
text, but in 1931 abbreviated it and changed the conclusion to read:
"who causes His holy spirit to rest upon Zion." However, *FOP*(77)I
has gone back to the traditional text, so that the last two sentences of
its translation read: "Our eyes look forward to Your return to Zion in
mercy! Blessed are You Lord, who restores His presence to Zion."
Finally, it is interesting to note that Rabbi André Zaoui, in his *La
Montagne de Dieu* (1968), inserted into the *hatimah* the word mean-

ing "and His people," so that the translation reads: "Sois loué, Eternel, qui rétablis ta Schekhina *et ton peuple à* Sion." The same interpolation is found in the new (1981) prayerbook of the Israel Progressive Movement. Thus a prayer which began as a supplication for God's acceptance of the Jewish people's (sacrificial) worship has become an endorsement of the Jerusalem Program of the World Zionist Organization!

10. PEACE FOR ISRAEL OR HUMANITY?

The last benediction of the *Tefillah* is known as *Birkat Kohanim*, "The Priestly Benediction," or Birkat Shalom, "The Blessing about Peace." Traditionally, it ends by praising God "who blesses His people Israel with peace." But there is also a universalistic variant of this *hatimah*, found in an ancient Midrash (Lev. R. 9:9) and preserved in the Cairo *Genizah*, which is still used in the Ashkenazi Rite during the Ten Days of Repentance; it praises God simply as "the Maker of peace." The latter version was considered preferable by the compilers of *UPB*, *LJPB* as well as *SOH*(67), which also inserted one or two references to "mankind" in the body of the benediction. *GOP*(75), however, reverted to the traditional particularistic text, which is likewise found in *FOP*(77), as in its predecessors. On the other hand, the prayerbook of the Israel Progressive Movement, not only uses the universalistic *hatimah* but also inserts "and all peoples," in the preceding sentence.

11. NOT LIKE THE NATIONS

Professor Petuchowski (op. cit.) devotes a whole chapter to "The Problem of 'Particularism' in the 'Alenu Prayer.'" The problematic passage powerfully emphasizes the uniqueness of the Jewish people as the world's only worshippers of the true God, and consists of three clauses: (a) "For He has not made us like the nations of other lands, and has not placed us like other families of the earth, since He has not made our portion like theirs, nor our lot like that of all their multitude." (b) "For they bow down before vanity and emptiness, and pray to a god who cannot save." (c) "But we kneel, bow down and give thanks before the supreme King of kings, the Holy One, blessed be He." Clause *b* has long been omitted from Ashkenazi prayerbooks because of its alleged offensiveness to Christianity. (Of course it was directed, in phrases taken from Isa. 30:7 and 45:20, against idolatry.) But some compilers of Progressive prayerbooks have experienced difficulty with Clause *a* as well and either omitted it altogether (so *UPB* and *LJPB*) or substituted a positive restatement of the theme. Thus *FOP* has since 1841 substituted, from the blessing before the reading of the Torah, "who has chosen us from all peoples by giving us His Torah," while *SOH*(67), using some phrases from the traditional text, has: "for he chose us to make known his unity, and called us to proclaim him King." On the other hand *GOP*(75), which offers several versions of the *Aleinu*, restored the traditional Clause *a* in one of them. The prayerbook of the Israel Progressive Movement does likewise but offers this interesting alternative, quoting from Micah 4:5: "For He has separated us from those who go astray, and given us a true Teaching, and planted eternal life within us. For all the peoples walk each in the name of its own god, [but we . . .]."

12. THE QUESTION OF PEACE AGAIN

The great doxology called Kaddish ends with a phrase based on Job 25:2: "He who makes peace in His lofty heights, may He make peace for us and for all Israel." Most Progressive liturgies have let that stand. Only the compilers of *LJPB* and *SOH*(67) seem to have been bothered by the thought that peace is indivisible (cf. Jer. 29:7) and have therefore added: "and for all mankind."

Novel Passages

The foregoing examples have illustrated sufficiently how the prayerbook revisers have dealt in various ways with traditional liturgical texts which seemed to them overparticularistic. It needs to be added that they have also innovated *positively* by introducing passages previously unutilized liturgically, some culled from ancient and modern Jewish (and, rarely, non-Jewish) literature, some newly written.

Of these, some might be said to be particularistic. For instance, in the prayerbooks, such as *UPB* and *LJPB*, whose "spiritual ancestry" can be traced back to David Einhorn's *Olat Tamid*, there has always been a strong tendency to stress Israel's chosenness, but understood as implying a "mission" to humanity, a concept which therefore serves as a "bridge" between particularism and universalism.

In the new generation of prayerbooks, beginning with *SOH*(67), there are, of course, many references to mid-twentieth century events, both tragic and triumphant, that focus attention on the Jewish people, such as the *Sho'ah* (Holocaust) and the establishment of the State of Israel. But in addition, one detects in them, compared with the liturgies they replaced, a more confident affirmation of Jewish peoplehood. Transliterated Hebrew words tend to be preferred to translations and anglicizations: "Torah" rather than "Law," "Shabbat" rather than "Sabbath," Sukkot" rather than "Tabernacles," etc. Yiddish poetry makes its appearance. There are passages which sound a new note of Jewish self-respect, such as: "We were beset by the weaknesses and faults common to all humanity: yet it has been our glory to testify to the unity of God, to hold up before the world an example of courage, and to keep alive in dark ages a vision of humaneness and brotherhood" (*SOH*(67), p. 80).

There are also many novel passages that express general human concerns and aspirations or that emphasize the unity of mankind, the mutual responsibility of all men and women, and even the hope for harmony between people of different religions. A striking example is a series of prayers Rabbi Israel Mattuck wrote for the first (1923) edition of the High Holyday volume of *LJPB*: "We pray for all members of the house of Israel, who, though scattered over the earth, are yet bound to one another . . . We pray for all mankind. Though divided into nations and races, yet are we all thy children . . . We pray for all who come together for thy service . . . Strengthen the spirit of brotherhood among the men of diverse faith and increase mutual understanding between them." Such sentiments are also expressed in the more recent prayerbooks. *FOP*(77) makes an important addition to the Thanksgiving after Meals, with the short prayer (in Hebrew and English): "We have eaten and been satisfied. May we not be blind to the needs of others, nor deaf to their cry for food. Open our eyes and our hearts that we may share Your gifts, and help to remove hunger and want from our world."

Summary and Conclusion

The relationship between the Jewish people and the rest of humanity, and hence the issue of particularism versus universalism, always problematic, has several times changed complexion. In ancient times the question was how a monotheistic people should relate to a polytheistic world, and a conquered nation to its conquerors. In the Middle Ages it was how a scattered and persecuted minority should relate to a monotheistic but hostile majority church. Until the Emancipation it was therefore difficult for Jews to entertain favorable sentiments about non-Jews. Although individual proselytes were welcomed, and tolerant rulers appreciated, gentile humanity as a whole was not generally thought of as playing a positive role in the divine scheme except in the far-distant eschatological future. With the Emancipation it became possible to envisage a new relationship in which Jews would no longer be exiles waiting for a return to their own national existence in another land, but partners with their Gentile neighbors in a common human enterprise. Not all Jews espoused such a changed perception, but those who did found pre-Emancipation, Rabbinic Judaism, now perpetuated under the name of Orthodoxy, and especially its liturgy, both excessively particularistic and insufficiently universalistic. To remedy this was a major preoccupation of the Jewish Reformers throughout the nineteenth century and well into the twentieth.

But after World War II, the old Progressive liturgies no longer seemed adequate. Too much had changed. On the one hand, the Holocaust and the establishment of the State of Israel induced a widespread disillusionment with European civilization and a correspondingly confident, even defiant, reassertion of Jewish identity and peoplehood. On the other hand, the increasing economic and political interdependence of the nations, the proliferation of international institutions, the accelerating speed of travel and information, and the awareness of common dangers (not least ecological ones) facing humanity tended to make for a new cosmopolitanism. And some developments pointed in *both* directions. For instance, the emergence (not least in Britain) of multiracial, multicultural and multireligious societies created an atmosphere in which, on the one hand, minorities felt freer to maintain their distinctive traditions, but on the other, social contact and interfaith dialogue engendered respect for religions other than one's own. The resultant picture is a complex one, with some tendencies favoring particularism and others universalism.

There was, therefore, a felt need for new ways of balancing and expressing the conflicting claims of particularism and universalism and, incidentally, also for a more contemporary *language* of worship. As it happens, it was in Britain, in 1967, that this need first led to the compilation of a new generation of Progressive Jewish prayerbooks. There ensued a period of remarkable liturgical creativity in which both of Britain's Progressive movements, Reform and Liberal, distinguished themselves, but which was soon emulated and further developed in the United States of America and other countries.

We have examined how these new liturgies, compared with those which they replaced, have handled the issue of particularism versus universalism. We have observed, as was to be expected, divergencies between the more conservative and the more radical wings of Progressive Judaism. We have noticed inconsistencies, infelicities, and retrogressions. It is very clear why the *partial* Ingathering of the Exiles that has taken place should be celebrated, and why it should make former repudiations of Jewish national aspirations seem overcategorical. It is less clear why communities long accustomed to more universalistic formulations should suddenly find it appropriate to pray for healing and peace on behalf of Israel alone, or for the return of the *Shekhinah* to Zion. And yet there is a broad consensus on many issues. There is little or no emphasis on a personal Messiah. There is no wish for a restored Davidic dynasty, or a rebuilt Temple, or the *total* Ingathering of the Exiles. It is taken for granted that the Diaspora will continue, and that there, as well as in the State of Israel, the Jewish task is to live and work with non-Jews for the benefit of humanity, strongly affirming at one and the same time *both* their Jewish particularity *and* their identification with the larger human family.

At the very least we have seen a valiant wrestling with the problem of the respective roles of Jews and Gentiles in the divine scheme, a sincere desire to achieve the right balance between particularism and universalism, and a serious attempt to express that balance in appropriate liturgical language.

10. Recent Theological Developments in Liberal Judaism

William E. Kaufman

Pluralism has always been a factor in Jewish religious life. The Bible, the Talmud, the Midrash—the major sources of Judaism—all bear witness that within Judaism throughout its history there have been differences of views and conclusions. The term "Judaism" thus encompasses a wide range of alternative interpretations of a common core of beliefs and attitudes, which is itself not monolithic.

Recognizing the pluralistic nature of Judaism, my purpose in this paper is to delineate and critically evaluate recent theological developments in American liberal Judaism.

There are four major religious movements in American Judaism—Reform, Conservative, Orthodox, and Reconstructionist. Orthodoxy by definition is traditionalism anchored in religious authoritarianism. "Liberal Orthodoxy" would be an oxymoron. Reform and Reconstructionist are by definition liberal in the sense of favoring progress and reform and "having, expressing, or following views or policies that favor the freedom of individuals to act or express themselves in a manner of their own choosing."[1]

Conservative Judaism today includes a right-wing component, the Union of Traditional Judaism, that holds to an authoritarian stance on Halakha or Jewish law and which, by no stretch of the imagination, could be considered liberal. By definition, Conservative Judaism is that branch of Judaism that strives to conserve the Jewish tradition by evolutionary, rather than revolutionary, adaptation to the changing circumstances and conditions of modernity. We will be interested in that aspect of the Conservative movement that represents reverence and respect for Halakha but which is also concerned with autonomy, the freedom of the community to choose which traditions and theologies to accept and which to reject.

Since our aim is to delineate the differences in approach to liberal Judaism in Reform, Reconstructionism, and Conservative Judaism, we shall be concerned with theological, rather than organizational, developments in these movements. This is for the simple reason that the differences between the movements flow mainly from divergence in theological outlook rather than variations in organizational polity, as in Christian Protestant movements. Suffice it to say that liberal Judaism in its various forms encompasses well over two-thirds of religiously affiliated American Jews and directly affects a very high percentage of the unaffiliated.

Covenant Theology

Eugene B. Borowitz has been called "the premier thinker of liberal Judaism in America."[2] He is indeed the most forceful thinker articulating Reform Judaism today. He is the author of twelve books, including *Exploring Jewish Ethics, Choices in Modern Jewish Thought, Liberal Judaism*, and most recently *Renewing the Covenant: A Theology for the Postmodern Jew.*

Borowitz is a spokesman for Reform Judaism in particular and for liberal Judaism in general in his insistence "on the legitimacy of a nontraditionalist approach to Jewish belief and practice, without drifting down the slippery slope into radical relativism and anarchy."[3] Since our concern is indeed liberal or nontraditionalist Judaism, it is instructive to follow closely how Borowitz delineates this liberal approach and argues for its legitimacy.

Borowitz is a fideist: he considers faith in a personal God to be the cornerstone of Jewish existence. He is therefore radically opposed to any conception of Judaism and the Jewish people which minimizes the role of faith. Accordingly, he excoriates proponents of secularism in Jewish life, especially when they are found in the synagogue. About such secularists Borowitz writes:

"Those, then, who consciously or unconsciously are turning the synagogue into an effectively secular institution are blaspheming a sacred history of millennia, indeed, all the history the Jewish people has ever cared to remember until recent years."[4]

We see that Borowitz espouses *Heilsgeschichte*—sacred history, and holds that such a theological and teleological view of history still holds for our time. The specific concept Borowitz defends is "Covenant Theology."

Covenant theology emphasizes the relationship between God and the Jewish people. The term "covenant" denotes the nature of this relationship, defined by Borowitz to signify that throughout the ages "the one God of the universe was using the Jews in a unique way to carry out His purpose in history. The Covenant exists to bring the Messianic Era, to create and await the kingdom of God."[5]

Covenant theology involves "the scandal of particularity": the idea of a universal and timeless God selecting a *particular* people, Israel, as the instrument of His salvation, which is a scandal to the philosophic mind. To the philosophic mind, truth is universal and timeless; and it is scandalous to the philosophic mind to assert that one particular people is the embodiment of truth and redemption.

What are the terms of the covenant? Borowitz writes: "God's responsibility in that relationship is, among other things, to save his people."[6] Borowitz does not mean that God will save his people from particular catastrophes. He is rather asserting that God will always preserve a saving remnant and ultimately vindicate the Jewish people.

What is the human side of the covenant? Borowitz acknowledges that "The Covenant did not begin with me. I came into it when I was born. It was, so to speak, there waiting for me." But he interprets the covenant, not in the traditional collective halakhic way but rather "in personal rather than legal terms."[7] What does this mean?

To understand Borowitz's notion of interpreting the covenant in personal rather than legal terms, one must bear in mind that Borowitz's methodology is that of religious existentialism. But it is not religious existentialism *simpliciter*, but religious existentialism in dialectic relationship with an open traditionalism. Borowitz explains:

> In the case of society and history it seems to me the existentialists are wrong and need the interpersonal, time-oriented vision which Jewish faith provides. In the case of law, I dissent from both positions. That leads me to a Jewish sense that all authentic existence must be structured, an understanding foreign to existentialism. Yet I am also moved to an existentialist reworking of Jewish law in personalist terms it could not traditionally tolerate.[8]

Clearly, Borowitz is striving to develop a liberal, *nonhalakhic*, personalist interpretation of covenant theology. On the face of it, this would seem to be a most difficult task, for "covenant" is more a collective than a personalist concept.

Nevertheless, Borowitz, in his most recent major work, attempts to negotiate this task by means of his notion of the Jewish self.[9] Borowitz explains that "the Jewish self has its roots in the Jewish people's historic relationship with God. The Covenant-Jew is no schizoid person-in-general who incidentally though gratefully participates in Jewish ethnicity but is a Jew/person at once, in utter existential depth."[10]

Borowitz here is striving to develop a liberal postmodern Jewish theology—postmodern in the sense that his source of truth is not universal but the particularism of the historic Jewish experience, and the method of arriving at truth is not the rationalism of pure intellect, which he rejects, but religious existentialism or the experience of the person as a whole.

Borowitz believes that the Holocaust shattered our faith in man, in collective human reason, not our faith in God. For him, the Holocaust demonstrated the weakness of what he considers the project of modernism: reason and science. Thus, Borowitz opts for what he calls a liberal postmodern theology based on the relationship of Jewish selves to God mediated through covenant. Borowitz holds that no human ground of ethics or value can be discovered. Jewish duty and ethics can only flow from God, the Jewish covenant partner, in relationship to the Jewish people.

What can be said about Borowitz's program?

The fundamental premise of Borowitz's methodology can be discovered in an essay he wrote on "The Idea of God."[11] In this essay, Borowitz lists various criteria necessary for an idea of God to be an authentically Jewish concept of God.

First, an idea of God must be such as to make possible for the Jew the life of Torah, moving him/her to fulfill the Torah by showing the cosmic authority from which it stems and the meaning and significance of the religious acts it requires. Second, a Jewish idea of God must imbue the Jewish mind with an assurance of the value of the continuing significance of Israel, the Jewish people, by virtue of the covenant—the bond between God and people. Thus, the idea of God must make life with God possible for the Jew as an individual—that is, the life of piety.[12] Clearly, then, this must be the idea of a God who cares for human beings, whose standards are ethical and who is the master of human history and destiny.[13]

How shall we evaluate Borowitz's covenant theology? One cannot but have great respect, on one level, for the strength of his faith in a God of history, a faith which can still hold to this belief *after* the Holocaust, since for Borowitz "the Holocaust was shattering but not determinative."[14] However, the requirements he lays down for an idea of God to be a *legitimate Jewish* concept leave little room for theological and philosophical inquiry. It is apposite in this regard to recall the medieval Jewish philosopher Saadya's concept of the four roots of knowledge—namely, knowledge gained by direct observation, intuition of the intellect, knowledge inferred by logical necessity, and knowledge derived from reliable tradition.[15] In Saadya's view, knowledge derived from reliable tradition is only one of four sources of knowledge. One problem with Borowitz's covenant theology is that tradition and a subjective, existential faith in the God of that tradition must carry all the weight. Borowitz would doubtless reply that he is doing theology, not philosophy. Of course, epistemology is more central to philosophy than to theology. But for theology to discard epistemology and science weakens its credibility. And it is precisely the credibility of belief in a God of history, a God of the covenant, that is problematic for a Jewish theology to be post-Holocaust as well as postmodern.

However, let us assume that Borowitz's rational exposition of his nonrational, existential faith-commitment to the God of the covenant will be convincing to those who share his uncompromising insistence that a personal God is real and is involved with the world. What, then, is the nature of authority in Judaism? Halakha is rejected in principle; what authority remains? Borowitz seems to rely on a Jewish inborn sense of duty and conscience. But if everything is left to the personal autonomy of each individual Jew, what precisely does the covenant obligate the Jew to do? Despite these considerations, Borowitz is forceful in his convictions and a dynamic spokesman for liberal Judaism.

Polydoxy

Diametrically opposed to Borowitz's covenant theology is Alvin Reines's polydoxy. Polydoxy is the direct antithesis of orthodoxy. Whereas orthodoxy represents conforming to established and conventional doctrine ("orthodox" means literally straight or right opinion, implying one right way of thinking or doing), polydoxy implies a plurality of views. Reines's Polydox Judaism is "a religion of profound personal freedom. In Polydox Judaism persons have the right to accept only beliefs they are convinced are true, and to keep only observances they regard as meaningful. The fundamental principle of Polydoxy may be stated in the form of a covenant. This is the Freedom Covenant, which declares: Every adherent of Polydox Judaism pledges to affirm the freedom of all others in return for their pledges to affirm her or his own."[16]

This is worlds apart from Borowitz's covenant theology. Whereas

Borowitz's fundamental concern is Jewish authenticity, Reines, a philosophical rationalist, seeks truth. The Polydox Jewish Confederation provides American Jewry, and Jews everywhere, with a liberal religion of explicitly stated principles and a clearly defined identity.

Polydox Judaism has its origins in the method and conclusions of scientific research into the Jewish past which was initiated by Jewish scholars in the nineteenth century and continues until the present day. The method of Jewish scientific research presupposes the right to free inquiry or freedom. It follows that the Jewish Scriptures are considered to be at least in part, and perhaps entirely, of human authorship and therefore fallible; and that Jewish religious systems have changed over the course of time (that is, Jews in every age have reformulated their Jewishness to respond to new intellectual, social, political, and economic conditions). "Polydoxy is a contemporary reformulation of Jewishness that elevates the freedom presupposed by Jewish scientific scholarship to a basic right of the entire community and thereby releases the creativity necessary to deal with the novel conditions of the present age."[17] An obvious question is: What makes Polydoxy Jewish? Reines answers: "Historically, a religion has been acknowledged as Jewish, that is, a religion is a 'Judaism,' if it has been created by Jews as a response out of their ultimate concerns. New Jewish religious systems arise when the Jews of some particular age find that the Judaism they have inherited is no longer responsive to their ultimate concerns. Thus prophetic ethical monotheism was a new religious system superseding an earlier Israelite polytheism and henotheism; Pharisaic Judaism, with its belief in an afterlife and *Halakha*, differed radically from the Sadducaic Judaism it replaced; and the philosophic Judaism of a Maimonides or Gersonides is a totally different system from Hasidic Judaism. Thus, based on the realities of Jewish history, the rule can be laid down that any given 'Judaism' of an age is that which Jews of the age say it is."[18]

Here is the hallmark of Jewish liberalism—the recognition that Judaism evolves and that in fact there have been many "Judaisms." Contemporary Jews therefore have a right to adapt, change, re-fashion, re-form, or reconstruct Judaism to meet the ultimate concerns of the contemporary Jew.

Reines's use of the term "ultimate concern" manifests the influence of Paul Tillich on his thought. In fact, one can see the influence of both Paul Tillich, the Harvard Protestant theologian, and Alfred North Whitehead, the British-born mathematician and Harvard philosopher, on Reines's theology.

Reines develops a concept of God as "the enduring possibility of Being." Like Tillich's notion of God as the Ground of Being or Being-Itself, this is an impersonal, nonmoral Divinity. And similar to Whitehead's process philosophy (in particular, his notion of the primordial nature of God—that is, the ground of possibility and novelty), is Reines's notion of the *enduring possibility* of Being. What this means is simply the identification of God with the possibility of new things coming into being.

Since, according to the Freedom Covenant of Polydoxy, every Jew is entitled to his or her own God-concept, Reines is not necessarily advocating others to adopt his concept. Nevertheless, it is important to evaluate his God-concept, since Reines believes that the essential criterion of a God-concept is that it be *true*.

How to evaluate it? I suggest that we examine God-concepts utilizing two criteria: Is it credible? And is it inspiring? Let us utilize these criteria to contrast the God-concepts of Reines and Borowitz. Reines's concept of God is credible. Who would deny that new things are constantly coming into existence in our universe? This is true. But his concept is uninspiring. The skeptic can always ask: Why call it "God"? To which Reines would reply that according to the Freedom Covenant of Polydoxy every member of the polydox Jewish community, including himself, has the right to view the word "God" as he or she chooses.[19]

On the other hand, Borowitz's idea of God is inspiring but not very credible. The idea that there is a supernatural supreme being who created the universe and that the Creator made a covenant with a particular people, the Jewish people, and is directing all of history toward a goal in which the Jewish people plays a prominent role is surely *very* inspiring but not very credible, since it involves the scandal of particularity, a scandal to the philosophic rational mind.

The key to an intellectual and emotionally satisfying Jewish theology therefore is to develop a God-idea that has just the right balance of credibility (truth value) and "inspiration"—i.e., informing us about an exciting, nontrivial, nonobvious aspect of the universe.

Religious Rationalism and Naturalism

Seeking this balance, we turn to a third "option" in recent Reform liberal theology: the religious rationalism and naturalism of Roland Gittelsohn. His major work is *Man's Best Hope*.[20]

Gittelsohn's method strikes a nice balance between faith and reason. He writes: "Reason without emotion and intuition may be compared to food which is entirely without seasoning. What is needed is a properly proportioned admixture of condiment."[21] Gittelsohn admits that we need faith to carry us beyond the bounds of reason, but he adds an important qualification: "But that faith must be built on a foundation of reason, must be consistent with the reasonable and the known, not contradictory to them. If the direction of the knowledge yielded by experience and reason be represented by a solid line, faith must be a dotted line which continues in the same general direction, not one which goes off at a capricious and contradictory angle."[22] In other words, faith must be a reasonable extrapolation from the known to the unknown. Utilizing this exemplary method, what concept of God does Gittelsohn develop?

The influence of Whiteheadian process philosophy and theology on contemporary Jewish liberal theology is wide ranging. Gittelsohn follows the founder and seminal thinker of Reconstructionism, Mordecai M. Kaplan, in seeking to develop a notion of God as an immanent "transnatural" cosmic process operating within and through nature rather than a supernatural Being activating the universe from without. This is surely sensible, for the universe is so all-encompassing that we cannot conceive of what it would mean to posit a Being "outside" the universe.

Gittelsohn attributes the traditional notion of God as a transcendent spiritual person to primitive man's tendency to personify the forces of nature. What should the modern, scientifically oriented Jew believe? Gittelsohn asserts: "The purposeful order we perceive in nature . . . the exciting though sometimes excruciating development from protozoan to man . . . the principle of organization which permeates and unifies every manifestation of existence from the remotest galaxy to the minutest cell within our bodies: all this we should now be able to conceive as Energy or Power or Force or Intelligence rather than Person."[23] In short, for Gittelsohn God is to nature what energy is to matter. Since God is not a person, "he/she" cannot intervene in the course of nature to work supernatural miracles, such as the parting of the Red Sea. What a naturalistic theology such as Gittelsohn's entails is a reinterpretation of traditional theological concepts: "God's will" means the nature of the universe and myself; "What God wants me to do" refers to my inescapable responsibility to conform to the nature of the universe and myself; "God watches over me" refers to the laws of nature which are changeless and dependable, "prayer" reminds me of my relationship to the universe of which I form a part.[24]

It is interesting that in a more recent exposition Gittelsohn indicates that he has modified the stance on prayer he took in *Man's Best Hope*. He explains: "I can now confess, as I could not have done earlier in life, that despite my rejection of older, outmoded frames of reference, despite my newer, more sophisticated ways of thinking, I often pray *as if* God were a listening Person. There is at best—let me say it once and for all—there is an inevitable, ineradicable gap between head and heart."[25]

Here is highlighted the crucial problem of Jewish theology—and indeed, of all theology. It is the gap between head and heart. It is the effort to articulate a theology which is both inspiring (appealing to the heart) and credible (acceptable to the intellect). This crucial issue is also manifested in recent developments of another liberal movement in Judaism—Reconstructionism.

Reconstructionism

Reconstructionism originated as a liberal school of thought within Conservative Judaism, articulated by Mordecai M. Kaplan, a professor at the Jewish Theological Seminary of America, the Conservative seminary. Reconstructionism became an autonomous fourth movement in Judaism in 1968 with its own school, the Reconstructionist Rabbinical College, in Philadelphia.

How does Reconstructionism differ from Reform? Kaplan's famous phrase "the past has a vote but not a veto" articulates the fact that Reconstructionism upholds more of the traditional customs, ceremonies, and rituals of Judaism than Reform. Kaplan simply gave Jewish observance a different rationale: namely, the Jew should observe the customs of Judaism because they are folkways by means of which Jews identify with the historic experience of the Jewish people—*not* because they are commandments issued by a supernatural god.

Kaplan's view was that Judaism is the evolving religious civilization of the Jewish people. Therefore, each age has its own "Judaism." But Kaplan was far more concerned about Jewish continuity than Reines, who also saw Judaism as evolving. Therefore, Kaplan emphasized the notion of *sancta*—Jewish sacred institutions such as the Sabbath and dietary laws that should remain constant throughout the ages.

Nevertheless, theologically Kaplan was just as radical as Reines. Take, for example, Kaplan's famous formulation: "It is sufficient that God should mean to us the sum of the animating, organizing forces and relationships which are forever making a cosmos out of chaos."[26]

Kaplan's most renowned disciple, Milton Steinberg, although agreeing with Kaplan's concept of Judaism as a civilization, parted company with his theology, indicating that it made a great difference to him who was adding up the sum total of all the animating and organizing forces in the universe—humankind or God? Steinberg was also troubled by Kaplan's definition of God as the power that makes for salvation, because he saw Kaplan as sidestepping the metaphysical issue. [I have argued that Kaplan has not sidestepped metaphysics but rather has an ambivalent attitude toward it and has a metaphysics of his own.][27]

Another disciple of Kaplan, Harold M. Schulweis, represents the most authentically Kaplanian recent development in liberal Reconstructionist theology. Kaplan argued that it is instructive to explain the idea of Divinity in terms of predicates or adjectives: "We therefore learn more about what God or Godhood should mean to us when we use those terms as predicates of sentences than when we use them as subjects. We learn more about God when we say love is divine than when we say God is love."[28] On this basis, Harold Schulweis has developed a full-fledged Predicate Theology as a theological option for the liberal Jew.

In an article entitled "Predicate Theology: Feuerbach's Copernican Revolution,"[29] Schulweis explains this option by utilizing an insight of the famous critic of theology, Ludwig Feuerbach, who had argued that theology is anthropology—that man simply projects his own highest qualities onto an imaginary being, who is simply a projection of the human mind. Schulweis holds that while much of Feuerbach's Copernican revolution suffers from a far too simplistic reductionism, it does contain perceptive insights that point the way to theological reconstruction. Accordingly, Schulweis maintains:

> We consider Feuerbach's inversion proposal as a pedagogic and methodological principle: 'That which in religion is the predicate we must make the subject, and that which in religion is a subject we must make a predicate. The first shall become last and the last, first. The predicates are no longer seen as qualities which derive their meaning from the Subject. The predicates are now the proper subject of theology. They assume a new status. We look to them to understand the character of divinity. The theological task changes accordingly. The aim is not to prove the existence of the Subject but to demonstrate the reality of the predicates. . . . The critical question for Predicate theology is not "Do you believe that God is merciful, caring, peace-making?" but "Do you believe that doing mercy, caring, making peace are godly?"[30]

This is nothing less than a new way of thinking about God and Godliness. Schulweis admits that for some his theology is too prosaic.[31] To use Gittelsohn's terminology, it appeals to the head but not the heart. Most people need to individuate the object of their prayer. The virtue of Schulweis's approach is that it erases all the problems of theodicy. It no longer makes sense to say, after a tragedy, why did God do this to me? Schulweis's Predicate theology is extremely clever. But, again, most people who have religious needs seek a sense of mystical communion with a unitary being, force, dimension, or creative process.

It is interesting that this mystical dimension was not entirely absent in Kaplan. Writing about Kaplan, Arthur Hertzberg states: "It is possible to discern a deep current of personal mysticism—an echo of Spinoza's awe at moments of immortality in this life, a sense that one's individuality ultimately belongs, at best and most creatively, to the very web of the universe, to its ongoing createdness and creativeness."[32]

Arthur Green, like Kaplan, utilizes the language of process in articulating his God-concept, maintaining that "God is both being and becoming, noun and verb, stasis and process. All of being is One in a single simultaneity in God, and yet God is at the same time process without end. . . . God evolves as life in the universe and on the planet evolves. The divine force that resides in the molecular structure of beings, or in DNA as well as in the stars and the sky, continues to grow and change along each step of the evolutionary ladder. But that same Y-H-W-H is also the eternal and unchanging One. We may depict divinity on the one hand as a configuration of spiritual molecules involved in a process of constant change, ever rearranging themselves like a cosmic kaleidoscope. But the same deity is also the great ocean in which those ripples of change mean nothing at all, and which one day will be still again."[33]

Once again we see the "process motif" in contemporary liberal Jewish theology. Green's dual aspect concept of God is similar to Whitehead's bi-polar God with its Primordial and Consequent Natures, which in turn is similar to the kabbalistic concept of the *En-Sof* (the infinite) and the *Sefirot* (the manifestations or emanations of the Godhead). The project of a fully elaborated Jewish process theology thus seems to be a desideratum for contemporary liberal Jewish theology.[34]

Liberal Conservative Theology

The most articulate spokesman of the liberal wing of Conservative Judaism is Neil Gillman, an associate professor at the Jewish Theological Seminary of America.

In his book *Conservative Judaism: The New Century*,[35] Gillman describes the formation of a commission to write up a Statement of Principles for Conservative Judaism. Robert Gordis, a leading Conservative scholar was appointed chairman. The commission's final document was entitled *Emet Ve-Emunah (Truth and Faith)*, forty pages in length. This was a historic document: the first time a theological underpinning for Conservative Judaism's ideology was officially promulgated.

Central to the ideology of the Conservative movement is the issue of the halakhic process—namely, how changes are to be made in Jewish law. The document unanimously affirms that in Conservative Judaism "*Halakha* is indispensable . . . because it is what the Jewish community understands God's will to be."[36] Needless to say, the right wing of Conservative Judaism, the Union for Traditional Judaism, would not agree that Halakha is merely what the Jewish community understands God's will to be. The emphasis on the *Jewish community* as the arbiter of Halakha, rather than seeing the details of Halakha as divine, is precisely the characteristic of liberal, as opposed to right-wing, Conservative Judaism. With respect to changes in Halakha, the document states that "some within the Conservative movement community are prepared to amend the existing law by means of a formal procedure of legislation. Others are willing to make a change only when they find it justified by sources in the Halachic literature (p. 24)."[37]

Gillman provides a helpful summary of what the document states with respect to the theological underpinnings of Conservative Judaism:

No human being can say precisely and objectively what God is. That's what makes God God (i.e., totally other than anything within human experience). All of our characterizations of God, then, are metaphors, human approximations of a reality that remains beyond human understanding. As a result, any statement about God as revealer of Torah is also metaphorical. God could not really "speak" at Sinai because to attribute speech to God is another one of the classic Jewish metaphors. But if God did not speak at Sinai, then the words of Torah are human words—whatever God's role in revelation may be—and Torah as it has come down to us is legitimately a human document. It can be studied as any other human document, and its authority rests in the community, for in the last analysis, it is the human community, not God, that formulated the contents of that document. *Halakhah* is thus the community's understanding of God's will, not, note well—God's will, but, rather, Israel's understanding of that will.[38]

To conclude this essay, it must be stated that the whole emphasis on what the *Jewish community* takes to be the Halakha breathes the spirit of what Mordecai Kaplan considered his Copernican revolution in understanding Judaism—namely, placing the center of gravity in the *Jewish people* rather than a supernatural God and a supernatural revelation. It is precisely Kaplan's definition of Judaism as "the evolving religious civilization of the Jewish people" that is the cornerstone of liberal Judaism in America—the liberal wing of Conservative Judaism, Reconstructionism, and Reform. The unresolved problem for liberal Judaism is: Who *represents* the Jewish community and is the source of authority?

Another future task of liberal Judaism is to develop the ramifications of Kaplan's concept of God as the creative process or power that makes for salvation, as the basis for a new "Judaism," a new Jewish religious system. This will entail further exploration of the process philosophies of Alfred North Whitehead and Charles Hartshorne and close study of Jewish sources, both ancient and modern, to note adumbrations of the "process motif." This is a task Mordecai M. Kaplan has called "a greater Judaism in the making," by which he surely meant a greater *liberal* Judaism in the making.

NOTES

1. *The American Heritage Dictionary of the English Language* (Boston: Houghton Mifflin Co., 1959), 753.
2. Jacket cover of Eugene B. Borowitz, *Renewing the Covenant: A Theology for the Postmodern Jew* (Philadelphia: The Jewish Publication Society, 1991), comment by David Novak.
3. Op. cit., comment by Neil Gillman.

4. Eugene B. Borowitz, *A New Jewish Theology in the Making* (Philadelphia: The Westminster Press, 1968), 49.

5. Ibid., 41.

6. Borowitz, *How Can a Jew Speak of Faith Today?* (Philadelphia: The Westminster Press, 1969), 43.

7. Ibid., 68.

8. Borowitz, *A New Jewish Theology*, 208, 209.

9. Borowitz, *Renewing the Covenant: A Theology for the Post-Modern Jew* (Philadelphia: Jewish Publication Society of America, 1991).

10. Ibid., 215.

11. Borowitz, "The Idea of God," in *Reform Judaism: A Historical Perspective*, ed. Joseph L. Blau (New York: Ktav Publishing House, Inc., 1973), 167–84.

12. Ibid., 174, 175.

13. Ibid., 177.

14. Borowitz, *How Can a Jew Speak*, 52.

15. Saadia Gaon, *The Book of Beliefs and Opinions*, trans. Samuel Rosenblatt (New Haven: Yale University Press, 1948), 16–26. See also Saadya Gaon, "The Book of Doctrines and Beliefs," in *Three Jewish Philosophers*, ed. Alexander Altman (New York: Meridian Books, 1960), 36–43.

16. Dr. Alvin J. Reines and the St. Louis Institute of Creative Judaism Research Society, *Questions and Answers on Polydoxy*, 1.

17. Ibid.

18. Ibid., 2.

19. *Polydoxy, Journal of the Institute of Creative Judaism* 4, no. 1 (1979): "Credo," 1.

20. (New York: Random House, 1961).

21. Ibid., 61.

22. Ibid., 62.

23. Ibid., 109.

24. Ibid., 121, 122, 164.

25. Roland Gittelsohn, *Here Am I—Harnessed to Hope* (New York: Vantage Press, 1988), 198.

26. Mordecai M. Kaplan, *The Meaning of God in Modern Jewish Religion* (New York: Reconstructionist Press, 1962), 76.

27. See, for example, William E. Kaufman, *Contemporary Jewish Philosophies* (Detroit: Wayne State University Press, 1992), chap. 9, and "Kaplan's Approach to Metaphysics," in *The American Judaisms of Mordecai*

Kaplan, ed. Emanuel S. Goldsmith, Mel Scult and Robert M. Seltzer (New York: New York University Press, 1990), 271–82.

28. Kaplan, "The Meaning of God for the Contemporary Jew" in *Essays on Jewish Thought and Life* (New York: Schocken Books), 71.
29. *The Reconstructionist*, 49, no. 7 (June 1984).
30. Ibid., 8.
31. Schulweis, *Evil and the Morality of God* (Cincinnati: Hoc Press, 1984), 140.
32. Introduction to Mordecai M. Kaplan, *Judaism as a Civilization* (Jewish Publication Society and Reconstructionist Press, 1981), xxi.
33. Arthur Green, *Seek My Face, Speak My Name: A Contemporary Jewish Theology* (Northvale, New Jersey: Jason Aronson, Inc., 1992), 19, 20.
34. I have begun to develop a Jewish process theology in my recent books *The Case for God* (St. Louis, MO: The Chalice Press, 1991), and *A Question of Faith: An Atheist and a Rabbi Debate the Existence of God* (Northvale, New Jersey: Jason Aronson, Inc., 1994).
35. (New York: Behrman House, 1993).
36. Gillman, ibid., 157, quoting *Emet Ve-Emunah*.
37. Ibid., 156.
38. Ibid., 158.

11. A Secular View of Religion in Israel

Saul Patai

I was invited to write a paper for this conference from the secular point of view. I accepted this invitation, assuming that the term "secular" includes several of its synonymous or related meanings as given in *Roget's Thesaurus*, among them being "laical" and "nonprofessional." On the other hand, I certainly will *not* make use of the definition of the *Concise Oxford Dictionary*, according to which "secular" means also "going on for ages or for an indefinitely long time." Thus, this paper will present the views of a man-in-the-street on those aspects of religion which intimately or remotely influence the life of the total Jewish (both religious and nonreligious) population of Israel.

Some Israeli Statistics[1]

a. *Division according to religion:*
The latest available population count of Israel is from the end of 1988. According to the Central Bureau of Statistics (July, 1989) the division according to religions was:

TABLE 1

Religion	Number	Percentage
Jews	3,659,000	81.7
Moslems	634,800	14.2
Christians	105,000	2.4
Others (Druse, etc.)	78,000	1.7
Total	4,476,800	100.0

b. *Division of the Jewish population according to traditional attitudes*
No official statistical data exist on this subject, and it is doubtful whether data can be obtained at all and if so, what their reliability would be. The primary problem is the lack of definition for various grades of religiosity or of observance of tradition. There is an enormous variety of Jewish communities by geographic origin (European, North African, Asian, American—each with subdivisions according to countries, such as Algerians, Moroccans, Tunisians, etc., each of these having separate and distinct characteristics, traditions, usages, prayer books, etc.).

In addition, some smaller Jewish communities lived in isolated diasporas (such as the Ethiopian Jews or the "Bene Israel" of India). Although there seems to be a process of assimilation among these different communities after they reach Israel (as e.g., shown by the rising percentage of intermarriages), for the time being they still retain their distinct individual characteristics. Hence the definition of "religiousness" will be very different according to different communities, and some Jews who define themselves as "very religious" within one group may be viewed as nontraditional by the members of another.

Nevertheless, a few surveys have been carried out, especially by the Israel Institute of Applied Social Research ("Guttman Institute"). The latest of these (January, 1989), based on a sample of six hundred, gave the following results:

15 percent declared that they live completely according to the religious tradition.

17 percent declared that they obey most religious laws.

40 percent declared that they obey part of the religious laws.

28 percent declared that they obey no religious laws.

In addition to the subjective natures of these responses, it has to be considered that some very religious Jews will decline to answer any questions which have the nature of a census or statistical study.

All these limitations notwithstanding, the number fifteen percent pops up again and again as the percentage of the religious population in Israel, as we will see in the data on elections and on education.

Two nonquantitative but important conclusions emerge from most studies: (a) There seems to be an inverse relationship between social, general (nonreligious!) educational or vocational *achievement and religiosity*, and (b) almost the whole of the Jewish population appears to agree that a minimum of traditional Jewishness, such as *kashrut* in the army and government institutions, complete work stoppage on Yom Kippur, *mezuzot* on public and private buildings, Bible readings on the radio and television, is acceptable and not to be equated with "religion" but rather with "national heritage." While active pressure to base all life in Israel on religious laws does come from the religious sector, up to now this pressure has been in practice carefully regulated so as not to bring matters to the breaking point. On the other hand, the nonreligious sector, while insisting on its right not to obey religious laws, does not wish to intrude into the way of life, customs, and traditions of the religious sector. On the whole, both sides seem to be anxious to avoid a *Kulturkampf*.

c. *Religion and elections*

The results of the parliamentary elections demonstrate rather clearly what percentage of the population shows allegiance to the religious parties. The relative strength of the two big blocks (Labor, including at various times also Mapam, Ahdut Haavoda, etc., and

Likud, including mainly Herut and Liberals) in various elections underwent very considerable changes: Thus the Mapai-Mapam-Ahdut block in 1961 had fifty-nine mandates (42+9+8), it had only thirty-one in 1977, and again forty-four in 1984. The Likud block had thirty-four mandates (17+17) in 1961, forty-two in 1977 and forty-one in 1984. At the same time, various small parties appeared and disappeared with 2 to 3 and in one case (Shinnui, 1977) even eight mandates.

The political allegiance of the religious voters seems to be much more constant, as shown in the following Table:

Table 2

Parties	1961	1969	1977	1984	1988
National religious	12	12	12	5	5
Shas	—	—	—	4	6
Aguda + PAI	6	6	5	3	5
Tami	—	—	—	1	—
Degel Hatorah	—	—	—	—	2
All religious parties°°°	18(15%)	18(15%)	17(14%)	13(11%)	18(15%)
Ma'arakh	59	56	31	44	42
Likud	34	26	42	41	40
	111	100	90	98	100

°°° (means out of 120)

The constancy of the religious voters at about 15 percent made it almost obligatory for every Israeli government to include the religious parties in order to achieve stability. Indeed this was the case up to now with every government without exception. This of course meant and means that the requirements and demands of the religious parties have to be considered in the Knesset and its legislation well over what is objectively due to the percentage representation of the religious parties.

d. *Religion in the educational system*

TABLE 3

Jewish primary schools (age group 5–13)

	1960 %	1970 %	1980 %	1988 %
State	66.9	65.6	74.2	72.2
State religious	26.5	27.8	20.1	21.0
Independent (Aguda)	6.6	6.6	5.7	6.8
Haredi (Talmud Tora + Bet Yakov-girls)	~2.0	~2.0	~2.0	
(Total)	(358,000)	(376,000)	(425,000)	(472,000)

Jewish intermediate schools (13–15)

State	62.5	75.6	82.7	
State religious	37.0	23.0	16.7	
(Total)	(8,000)	(73,000)	(113,000)	

Secondary (high) schools (16–18)

State	74.4	73.8	75.5	
State religious	21.9	22.2	18.9	
Independent	3.7	4.0	5.6	
(Total)	(130,000)	(144,000)	(199,000)	

The nature of the supervision shows strong differences in the emphasis laid upon various subjects in different schools, in the twelfth (prematriculation) grade. This is, at least theoretically, the decision of the pupils themselves and it is impossible to assess to what extent (if any) the teaching staff or the home environment is responsible for these differences (note that the subjects can be studied at various levels, expressed in "study units" between 1 [minimum] and 5 [maximum]).

Among the compulsory subjects, the sciences—geography, physics, chemistry, biology, and mathematics—are preferred roughly to the same extent in general and religious schools, and the same is true for English. Naturally, Bible studies are preferred in religious schools (98.5 percent take 3 to 5 units, compared to only 45 percent in general schools), and the corresponding numbers in the study of "Oral Law" are 99.8 percent in religious schools, compared to 1.2 percent (!!) in general ones. Pupils of general schools tend to learn more history and literature, while social sciences are chosen between 1 to 5 units in the general schools by 77 percent of the pupils and only by 15 percent of the religious pupils.

Some interesting trends are shown in the optional subjects:

TABLE 4

Subjects	General schools %	Religious schools %	Units
Computer	24	49	1–4
Philosophy	5	62	1–2
(incl. Jewish thought)	—	10	3–5
Land of Israel	8	13	1–5
Arabic	43	17	1–5
French	26	5	1–5
Music	9	0.3	1–5
Plastic Arts	11	5	1–5

Computer studies seem to be an exception which proves the case, but in the other optionals it is obvious that religious pupils are much more interested in Jewish subjects (which, due to their background, are also easier for them to study) and less interested in languages other than Hebrew.

e. *Higher education*

The number of university students in Israel in 1987–88 was about seventy thousand. Naturally, the background of the students influences their choice of subjects, and it can be assumed that the number of religious students in Bible, Talmud, Jewish philosophy, and related subjects will be relatively higher; however, no statistics exist. All departments are closed on the Sabbath and holidays, although staff and advanced students can obtain keys and have access to laboratories and libraries, as far as safety laws permit. Most sports facilities (e.g., swimming pools) are open. Restaurants, mensa and faculty clubs are kosher.

Bar Ilan University is the only university in Israel that is run according to traditional lines and integrates traditional learning with secular studies. Nonreligious (also Arab) students are accepted. There are nearly ten thousand students, about half religious, and about two hundred Arab students. All Jewish students are obliged to devote about 15 to 20 percent of their study time to Jewish, religious, and traditional subjects, according to individual study-plans prepared for them by staff members. These studies include Bible, Talmud, Jewish philosophy, etc. During these lessons (but not during others and not generally on the campus), they are expected to have their heads covered and to behave "generally in accordance with Jewish customs and traditions honoring the values of the institution." The staff includes a rabbi, who works in close cooperation with the dean of students. Together they organize seminars and study-days on traditional subjects and problems in Jewish law. Attendance in these is very good, and the staff sociologists believe there is a definite meeting of minds between the religious and nonreligious, including new immigrants coming from completely areligious milieus.

There are many Arab girls who wish to be accepted, since their parents prefer them to study in a religious (traditional, moral) atmosphere, albeit Jewish.

e. *Publications*

In 1986–87, 5,300 books (including textbooks) were published in Israel. Among these, only 168 or circa 3 percent were classified as "Judaism" (e.g., compared with 207 in social and behavioral sciences and 135 in economics). These numbers can be seen as indicative of the secular nature of Israel, or at least of the Israeli publishing trade.

Laws and Legislation

Jewish religious laws in the Bible and in the Talmud embrace in enormous detail all aspects of life. Following these laws almost certainly ensured the survival of Judaism throughout the ages. However, the appearance of Zionism and the creation of the State of Israel made it possible for Jews (and especially for Israelis) to feel and declare themselves definitely Jews and/or Israelis, even if completely secular. This dichotomy is strongly felt in many aspects of Israeli life and strongly influences even an institution as secular as the Israeli Knesset.

Thus, one of the first laws enacted by the first Knesset, in 1948 in the very first months of statehood, was the law of kosher food for soldiers. About two years passed before the proclamation of the Law of Return, which already contains the seeds of the controversy over who is a Jew (and therefore who is entitled to claim Israeli citizenship by virtue of the Law of Return). The law defining the jurisdiction of the Rabbinical Courts (1953) decreed that all Jewish marriages and divorces are subject to this court, and through it, to religious laws. Some of the most controversial issues are included in this provision,—e.g., the *Halitzah*, according to which a man is obliged to marry the childless widow of his brother, unless he submits to a ceremony in which the widow removes his sandal and spits at him. Again, a Kohen is not allowed to marry a divorced woman (even though the marriage, once performed, remains valid), and a woman, whose husband is missing but was not proven dead to the satisfaction of the Rabbinical Court, cannot remarry.

While in theory in Israel only religious marriages exist, in practice civil marriages contracted abroad are also acknowledged. Such marriages were usually performed in Cyprus, this being the nearest available country, although a civil marriage is possible even without travel, by sending a power of attorney abroad. Lately, Shulamit Aloni, M.P. has advocated that couples not willing to undergo a religious marriage ceremony should enter into a civil contract regulating the personal and financial relationships between them.

Since a (religious) divorce is impossible without the consent of the husband, the Rabbinical Court is empowered to (and often does) send a husband to jail until he agrees to a divorce. This usually (although by no means always) helps.

Burials do not have to be performed according to religious rituals, since no such legislation exists. However, in practice there is no other way of burial but through the religious burial societies, in the cemeteries maintained by them.

Opting out from Judaism is difficult, almost impossible. The religious principle is that "A Jew, even if he sins, remains a Jew." According to the British Mandatory law, a change of religion was possible if the accepting religious authorities sent an official notice to the State, when the person was registered in his new religion. This procedure, however, was not and is not recognized by the rabbinate.

The "prohibition of pig breeding" law (1962) is in force in all of Israel, except areas where the majority of the population is not Jewish. The sale of pork (in shops and in restaurants) is usually prohibited by municipal laws. Nevertheless, throughout Israel, even in purely Jewish quarters, pork is freely available and is served in a large number of the restaurants.

Rabbinical Courts or Rabbinical Councils deal also with matters of circumcision, and practically every Jewish child is circumcised, although a growing percentage is done in hospitals (by doctors, not by *Mohalim*). Supervision of *kashrut* and granting of *kashrut* certificates is also the responsibility of the rabbinate, and often this has assumed wider powers than was intended in the law (e.g., *kashrut* certificates were withdrawn from a hotel restaurant because the appearance of a belly dancer, which is not relevant to the issue).

On the whole, it can be said that there is a tendency, on the part of the legislature, to incorporate the principles of Jewish law into new laws enacted by the Knesset, after studying them carefully and ascertaining whether such laws can be kept in a modern state. Thus, there is no controversy regarding the basic principles of not working on the Sabbath, while at the same time it is quite clear that this cannot and should not mean the interruption of public services such as electricity, water supply, etc.

Medicine

According to Jewish law, it is an overriding duty to save a human life, even if this involves work prohibited on holy days. Hence hospitals perform all necessary functions on holy days, although religious hospitals will tend to cut down activities to a minimum and employ non-Jewish personnel if possible.

If a religious doctor believes his presence is necessary at the side of his patient, he will (and is allowed by religion) drive on the Sabbath to reach the patient and attend to him. However, once the emergency has passed, he will either stay in the hospital until the end of the Sabbath, or walk home. Similarly, medical apparatus, elevators, etc., may be used in an emergency but not routinely.

The principle of "life-saving" is regarded differently by different religious communities. Thus, especially the extremely religious *Haredi* community has a rather fatalistic attitude, and believes that if a man's fate is to die, his life should not be prolonged by artificial means. This, in their view, includes also transplant surgery, which they forbid completely. Less extreme communities submit to the decision of the rabbinate, according to which it is allowed to transplant organs, on condition that the donor was dead and his family agreed.

Kohanim are forbidden to enter cemeteries or to approach dead bodies. This influences the architecture of hospitals, where the anatomy rooms and the mortuary will be separated from the main body of the building by revolving doors or double doors. This causes minor problems in the study, and later the practice, of medicine by *Kohanim*, who have to undergo ritual purification (by immersion in a *mikveh*) after they become impure by contact with dead bodies.

Everyday Life

As we have seen before, there are major differences in observances among the various more or less religious communities. State or municipal laws do not extend to all aspects of everyday life, and even when such laws do exist, they very often limit activities on paper only, but not in practice.

Commerce and industry: In the Jewish sector, Sabbath observance coincides with social legislation making a rest day obligatory. Thus the large majority of shops, factories, construction sites, etc., are closed. Nevertheless, permits for Sabbath work can be obtained, e.g., in the case of some production lines which cannot be shut down. Various minor enterprises operate without an official license, such as street vendors, farmers, and, of course, most hotel services. In kosher hotels, no food is prepared on the Sabbath, and meals are either kept warm from Friday evening or else served cold. Nonkosher hotels provide full services on holidays.

Public services: Electricity, water, telephone, radio, television—all work on the Sabbath. Post offices are closed—one can phone or send a facsimile on holidays but one cannot send a cable or a facsimile from the post office.

Transport: There are no rail services on holidays at all and no flights by ELAL, the Israeli airline. However, Ben-Gurion airport does operate normally for all other flights.

Buses run by the big cooperatives (Egged, Dan) do not run on Sabbath and holidays in most parts of Israel, except in Haifa, Nazareth, and East Jerusalem. Private companies run buses regularly between central Tel-Aviv and the Herzlia beach hotels, and on various other minor routes. In addition, excursion buses both for tourists and for Israelis run all over Israel.

A network of "shared taxis" (*sherut*) connects regularly all big (and not so big) cities in Israel and runs also within the major towns. About half of the service stations are open on holidays.

Museums and galleries are usually open, although as a rule, not the ticket offices. Tickets can be bought in advance and in most cases also from an "unofficial" ticket vendor who operates near the entrance.

Movies, theaters, and concerts: A growing number of movie theaters are now operating on Friday nights also, both in the regular commercial movie houses and in the so-called cinematheques. In many places, municipal legislation forbidding this exists, but is not enforced. The major theaters do not perform on Friday night, but the minor ones (especially "theater-clubs" and such) do. Similarly, there are no major concerts on Friday night.

Restaurants: All nonkosher restaurants are open on holidays. In most hotels, kosher meals are also served but only to customers paying in advance.

Places of outdoor entertainment: Tourist sites, zoos, safari parks, beaches, and playgrounds operate on the Sabbath and holidays, some with and some without licenses.

Some Special Cases

a. *The case of Brother Daniel*

Daniel Rufeisen was a Jew who converted to Catholicism and became a Carmelite monk. Since, according to the Rabbinical code, "a Jew remains a Jew even if he sins," his Jewishness, although debatable, could not be denied. Brother Daniel submitted to the Israeli authorities a request for Israeli citizenship, on the basis of the Law of Return (1950), and argued that since he was a Jew, it was his right automatically to become, upon immigration, an Israeli citizen. The religious authorities did not express an opinion on the case, but if pressed, would probably have had to accept Brother Daniel's argument. The case reached the Supreme Court, which by majority vote decided that the term "Jew" for the purposes of the Law of Return, does have to be interpreted according to its popular, commonsense meaning, so that a Catholic priest cannot be a Jew and the Law of Return does not apply to Brother Daniel. Brother Daniel later, nevertheless, became an Israeli citizen, after he resided the required number of years in Israel.

b. *The case of Judea and Samaria*

In July 1989, the Chief Rabbinate issued a "halakhic decision" that the Torah did not permit making territorial concessions in the Land of Israel, including all territories liberated in the Six-Day War of 1967, not even for the sake of obtaining peace. This decision extended a previous ruling issued many years before and related to the 1948 borders of Israel.

Controversy raged among various religious camps and communities. Former Sephardi Chief Rabbi Ovadiah Yosef was reported by the newspapers to have told Egyptian President Hosni Mubarak, that

Yosef did not agree with the rabbinate's ruling and was quoted to have said, "By the law, we must hold on to all territories now under Israeli rule. However, since you are willing to kill Jews unless we retreat, then we must withdraw so as not to lose lives." In a reaction to this, the Chief Rabbinate rejected Yosef's view and reiterated that Israel had to be kept whole even in the face of "danger to life" (*piquah nefesh*), when most other laws could be broken.

Later, again according to the press, the Chief Rabbinate explained that the ruling was only one expanding the religious law and did not necessarily apply to political realities.

Conclusion and Hope

Both the religious and nonreligious camps in Israel will claim in the press, electronic media, and public debates, that the influence of the other side is constantly growing in the country. It is our belief that only an extremely small minority of each side (*Haredim* and violent anti-religionists) negates the rights and views of the other side. The over-whelmingly large majority, while often quarreling, quarrel as brothers do, not forgetting the brotherhood, albeit a brotherhood with widely divergent views and attitudes. In the quarter where I live, my neighbors often tell me that it is becoming "overrun by the religious," but I do not believe that statistical study would show more than a minor population movement from more religious to less religious quarters. What is true is that, in the last ten years or so, the percentage of religious immigrants has grown. However, I have yet to meet an Israeli who would prefer that the religious Jews should remain in the Diaspora!

I have spent a lifetime in Jerusalem and have seen many Jews coming to the city and leaving it in the course of fifty years. I felt the repercussions of five wars, saw more troubled times and less troubled times, and even though I never saw real peace in Jerusalem, the "City of Peace," I am still an optimist. I believe in the fulfillment of the Zionist ideal and in a future in which religious and nonreligious Jews will live in harmony side by side, as well as with their Muslim and Christian neighbors.

NOTES

1. Most of the numerical data in this paper have been taken from the *Statistical Abstract of Israel*, no. 39 (1988), published by the Central Bureau of Statistics, Jerusalem, Israel.

12. Toward a Post-Zionist Model of Jewish Life

David M. Gordis

Any attempt to characterize the history of a complex group in one-dimensional terms runs the risk of reductionism and distortion. This is certainly true of Jewish history. Salo Baron warned against the inadequacies of the "lachrymose conception of Jewish history" which viewed the record of the Jewish past as nothing more than a series of devastating catastrophes. Among other things, this limited understanding of Jewish reality ignored the internal intellectual and spiritual life of the people. Purely economic interpretations of Jewish history and even social histories are similarly incomplete accounts of the rich and multifaceted phenomenon of Jewish reality.

Jewish History as a Series of Transformations

It is not only the intricacy of the Jewish experience at any one time that challenges the observer but also the dynamic quality of Jewish reality. Jewish history ought to be viewed as a series of transformations in the political, intellectual, and social conditions of the Jewish people; its internal structures and mind-sets together with its inter-relationships with the larger society. Exiles and expulsions transformed demographic realities; the repeated encounters with new cultures restructured Jewish institutions, transmuted the approach of Jews to fundamental questions of human existence, and even altered their linguistic patterns which constitute not only semantic conventions but also the categories by which reality is conceived and manipulated. Some of the most tragic and cataclysmic transformations were inflicted on the community from without. However, those transformations which were the product of internal dynamics were often of the greatest fundamental significance because they represented paradigmatic shifts in the perception of the essence of Judaism and of what community priorities should be. These transformations were sometimes dramatic and visible. At other times they were more subtle. Some transformations imposed themselves on the consciousness of members of the community; others tended to be overlooked. Whatever their nature, it may well be that the only persistent pattern in Jewish history has been that of transformation itself.

The mutability of Jewish history is of more than historical interest. The Jewish people wishes to ensure for itself a secure and creative future. Its success will depend on its ability to maintain sufficient elements of continuity in communal and personal patterns of thought and behavior, to sustain a recognizable Jewish character while at the same time assimilating change and adjusting to it. This composite ability has been the key to Jewish survival in the past, and it continues to be the key for the future. A community which ignores change and fails to adjust appropriately while still maintaining its fundamental character is a community whose survival is at risk. Insufficiently alert to changing realities, both within itself and outside, which affect its vital concerns, such a community retains obsolete institutions, rather than reshaping and remolding them. It preserves outdated slogans and formulations which become increasingly irrelevant. Finally, it freezes ideological mind-sets in ways that preclude effective planning, all this producing a pattern of communal decision making which cannot sustain the community's existence and vitality.

Zionism as a Radical Transformation of Jewish History

The appearance of the Zionist movement represented a radical transformation of the Jewish people's self-understanding. Its impact on the Jewish community was revolutionary because it offered a new, secular alternative to the earlier traditionalist religious ideologies which had already been undermined by the twin battering rams of Enlightenment and Emancipation. It proferred at least the beginnings of a new Jewish political theory, one in which Jews were to return to the stage of political history from their earlier primary role as principals in a purely celestial drama of redemption and messianism. The new political theory, a Jewish version of modern nationalism, required a drastically revised Jewish historiosophy and historiography; history as the playing out of the divine plan no longer sufficed. Catastrophe could no longer be satisfactorily explained as the divine response to human sinfulness, and redemption could no longer await the divine reward for the people's return to God's path. Imposed in part, to be sure, by the failure of Jewish emancipation and integration to solve the "Jewish problem" and by the continued vigor of anti-Semitism, it became a profoundly important new ideology because it transformed the Jewish people's self-image radically and ultimately required of it a totally new program with new structures to implement it.

Zionism was a stunning success in its fundamental objective, the reestablishment of sovereign Jewish national existence, even though the path was arduous and formidable. Political, social, and economic instruments had to be created to advance the program. Platforms were devised, political forces mobilized, economic means generated, heroes sprung, language formulated, and organizational skills honed. The vast majority of the Jewish people was exhilarated by the vision and motivated to achieve its realization. The efforts were crowned with triumph; the State of Israel was established. Indeed, not only was the state created, but also her achievements and successes have been remarkable, though at times like these they are too often underestimated or overlooked. Despite enormous burdens of defense and absorption, a modern economy has been created which provides a high standard of living for its citizens. This achievement deserves a greater degree of appreciation than it receives, for awareness of it is sometimes overwhelmed by the persistence of imposing economic problems. Creating and maintaining both democratic institutions and an awesome military capacity with limited resources and under constant threat of war are similarly remarkable achievements. Without doubt, the most significant accomplishment, both politically and sociopsychologically, is that by reestablishing Jewish national existence, the Zionist movement empowered the Jewish people and restored it to the stage of world history. This radical transformation from powerlessness to power was anticipated in part by the Zionist movement but certainly not to the extent that it has been realized. It was certainly expected that the Jewish people would attain a more normal life and solve, at least in part, the problem of its existence as alien appendages to inhospitable and hostile host societies. It was not anticipated that through the State of Israel the Jewish people would become a major player in world events.

To this day, the Jewish people has not come to terms sufficiently with this fundamental transformation. To a great extent, the Jewish self-perception remains grounded in a sense of Jewish powerlessness, understandably conditioned, no doubt, by the impact of the Holocaust. Thus, Jewish organizations in the United States spend vast sums on anti-Semitism-related projects, far more than is necessary to maintain vigilance and deal effectively with the problem as it exists there. Criticism of individual Jews or of one or another Israeli policy often invokes exaggerated responses from Jewish communal organizations, responses which seem to reflect a vacillation between an unrealistic self-confidence bordering on triumphalism on the one hand and an exaggerated sense of helplessness and vulnerability on the other. In short, the community has not developed a balanced and coherent response to Jewish empowerment. Nevertheless, the transformation has occurred, and the Jewish people must adjust to this new reality if the structure of Jewish life, its agenda and its program, are to be appropriate to its present condition and effective in dealing with that condition and planning for the future.

The Meaning of Zionism After the Establishment of the State of Israel

Coinciding with the establishment of the State of Israel, there began the debate over the meaning of Zionism and its continuing relevance after the achievement of its fundamental objective. A program for the Zionist movement was formulated soon after the establishment of the state and was debated for twenty years before being redrafted and adopted by the 27th Zionist Congress in Jerusalem in 1968. This "Jerusalem Program" remains current as the only formal, widely accepted statement of the Zionist program.[1] Its five principles are as follows:

1. The unity of the Jewish people and the centrality of Israel in Jewish life.

2. The ingathering of the Jewish people in its historic homeland through immigration from all countries.

3. The strengthening of the State of Israel based on the prophetic values of peace and justice.

4. The preservation of Jewish identity and the unique character of the Jewish people through education in Hebrew language, Jewish culture, and Jewish spiritual and cultural values.

5. The protection of Jewish rights.

The platform is noteworthy both for what it contains and for what it omits. It asserts centrality for Israel but omits reference to the status of the Diaspora. It affirms the principle of the ingathering of the Jewish people, but it is silent over the fundamental question of whether *aliyah* is a personal obligation of every would-be Zionist. It calls for the preservation of Jewish identity, but takes no position on the nature of that identity, a fundamental concern of earlier Zionist ideologists, many of whom viewed the Jewish identity forged in the

Diaspora in the period between the Biblical age and the dawn of Zionism as historically aberrant, and Zionism as a radical rejection of that Judaism.[2]

The omissions are neither accidental nor unimportant, for they spring from a fundamental question about the continued valence of Zionism as a movement in the State of Israel age. The crux of the matter lies in the meaning of two of the five paragraphs in the program: the centrality of Israel and the ingathering of the exiles. The two are interrelated and in their classical Zionist meaning are rooted in *shelilat hagolah*, the "negation" or "rejection" of the Diaspora, implying its denigration. No less a figure than David Ben-Gurion suggested that the Zionist movement in the Diaspora was obsolete, since a Zionism without *aliyah*, even if well intentioned and strongly supportive of Israel theoretically and ideologically, was empty rhetoric. A Jew who lived in the Diaspora could be a "Lover of Zion," but not a Zionist. A Jew who settled in Israel was a living embodiment of Zionism fulfilled and needed to deal with problems of building the Jewish state and not with the polemics or politics of an outdated movement. Much has been written and said since Ben-Gurion on these two related issues, centrality and *aliyah*, but I think it is fair to say that nothing radically new has emerged. The issues of *aliyah* and centrality were joined; they remain now where they were then.

Zionist organizations and their umbrella body, the World Zionist Organization, have struggled to formulate a "Zionist Program" for Israel and for the Diaspora. By-and-large, the efforts have been a failure, not because the individual program initiatives have been poorly conceived or implemented. On the contrary, many of the individual programs are of excellent quality and involve talented and able people.[3] The individual programs have not come together to form a coherent "Zionist Program" because the Jerusalem Program and subsequent efforts fail to deal adequately with the specifically "Zionist" issues of *aliyah* and the centrality of Israel, and because the remaining thrusts of these programs have been Jewish rather than uniquely Zionist. This leads me to suggest that past efforts to redefine Zionism for a State of Israel age have not worked because they have been built on a foundation of unresolved issues.

The Jerusalem Program is a good example. Its five paragraphs can be divided into two types: "Zionist" assertions on the one hand and Jewish planks on the other. The two fundamental "Zionist" assertions, "centrality" and "ingathering," need to be reexamined and recast and need to become integrated into basic Jewish ideology and program. Two of the remaining three paragraphs, preservation of Jewish identity and the protection of the Jewish rights, are Jewish rather than specifically Zionist tasks in the first place. Finally, even the strengthening of the State of Israel based on the prophetic values of peace and justice should be taken as a challenge to the entire Jewish people, not limited to a segment that calls itself Zionist.

Re-integrating Zionism into Jewish Life

The discussion of a specifically Zionist program after the establishment of the State of Israel suggests a distinction between Jews who are Zionists and those who are not. Retaining an implied separation between Judaism and Zionism, or suggesting that there is a Jewish approach as distinguished from a Zionist one, is, in my view, no longer useful or constructive. I advocate instead the integration of the component of Jewish national existence into our broad understanding of Jewish life generally, and the abandonment of the effort to define a specifically Zionist ideology as opposed to a presumed non-Zionist or anti-Zionist one. The unique task of Zionism was to create a Jewish state. This is not to suggest that Zionist ideology did not embrace a range of objectives, including salvation and regeneration. But the essential instrument for realizing those broader objectives was the creation of the sovereign Jewish state. That task has been accomplished.

It is the task of *Judaism* rather than Zionism as such to supply the ideological, philosophical, and theological foundations for Jewish existence throughout the world. Israelis will conduct the affairs of the State of Israel; Diaspora Jews will take responsibility for organizational and political matters in the Diaspora. However, all Jews should participate in articulating modes of positive Jewish attachment and involvement, finding ways to build the connections between Israel and the Diaspora and among Jews around the world. All Jews should seek to foster Jewish unity without insisting on uniformity and to nurture the cultural, religious, and intellectual creativity of the Jewish people. These roles must be common to all Jews wherever they live. An empowered but not invincible people, a vulnerable but not helpless people must adapt from its past and create new instruments and formulations to deal constructively with its new reality.

Preserving the language of an outdated movement whose instrumental mission has been accomplished contributes to divisiveness and serves no useful purpose. Instead, it makes the pursuit of a meaningful Jewish existence in the contemporary world more rather than less difficult. New approaches need to be devised that reflect the new Jewish reality.

The Centrality of Israel Re-Examined

Judaism requires the affirmation of the centrality of the land of Israel in Jewish life and the significance of the State of Israel as well. However, the meaning of "centrality" must be clarified, and some assumptions about "the centrality of Israel" need to be rejected if centrality is to be acceptable and meaningful to the Jewish people as a whole. Centrality implies, first of all, that the fate of Jews and Judaism is closely related to the fate of Israel, with all other meanings of "centrality" grounded in this assertion. What centrality means, appropriately, is that Israel must play a pivotal role in the life of the Jewish people ideologically, psychologically, and pragmatically. It asserts further, that Israel constitutes a unique mode of Jewish experience and offers possibilities for a kind of Jewish living not available elsewhere. It says also that Israel represents a dimension of Jewish existence which is vital; absent sovereignty in a national state, Jewish existence is incomplete and unfulfilled. Centrality refers also to psychological and sociological importance. It suggests that Israel should be a major focus of concern for Jews and a fulcrum around which a good deal of Jewish organizational life should revolve. "Centrality" affirms that

Israel is central to the Jewish people because all Jews have a stake in it and have a proprietary right to it, a right which has been invoked by hundreds of thousands who have escaped from lands of oppression, and by thousands of others who have opted for *aliyah* for other reasons. It suggests, finally, the Ahad Ha'am model of a religious cultural center, a place from which all Jews are nourished spiritually, culturally, and religiously, a place where Jewish culture can develop without the constraints of a larger non-Jewish society imposing itself upon Jewish life, with either hostile or benign intent.

Even momentary reflection suggests that centrality as described has been achieved to a great extent in contemporary Jewish life. This applies both to those groups in Jewish life who call themselves Zionists and those who do not. Rather than forming a plank in a specifically Zionist program, centrality of Israel has become a palpable Jewish reality. Much of Jewish organizational life, locally, nationally, and internationally, is Israel-centered. Israel is a central focus of Jewish fund raising and the dominant feature of Jewish political activism. Israel is a major center of Jewish scholarship, and religious, academic, and communal leadership training programs all include substantial Israel components. Support for Israel and concern for Israel occupy a prominent place in the mind of world Jewry, and this persists without regard to political or strategic vicissitudes. These are not Zionist realities; they are Jewish realities.

In contrast to the above, there is a classically Zionist meaning of the centrality of Israel, but precisely that sense of centrality needs to be reexamined and abandoned because it is neither historically accurate nor ideologically persuasive: that is the meaning of centrality which suggests that Israel is the exclusive arena for the working out of Jewish history, that the Diaspora is both fragile and lacks Jewish authenticity, and that the only legitimate option for the Jew is *aliyah*. This kind of centrality is clearly closely related to the other "critical" ("Zionist") paragraph in the Jerusalem Program: the ingathering of the Jewish people. This later idea has had a complex history in Zionist thought. That history includes the expectations of Herzl and Pinsker that the Diaspora would rather quickly wither away and disappear after the establishment of the State. Klatzkin saw the process as more gradual but no less inevitable. As mentioned above, Ben-Gurion was particularly scornful of the attempt to reformulate a Diaspora Zionism without the element of *aliyah* as central.[4] What is common to all the formulations and articulations of the idea is the element of *shelilat hagolah*, "negation" of the Diaspora, referred to above. Either overtly or subtly, Diaspora Jews are accused of characterological and Jewish weakness because they opt to remain in the Diaspora. The emptiness of Diaspora Judaism is supposedly revealed in Diaspora Jews' preference for the fleshpots of affluence over the unique spiritual and cultural fulfillment of Israel.

It seems that in recent years it has become fashionable to submerge or camouflage references to this idea. Frequently the argument is voiced that we should "agree to disagree" with our Israeli counterparts on the issue of "denigration of the Diaspora," i.e., to bracket the discussion of this issue in order to minimize that friction that reference to it inevitably generates, and thus to avoid alienation of Diaspora Jews. The suggested diplomacy is primarily for pragmatic considerations, because the risk of alienation carries with it the risk of reducing the level of political and financial support from the Diaspora to Israel. But the issue cannot easily be bracketed, for it is fundamental to the relationship of Israelis and Diaspora Jews and therefore to the future of the Jewish people. And so the issue must be joined. To the degree that centrality/ingathering are embedded in a model of Jewish life, which includes *shelilat hagolah*, they need to be rejected as a program for the Jewish people. Therefore, I am advocating the dismantling of the specific Zionist program, abandoning those elements of it which are either obsolete or invalid, and "Judaizing" those elements of it which are in fact central Jewish, rather than Zionist, concerns. It follows that the fact that *shelilat hagolah* is the only substantively "Zionist" inference to emerge from the Jerusalem Program, is a reason for abandoning the program altogether. Put differently, my argument for the assimilation of the Zionist program into the Jewish program is based on my assertion that the components of the program which are valid need to be adopted as the concern of the Jewish people generally and not limited to a specifically Zionist movement. Maintaining the distinction between Jewish and Zionist implies the recognition of the existence and even the legitimacy of non-Zionist and even anti-Zionist groups. The specifically Zionist component of the program, *shelilat hagolah*, needs to be reconsidered and abandoned in the light of the contemporary Jewish condition and postestablishment Jewish history. My advocacy of the rejection of *shelilat hagolah* is based on considerations of history, ideology, and pragmatism.

Historical Reasons for Rejecting "Shelilat Hagolah"

It is, first of all, apparent, that predictions of ingathering as the natural reaction of the Jewish people to the establishment of the state have not materialized. By and large, only Jews from areas of persecution and oppression have emigrated to Israel in large numbers. While several thousand Jews have emigrated to Israel in order to experience Jewish possibilities which were not available to them elsewhere, the overwhelming majority of Jews in Western countries show no interest in *aliyah*. This may in part be due to a unwillingness on their part to confront the hardships of life in a developing country facing problems of security and internal dissension. But there is a good deal more to it than that. Conventional Zionist explanations for the failure of *aliyah* from the West fail to comprehend the ties between Jews and their home countries. Israelis, for example, find it almost impossible to understand that American Jews are not simply grateful to America for its hospitality. Rather, they are patriotic Americans with feelings of love, loyalty, and commitment to the country, based in part on the remarkable opportunities which America has afforded them, but rooted also in shared values, a shared sense of history, and a sense of full participation in all aspects of American life. Similar attitudes prevail among Jews in other Western countries, but America, because of the size of its community and the unique nature of the American experiment, exemplifies a particularly close relationship of Jews with their country.

The relationship between American Jews and America needs to be seen as affirmation of America, not rejection of Israel. I have in mind a reason for the inability of Israelis to come to terms with and appreciate the American-Jewish relationship. Israelis view the failure of massive *aliyah* to materialize as a rejection of Israel on the part of American Jews, and therefore a "denigration" of what Israel constitutes and what it has achieved. *Shelilat hagolah* becomes a defensive stance, a reaction, in part, to what is viewed as *shelilat hamedinah*, "denigration of the state." Thus, the debate over the status of the Diaspora and the failure of mass *aliyah* to materialize has become an exchange of accusations and invective. Mutual criticism and defensiveness have become the dominant motifs in Israel-Diaspora conversations. Even though Israelis may be disappointed that mass *aliyah* from the West has not materialized, this development must be integrated in a model of Jewish life which is responsive to reality and attempts to understand it accurately and even sympathetically. "Zionism's" inability to come to terms with the affirmative character of Jewish-Diaspora relationships, its misunderstanding of the absence of Western *aliyah* as *shelilat hamedinah*, reinforcing other ideologically rooted attitudes of *shelilat hagolah*, are destructive vestiges of a separatist Zionist ideology which we would do well to discard.

However, the historical concerns go deeper. They relate to the two issues of security and creative vitality. A common Zionist argument is that security for Jews in the Diaspora is, of necessity, illusory, and that the only real security for the Jewish people is in the State of Israel. This position may be correct but there certainly exist no historical precedents to prove it. Tragically, Jewish history is replete with instances of national and communal disaster, and they occurred in sovereign Jewish states as well as in the Diaspora communities. We have lost Jewish commonwealths in the past, and we have lost Jewish communities in the Diaspora. Undoubtedly, a powerful and proud State of Israel reinforces the sense of Jewish security and strengthens all Jews psychologically in the knowledge that we are no longer powerless even in a military sense. But there is no absolute security for anyone in our world. Even the mightiest military powers express fear for their security, and what is more, their fears are not misplaced. With massive destructive force proliferating, the suggestion that the existence of even a powerful Jewish state guarantees Jewish security borders on the absurd. That Israel provides a welcome measure of security to Jews who are threatened is undeniable. That Israel is secure and that the Diaspora everywhere is threatened is certainly not supported by history. The best estimate is that Jewish security in Israel and in the Diaspora will continue to be the product of Jewish vigilance and constructive interrelationships with others who are sympathetic to the security needs of the Jewish people. These interrelationships require both a State of Israel and a Jewish Diaspora in the West.

Finally, there are historical considerations which relate to the creative role of the Diaspora in Jewish life. Classical Zionism emerged because it was seen as the only solution to the constant threats of physical harm and cultural and religious annihilation that Jews faced in the Diaspora. This was a necessary ideological stance prior to the establishment of the state; nothing short of it could electrify the Jewish imagination and generate the practical steps necessary to establish the state. But although it would be foolish to suggest that the tragedies of the Diaspora can be forgotten, the place of Diaspora in Jewish history needs to be reexamined now. Considered objectively, the conclusion is unavoidable that along with the dangers and vulnerabilities of the Diaspora there evolved also a universalization of the Jewish perspective, a dimension that is fundamental to the Jewish character today, wherever Jews live. This perspective is also essential if the Jewish people is to make progress in enhancing the quality of Jewish life and removing the many imperfections which it suffers.

Jewish culture has been enriched immeasurably by the creative interaction of Jews with other civilizations in the Diaspora. Virtually every significant creative product of Jewish history has represented a synthesis of the Jewish internal experience with the culture of others. The Bible represents a fusion and transformation of much that the Jewish community absorbed from the earlier Canaanite and northwest Semitic cultures, primarily in the Land of Israel. However, the phenomenon of cultural transfusion was primarily a Diaspora phenomenon. The Talmud provides countless examples of Greco-Roman institutions, concepts and styles which entered Jewish life during the

Hellenistic period. The great flowering of Hebrew poetry in the Middle Ages resulted from the encounter between Hebrew poets and their Arab counterparts. The burgeoning of Jewish philosophy emerged from exposure to classical Greek thought through the instrumentality of Arabic translation, and theological categories entered the Jewish mind through the encounter with Christianity. In the contemporary world, Jewish reality is the result of the interaction and confrontation of traditional Judaism with modernism following the Enlightenment.

Examples of this fertilization can be seen in language, which contributes to the way we structure reality. New dimensions were added to our ability to understand, interpret, and describe human experiences by our contact with a variety of linguistic traditions. The resulting Judeo-Arabic, Judeo-Spanish and Judeo-German languages all brought to the Jewish experience the richness of the cultures from which they have absorbed. And together, all these confrontations with different modes of thinking, speaking, writing, and social outlook have served to broaden the Jewish vision, to transcend parochialism and to make of the Jewish people a "world people." One fundamental characteristic of the Jewish Diaspora experience—"marginality" with respect to the societies and cultures surrounding the Jewish community—carries with it profound blessings along with the obvious dangers it presents as well. It has allowed Jews to transcend narrow concerns and to understand that national boundaries do not draw limits to the fact that all people, wherever they live, exist in a state of interdependence. This "marginality" has helped the Jewish people to generate universal values and has afforded it the opportunity to implement them in a wide range of social and political settings. In the past this was mostly the work of Jews who either left the Jewish fold or acted outside of it. The American experience, in particular, raises the possibility of Jewish involvement in general societal concerns *qua* Jews, or from a Jewishly informed perspective. In spite of the vulnerabilities and dangers, the historical record certainly does not permit the facile characterization of the Diaspora as aberrational, unproductive, or sterile. In the past, the Diaspora produced a major and positive dimension of the character of the Jewish people. Nothing in the historical record suggests that it cannot continue to do so.

Ideological Reasons for Rejecting *Shelilat Hagolah*

In line with the centrality of Israel in its meaning outlined above, the promotion of *aliyah* as a unique Jewish opportunity should become part of the Jewish program generally, not limited to "Zionists." Ideologically, it is necessary to stress the distinction between the encouragement of *aliyah* through formal and nonformal educational programs and through programs of public information on the one hand, and the assertion, implicit or explicit, that *aliyah* is the only legitimate Jewish option for those who wish to take part in the drama of Jewish history, on the other. Reference has already been made to the distorted and inadequate view of the Diaspora which attaches to this approach. What is sometimes overlooked is the ideological corollary of such assertions as: "We need you to come to Israel, because otherwise we will become Levantinized," or "What we need is 'Western' Jews, because if they don't come we are lost." Such assertions create expectations which are both unrealistic, and even more important, unwholesome. They suggest that the solution to Israel's problems is contingent upon the arrival from "outside" of masses of "European" Jews who will remedy the ills of the state and constitute a countervailing presence to its current population with its large and growing number of Jews from Arabic-speaking countries. I believe that the character of the State of Israel must be shaped by its citizens, and if major portions of the population are Jews from Middle Eastern countries then the state will and should take on a Middle Eastern character. The suggestion that salvation requires mass immigration from the "West" represents an unacceptably prejudicial view of much of the citizenry of Israel and a Eurocentric vision of what the country should be like. Moreover, the thesis that the solution of fundamental problems in the political, social, and religious areas must await a mass influx of Western Jews who are unlikely to come becomes an instrument of mass delusion for it suggests that confronting the problems and finding solutions for them can be put off to a different time. Sadly, the hour is late and the last thing the State of Israel can afford is further delay in confronting its deepest problems.

A second major line of argument of an ideological kind for rejecting *shelilat hagolah* relates to the centrality/ingathering motif in the context of modern nationalism. The emergence of post-Enlightenment and post-Emancipation anti-Semitism brought about a disenchantment with models of acculturation and assimilation as the solution to the Jewish problem. The record of modern nationalism should generate a similar disenchantment with the idea of nationalism as the solution for the Jewish problem or the human condition generally. Assimilation failed as a "solution" to the Jewish problem, but that did not demonstrate that degrees of acculturation and assimilation were impossibilities. The failure demonstrated only that the total assimilation of Jews into the larger society was impossible, and that their distinctiveness could not be lost. This was, of course, a mixed blessing, implying both continuity and vulnerability. Nationalism, too, is a mixed blessing, both promising and threatening. Clearly, the obvious excesses of nationalism do not imply that it is a wholly pernicious pattern of social organization, only that it needs to be balanced by interests and forces that transcend national interests in order to minimize the risks attendant to it in its extreme and unbridled forms. The catastrophes that our generation has witnessed as the result of extremist nationalist movements should constitute sufficient warning to those who would view nationalism, any nationalism, as an ultimate solution to the challenge of creating a viable structure of social interrelationships in the world. Despite the fact that Jews, tragically, are late arrivals in the world of national states, the warning applies to them as well.

In the attempt to defuse the dangers of the excesses of nationalism, a variety of approaches and techniques has evolved. International organizations are a serious but imperfect approach. Federation and commonwealth arrangements are another; treaties often contribute to a process of internationalization. I suggest that the Israel-Diaspora relationship constitutes a unique Jewish instrument for sustaining the international dimension of Jewish consciousness and insuring against the excesses of Jewish nationalism. The Diaspora Jewish marginality described earlier provides an international perspective within the Jewish community. The centrality of Israel in Diaspora Jewish life exposes the State of Israel to that perspective. This is a further major role for the Diaspora to play and an important reason for building a healthy Israel-Diaspora relationship. The perspectives of Jews throughout the world should be a fertile source for Israel, though, of course, the ultimate decision-making role on matters pertaining to the State of Israel belongs to her citizens. In addition, the Diaspora represents for Israel a significant connection with Jewish history in the period separating the second and third Jewish commonwealths.

A common agenda for Israel and the Diaspora, if adopted and taken seriously, helps to reduce the dangers of narrowness of perspective and parochialism which are always present in a small and beleaguered country. The relationship is therefore mutual. The centrality of Israel in the consciousness of the Diaspora reinforces Jewish identity and guards against the excesses of assimilation; the presence of the Diaspora contributes a dimension of breadth to the Israeli consciousness which mitigates the risks inherent in the excesses of nationalism. I would argue that the Diaspora has played that role in the recent period of uncertainty and tension in Israel, despite the fact that it appropriately claims no right of intervention in the actual decision-making process of the state.

Pragmatic Reasons for Rejecting *Shelilat Hagolah*

Finally, I come to my third category of argument for rejecting *shelilat hagolah*: pragmatism. Shelilat hagolah has not, in fact, encouraged *aliyah*. If anything, the argument has inhibited it, because it has stressed the "radically other" nature of Judaism in Israel as opposed to its continuity with Diaspora Judaism. Orthodox Jews are unaffected by the argument since, when emigrating to Israel, they generally create a life-style which is not significantly different from their life-style in the Diaspora. The nonorthodox Jews most likely to be attracted to the idea of *aliyah* are those who see it as a natural progression from their Jewish commitment in the Diaspora, rather than a rejection or negation of that commitment. In this they are interestingly and importantly different from the early secular Zionist founders of Israel. The state-sanctioned delegitimization of all but the Orthodox branch of Judaism continues to irritate and to act as a disincentive to those who might consider *aliyah*.

To summarize, then, in the light of past failures, what useful purpose is there in efforts to focus on a Zionist ideology in contrast to a Jewish ideology? In view of the fact that Israel is already a central feature in the life of the Diaspora and that no new Zionist formulation will suddenly generate mass *aliyah*, why maintain a distinction which serves no purpose other than to divide Jews from one another? Israelis may feel resentment at Diaspora Jews who fail to come to Israel, but why give ideological reinforcement to that resentment when nothing useful can come of it?

Three Settings for Contemporary Jewish Life

My appraisal of contemporary Jewish existence suggests that it is appropriate to view Jewish life as functioning in three distinct contexts: the sovereign Jewish state, the homogeneous national state, and the multicultural environment. Each of these contexts has its own characteristics, requires its own program, and presents its own challenges. There are tasks which are common to the Jewish communities of all three, but they differ in their capacities to fulfill these tasks.

We have already described the uniqueness of the Jewish reality under Jewish sovereignty. Israel faces specific Jewish challenges: How should it infuse the modern Jewish state with values and insights from Jewish tradition? Is Jewish tradition to be granted authority in some areas under Jewish sovereignty? If so, which aspects of the tradition and as understood by whom? Working out the relationship of contemporary realities to traditional norms is a unique, troublesome, but ultimately exciting and invigorating challenge for Israel, comparable to the need to balance security needs and the exercise of power with democratic, humanistic, and religious values.

Jewish existence in the homogeneous national state comes closest to approximating the conditions which gave birth to Zionist solutions. Jews remain outsiders in societies in which there is a dominant religious, national, or ethnic majority. Under these circumstances, the presence of Jews represents at the very least a potential irritant, with possibly disastrous implications. The fundamental task for Jewish communities in these countries is to negotiate maximum conditions of security and rights of free expression and to navigate between extremes of assertiveness and accommodation, isolation and assimilation. Here, *aliyah* must be considered with particular seriousness. Even if the present moment appears nonthreatening, the classical Zionist projection of ultimate instability and danger appears most convincing for Jewish communities of this type.

The multinational, multicultural setting is the most significant new setting for Jewish existence. Although there are no guarantees of security, there appear to be important relevant differences between this setting and the homogeneous national state. The United States is, of course, the most outstanding example of a multicultural environment. It is a country of minorities—ethnic, religious and national. It is not a country without intergroup tensions, or totally free of anti-Semitism, but anti-Semitism in the United States appears to be different from classical anti-Semitism in that it is not predominantly rooted in Christian theological doctrine, nor does it demonize or dehumanize Jews. Although it is difficult to generalize about a phenomenon as complex as anti-Semitism, in the United States it appears to be more the characteristic product of intergroup rivalry exacerbated by Jewish success and prominence than anything else.[5] Even more important, the election of Jews to high office in districts where few Jews live, Jewish participation as Jews in public fora in the United States, and even the high rate of intermarriage which is a great problem for Jews but which at the same time is an indicator of their acceptance, all suggest that the principal challenges to Jewish continuity in the United States are internal, that is, they relate more to the choices and decisions that Jews themselves make about their Jewishness than to the operations of external forces upon them.

While the United States is the most extraordinary example of the multinational, multicultural environment, it is interesting to refer at least briefly to two newly emerging settings, radically different from one another and probably diametrically opposite in the prognosis regarding their potential for a secure Jewish life in their midst: Europe and the former Soviet Union. We have referred to the polarities of nationalism and internationalism as appropriate and constructive tensions in Jewish life, with specific reference to Israel and the Diaspora. The United States, because of its size and its diversity, embraces regional particularisms and national consciousnesses. At the same time, because of its international role, it balances national and international perspectives in its world view. European countries were until recently the best examples of homogeneous national states where the dominance of a single national group projected the Jews as outsiders and contributed to the catastrophe of European anti-Semitism. Europe is currently moving to a mitigation of nationalist elements through the linking of economies and the weakening of national boundaries. It appears that Europeans will carry European passports, rather than those of their individual countries. Travel between European countries will be made easier and more accessible. Media news and entertainment will be increasingly shared. Thus the international dimension of political consciousness is bound to grow and will interact with the continuing modes of national expression, language, literature, and culture. It will be interesting to observe the impact of this change on European Jews, especially in France. Will the emergence of this kind of internationalist-nationalist model create greater opportunities for Jewish cultural development? How will it affect the Jewish self-image, which in Europe seems still very much in tension with the homogeneous national environment?

The former Soviet Union remains one of the most interesting and important enigmas of all. No one knows what will happen to the country generally, and few would dare to predict whether recent new options for Jewish self-expression for Russian Jews represent the beginning of a new phase of Jewish life there or momentary blips on the continuing descending curve of Jewish life. This question may be linked to the model of nationalist expression which emerges in Russia. A country which nurtures the free expression of its component groups, particularly one of the size and diversity of Russia, may nurture the rights of cultural and political expression of its Jews as well. Emerging nationalisms in Russia hold danger as well as promise for the Jews of that country, since they contain exclusionary and intolerant components. Nevertheless, a chance exists, however small, that the new patterns of political and cultural life in Russia will present a new model of nationalist-internationalist interaction, a model holding promise for the development of Jewish life and culture.

Conclusion

To summarize my thesis, I suggest that the maintenance of a separate "Zionist" ideology, as distinct from a program for Jewish life generally, preserves an outdated formulation and increases divisiveness within the Jewish community. The debate about whether Jews should continue to live in the Diaspora or should go on *aliyah* is a legitimate one, but need not be embedded in an ideological distinction which suggests that Israel not be a central concern for all Jews or that Diaspora life is inherently reprehensible.

The responsibility for protecting Jews, insuring Jewish rights, nurturing Jewish identity, and even helping those who choose *aliyah*, is not limited to a certain group of Jews, namely Zionists, with the rest of the Jewish people relieved of these responsibilities. At the same time, for historical, ideological, and pragmatic reasons, *shelilat hagolah* needs to be rejected, and the notions of "centrality of Israel" and the "ingathering of the Jewish people" need to be adjusted to new realities. Israel and the Diaspora should not view their interrelationship in competitive terms. Neither should be promoting its virtues by denigrating the other, and neither should bolster its sense of security by exaggerating the insecurities of the other.

An adjustment of Jewish ideology to the realities of Jewish life today is necessary. This adjustment requires an appreciation of the variety of settings in which Jews live, a patient but rigorous probing of the Jewish condition, thoughtful investigation of our problems, and imaginative and energetic programs for nurturing the creative energies of our communities and promoting their interrelationship. We need to inquire anew into the complex nature of Jewish identity. I sense that we will be less and less able to generate Jewish energy by promoting the perception among Jews of a hostile world arrayed against us. Nor will Jews around the world be energized by ideologies which are contradicted by history, unacceptable to them ideologically, and pragmatically ineffective. We need to dismantle structures that inhibit the process of identifying new modes of interrelationship among Jews and between Jews and Judaism. This is what is required for a post-Zionist model for contemporary Jewish life.

NOTES

1. It is cited in David Sidorsky, "Interpreting the Diaspora-Israel Relationship," in *Zionism Today: A Symposium* (New York: The Institute on American Jewish-Israeli Relations, The America Jewish Committee, 1986), 11.

2. For a discussion of this aspect of Zionism in the writings of such Zionist writers as Herzl and Jacob Klatzkin, and of the opposite view of Ahad Ha'am, see the introductory essay in Arthur Hertzberg, *The Zionist Idea* (New York and Philadelphia: 1960), particularly 64–72.

3. For a recent survey of these programs see *Report on Departmental Activities* (Jerusalem: World Zionist Organization, June, 1989).

4. See relevant passages from Herzl, Pinsker, Klatzkin and Ben-Gurion as well as the introductory notes in Hertzberg, *Zionist Idea*.

5. See the interesting discussion of the variety of phenomena which have been described as anti-Semitism by David Sidorsky, "Against the Idea of Anti-Semitism: Agenda Priorities, Empirical Disagreement and Conceptual Issue," in *Anti-Semitism, Proceedings of the Vidal Sasson Center for the Study of Anti-Semitism*, ed. Yehuda Bauer (Jerusalem: 1988).

13. The Reintegration of Middle Eastern Jewry

Guy H. Haskell

The Middle East was the cradle of, and has been the home to, Judaism and the large majority of Jews for over two-thirds of recorded Jewish history. It has provided the fertile ground for the development of the religion and the people and has shaped the nature of Jewish belief, praxis, society, culture, and world view. Yet since the late Middle Ages, the majority of Jews have lived elsewhere, and with this demographic shift, Jewish creative energies moved as well.

The cultural gap between Middle Eastern and Western Jewries has increased over time, until the dramatic events of our century reversed this trend with historically startling rapidity. In this paper we will briefly examine the development of the bifurcation of world Jewry into Eastern and Western and its subsequent reintegration in the light of recent events. We will also discuss the ramifications of this re-unification in the light of recent trends in Judaism and the structure of Jewish society, examining some of the conflicts and syncretisms this reunification has produced.

The origin of the Jewish Diaspora is popularly marked at 70 C.E., with the destruction of the Second Temple of Jerusalem which

219

deprived the Jews of sovereignty until the establishment of the modern State of Israel nineteen centuries later. However, even the casual student of Jewish history understands that the majority of Jews had chosen to live outside of Eretz Israel long before the ultimate end of Jewish rule over it.[1]

The reasons for this dispersion of the Jews outside the borders of their homeland are the subject of much debate and controversy, and I do not wish to enter the discussion by giving more weight to one factor over another. Suffice it to say that things were often tough in Eretz Israel and more attractive elsewhere. Simply put, Jews have exhibited a tendency throughout their history to place themselves where the social, cultural, political, and economic action was.[2]

With the fortunes of Israel varying greatly over time, the action was often to be found elsewhere. It may even be conjectured that the small and politically weak Jewish commonwealth managed to persist as an independent political entity as long as it did in part because of a well-placed partisan constituency spread throughout the centers of power in the surrounding empires and nations. Be that as it may, the final fall of Jerusalem found ancient and firmly established Jewish communities in all of the main cities surrounding Eretz Israel.

As the Middle East was the cradle of the Jewish people and the nursery in which its national religion grew and flourished, it was also the nexus of its transformation from a faith territory-bound to one unfettered by geographic limitations. Judaism, deprived of its heart and soul, of its Temple and its land, could be expected to have evaporated. Its metamorphosis into a self-contained, ever developing body of belief and practice, occurred partly on its own desecrated soil, but even more in the center of Middle Eastern power, Babylon. The academies of Sura and Pumbeditha served as exemplars of postnational Judaism, demonstrating its ability to thrive outside the Land of Israel.[3]

The rise of Islam in the seventh century was to transform the face of the Middle East with great speed and thoroughness. Islam provided the backdrop for Jewish existence in the Middle East for over a millennium, both enabling it to flourish and, ultimately, causing its destruction. The seeds of these seemingly contradictory trends are to be found in the very words of its founder, the Prophet Muhammad.[4]

No religious system can lay claim to consistency, and Islam is no exception. The pronouncements of Muhammed were often contradictory, and this is certainly the case in his references to the Jews. Alternating modest praise with vilification, Muhammed decreed both tolerance and persecution for the *Ahl al-Kitab*, "the People of the Book." Unlike Christianity, however, Islam did provide the usually stable, if despised status of *Ahl al-Dhimma* for Jews and Christians, which helped protect the Jews from some of the excesses that they were to experience in Christian Europe.[5]

These excesses, however, did not prevent a massive shift of Jewish population from the Middle East to Europe with the decline of Islamic civilization and rise of Christian Europe. Here again, the "where the action is" principle seems to have taken effect. Despite numerous savage depredations and expulsions, the center of Jewish population shifted to Europe, and that continent was to remain the preeminent site of Jewish activity in all fields of endeavor into this century.[6] The general decline of the Middle East was mirrored in the fading of Jewish vitality and creativity, and the virtual invisibility of Middle Eastern Jewry until recent events forced it back into the limelight.[7]

Although not always the case, it is often true that affluence, power, and stability lead to social tolerance. This was surely the case in the Muslim Middle East and North Africa. The flowering of Islamic civilization allowed the intellectual and economic flowering within the Jewish community.[8] The inverse is true as well; the economic and military decline of the Middle East led to constriction and defensiveness in all fields, as well as a marked decrease in religious tolerance.[9] In Europe, at the same time, greater economic and political stability in certain regions led to openings for Jewish labor and expertise, and the population shift was on.[10]

After the thirteenth century, there were several periods of immigration from Europe to North Africa and the Middle East. The most important of these population movements occurred after the Jews were expelled en masse from Spain and Portugal in 1492. The expulsion and the atrocities committed against the Jews in the years leading up to it constitute the most tragically seminal event in Jewish history to occur between the destruction of the Second Temple in 70 C.E. and the Holocaust in our century.[11]

The expulsion from Iberia brought new members and new vitality, as well as new tensions, to the Jewish communities of the Middle East and North Africa.[12] It did not, however, shift the center of population, power, or creativity away from Europe. There were other emigrations as well, as Jews fled persecution in Europe for the relative tolerance and safety of the Ottoman Empire.[13] Nevertheless, Europe continued to be where the action was, and the large majority of Jews continued to make it their home.

The short-lived Golden Age of Islamic civilization was followed by a long decline in intellectual, economic, and political power. The stirrings of the Haskalah movement in Europe in the middle of the eighteenth century produced little echo in the Jewish communities of the Middle East. Haskalah was not originally born out of Jewish thought, but was a Jewish reflection of the general intellectual trends which were shaping the gentile Enlightenment. Indeed, the *maskilim*, "enlighteners," saw the roots of their movement in the works of a Middle Eastern Jewish thinker of an earlier enlightened age, Maimonides.[14] But the Jews of the contemporary Middle East continued to live tradition-bound lives in their communities, based on Jewish law and lore. For them, the time of enlightenment had passed and was not to return until introduced from without, beginning in the nineteenth century.

Until the Haskalah movement began to challenge the very foundations of traditional Jewish life, the similarities between Jewish communities throughout the world were greater than their differences. Raphael Patai, in *The Jewish Mind*, finds these differences to be a veneer covering a basic unity of outlook:

> . . . in the essentials of both credo and ritual, and, more importantly, in the unquestioning acceptance of religiosity as the natural condition of Jewish life, there were neither intra-community nor inter-community differences. Whatever differences did exist between one Jewish community and another—in speech, *minhag*, material culture—were brought about largely by the absorption of Gentile influences, which

varied from place to place and from country to country, and which managed to penetrate even the most ghettoized and isolated Jewish community. However, beneath these surface differences, the same essential Jewishness lay everywhere.[15]

Haskalah changed this situation radically. No longer were those things which differentiated Jews limited to culture; now degree of adherence to the fundamentals of traditional Judaism created seemingly unbridgeable gaps. By the end of the eighteenth century, these gaps would divide the Jews of eastern and western Europe, but as Haskalah spread ever eastward, the differences became less pronounced geographically, and *maskilim* could be found within every community. For most of the Jews of the Middle East and North Africa, who experienced no similar intellectual transformation, the gap would remain largely intact until the dissolution of their communities a century and a half later.

This is not to say that Middle Eastern Jewry was totally isolated from the currents of European thought. But where the Enlightenment in Europe developed out of native intellectual trends, it was imposed on the Middle East from without. With the decline of the Ottoman Empire and European territorial conquest, ideas of enlightenment became popular among many urban Jews as well as Muslims, and the notion of religious freedom was particularly attractive to Jews. Thus an urban/rural, upper-class/lower-class, Europeanized/traditional split affected both Jews and Muslims alike.[16] But a later ideological import from Europe, modern nationalism, would herald the end of most of the Jewish communities of the Middle East and North Africa, while at the same time it provided the foundation for the creation of an independent Jewish state.

The beginning of the twentieth century found Jews in Europe in disunity and disarray. Virtually every community had its assimilationists, socialists, Bundists, Hasidim, Mitnagdim, Communists, Zionists, and adherents of numerous other ideologies and movements. In addition, the mass immigration to America split the communities geographically as well as ideologically. In the Middle East and North Africa, however, Jewish life continued to exist largely untouched by the great schisms of Europe, and Halakhah continued to be the guiding principle of Jewish life, even among the more Europeanized. With the contemporaneous rise of Jewish and Arab nationalism, however, the viability of Jewish existence would be threatened.

The introduction to the final chapter of Middle Eastern Jewish history was written in Europe, not in the Middle East. As Haskalah was one of the Jewish children of the Enlightenment, so Zionism was one of the offspring of modern nationalism. It is ironic that many of the very ideas that influenced the development of Zionism, such as romanticism, nationalism, and the idealization of folk and folklore, would produce the greatest enemy of the Jewish people, Nazism. It is also ironic that these ideas, imported from Europe, would serve the Arab world well in casting off the yoke of European imperialism.

Zionism, nationalism, enlightenment, and emancipation all challenged the traditional arrangement between Jews and Muslims in North Africa and the Middle East. The most important of these movements was Arab nationalism, for Zionism never became an important political movement in Middle Eastern Jewish society, even though a traditional outlook fostered messianic and spiritual Zionism. But it was clear that the status of second-class citizen would no longer be acceptable to the Jews, at the same time that the assertion of Arab nationalism was threatening the sovereignty of the protectors of Jewish emancipation. Add to this Arab resentment against Jewish nationalist aspirations and settlement in Palestine, and a clearly unstable situation is revealed.

The cataclysm of the Second World War and the Holocaust would unalterably change the course of Jewish history and radically alter the ratio between Eastern and Western Jewries. Numerically, the change is cold-bloodedly obvious. Of the 16.6 million Jews living in 1939, 9.5 lived in Europe, two million in North Africa and the Middle East (including Palestine), and 5.5 million in America and Oceania. By 1948, the world Jewish population was reduced by the Nazi slaughter to 11.5 million, with 3.7 million in Europe, 1.9 in North Africa and the Middle East, and 5.8 million in America and Oceania.[17]

As the Holocaust destroyed the continuity of Jewish life in Europe, so the increasing power of Arab nationalism was threatening the

Jewish communities of North Africa and the Middle East, paving the way for the mass exodus which was to occur as soon as the final piece of the puzzle was put in place.

In 1948, the third dramatic historic event occurred that led to the reunification of world Jewry. The establishment of the State of Israel provided a home for Jews displaced by the Holocaust and Arab nationalism, as well as for those who chose to make Israel their home out of either Zionist or religious conviction. While most of the Europeanized elite of Middle Eastern Jewry would move to Europe with the withdrawal of their patron powers, the impoverished and relatively uneducated masses of Jews sought refuge in the State of Israel.

By the mid-1960s, very few Jews remained in North Africa and the Middle East, and the longest continuous chapter of Jewish history came to a close. For the first time since the expulsion from Spain in 1492, Eastern and Western Jews faced each other in large numbers. In Jewish communities throughout Israel, Europe, and to a much lesser extent the Americas, Jews confronted other Jews who had different languages, customs, *minhagim*, and world views. This was the beginning of a long and fascinating process, until now largely unstudied, of conflict and accommodation.

This meeting of Jews long separated by geography, language, and culture, expressed itself differently depending on a number of factors: nature of the established Jewish community and the immigrant community; attitudes of the majority population; economic and employment prospects; religiosity of the two groups; linguistic and cultural differences; etc.

In general, I think that Patai's principle of the essential unity of Jewish identity, shaken by the Enlightenment, began to reassert itself under these new conditions, and the veneer of language and culture was quickly stripped away. What remained were the more fundamental differences in Jewish identity—degree and type of religiosity—which first developed during the period of the Haskalah. The spectrum of Jewish belief and practice within the European Jewish communities must have been startling and confusing to the new immigrants. No longer was there one standard against which an individual could measure himself. Suddenly a Jew was no longer simply a Jew. He was a secular, Reform, Reconstructionist, Conservative, Orthodox, or Ultra-Orthodox Jew, with limitless varieties and combinations of beliefs, attitudes, and practices.

One might expect, under the circumstances, that the new immigrants would isolate themselves from these confusing influences by creating their own insular communities. In fact, this is often what happened. Yet the dynamic of Jewish minority existence often broke down the barriers between Jewish communities fairly quickly, as they discovered that more bound them together than separated them. With the continued association of Eastern and Western Jews, the dividing lines between them began to tilt from the vertical to the horizontal. The primacy of doctrinal difference and the centrality of Halakhah took precedence over language or geographic origin as divisive factors. Jews of like belief banded together in opposing what was perceived either as heresy by the religious, or religious oppression by the secular.

A somewhat different dynamic developed in Israel. After all, state policy had to be created around definitions of Jewishness in the Jewish state, and the socioeconomic gap between Western and Eastern Jewries would produce profound and lasting conflict. Despite these differences, I contend that the end result of this historic meeting between Jews of East and West is similar in Israel and Europe.

As linguistic and cultural differences gradually weaken, a syncretistic Jewish, or in this case Israeli, culture is developing. In saying this I do not deny the vitality of immigrant culture or the persistence of the deeper elements of attitude and world view. But as in Europe, it seems increasingly clear that doctrinal differences are swiftly taking precedence over cultural differences in Israel as well, and as religious and political ideology become more and more intertwined, these differences will begin to pervade all areas of life.[18]

Until recently, I think it was fair to say that Jews of the Middle East in Israel were more religiously traditional than most European Jews, but that their religiosity was far more tolerant. A religious syncretism has been taking place, however, which is changing this situation. As religious Jews band together to fight the evils of secularism, they are beginning to think, behave, and even look more alike. Unfortunately, as religion and politics intertwine, it is usually the more strident, militant, and intolerant element that carries the standard. It is increasingly difficult to distinguish the religious leaders in Israel by ethnic origin, as they gradually adopt European religious dress and lack of tolerance. This trend is most readily visible in the policies of the new Sephardic religious parties and with the increasingly heterogeneous ethnic make-up of the National Religious Party.

The most important factor of all in the eventual disappearance of the gap between these two Jewish communities has not yet been mentioned, and that is the steady increase in exogamy. As linguistic and cultural differences fade, so does hesitation to intermarry, and this has been the case, both in Israel and in Europe. Marriage between members of a specific ethnic group, or between those whose parents came from the same country, are increasingly rare. Marriages between the children of Western and Eastern Jews, if not yet the rule, are hardly exceptional, with rates now reaching above twenty-five percent in Israel. It is rare to find an Israeli who has no close young relatives from other ethnic groups. Even the loudly proclaimed ethnic political divisions in Israel have been shown to be more fantasy than fact. Exogamy, then, will prove the final reducer of Jewish ethnic differentiation.

A final factor, which at present is working in favor of the balance of population between Eastern and Western Jews, is assimilation. Assimilation is most prevalent in those communities which are least traditional and most integrated into the surrounding Gentile community. From the foregoing discussion, it is clear that those Jews most prone to assimilation are the more nontraditional communities of the West, and that those most likely to remain identifiably Jewish are those of the more traditional North African and Middle Eastern communities. Thus, as assimilation continues at an ever increasing rate, demographics will work in favor of traditional Jewish communities. As the children and grandchildren of Jewish immigrants from the Middle East and North Africa become more assimilated into Western norms, both in Israel and in Europe, this relative trend may slow down, and rates of assimilation may begin to equalize.

I have isolated five main factors leading to the reintegration of world Jewry; three historic and two social. In quick succession, the rise of Arab nationalism, the Holocaust, and the establishment of the State of Israel created conditions for this phenomenon, and the trend toward numeric and influential equality among the two main divisions of world Jewry. Intermarriage between members of the two communities and differential rates of assimilation have aided this process.

In isolating these various factors, I have avoided questions of causality and discussion of the relationships between the various phenomena described. That the rise of Arab nationalism and the Holocaust played a role in the establishment of the State of Israel is fact; the attribution of causality or the degree of interdependence of these phenomena is a fascinating topic not directly relevant to the present discussion. That Arab nationalism would lead to the untenability of Jewish life in Arab lands I believe is true regardless of the establishment of Israel or the Holocaust; and that the Holocaust exterminated two-thirds of the Jews of Europe is fact regardless of Arab nationalism or the State of Israel; and Israel provided a locus for the integration of the Eastern and Western Jewish communities without regard to other factors.

A phenomenon as broad as that discussed here, which spans large chunks of time and space, is certainly not capable of being summarized in a few short pages. I hope that the foregoing will serve as a vehicle for stimulating discussion and debate on the larger picture presented by these drastic changes in the condition of world Jewry. Perhaps we may begin looking at the forest as well as the trees.

NOTES

1. Menahem Stern, "Diaspora," *Encyclopaedia Judaica* (Jerusalem: Keter, 1972).
2. Solomon Grayzel, *A History of the Jews* (Philadelphia: Jewish Publication Society of America, 1947), 138–42.
3. Raphael Patai, *The Seed of Abraham* (New York: Charles Scribner's Sons, 1986), 56–59.
4. Norman Stillman, *The Jews of Arab Lands* (Philadelphia: Jewish Publication Society, 1977), 3–21.

5. Bernard Lewis, *The Jews of Islam* (Princeton, New Jersey: Princeton University Press, 1984), 3–66.

6. Abba Eban, *My People* (New York: Behrman House, 1968), 161.

7. Stillman, *Jews of Arab Lands*, 64–86.

8. Lewis, *Jews of Islam*, 67–106; Patai, *Seed of Abraham*, 67–99.

9. Stillman, *Jews of Arab Lands*, 64–66.

10. Eban, *My People*, 161.

11. Yosef Yerushalmi, "Coping with Catastrophe: Jewish Reactions to the Expulsion from Spain," Sydelle Lewis Lecture in Jewish Studies, March 5, 1984, Indiana University.

12. André Chouraqui, *Between East and West: A History of the Jews of North Africa* (New York: Atheneum, 1973), 86–112.

13. Guy H. Haskell, *The Jews of Bulgaria* (Detroit: Wayne State University Press, 1994).

14. Yehuda Slutsky, "Haskalah," *Encyclopaedia Judaica* (Jerusalem: Keter, 1972).

15. Raphael Patai, *The Jewish Mind*, (New York: Charles Scribner's Sons, 1977), 265.

16. Chouraqui, *Between East and West*, 202–27; Stillman, *Jews of Arab Lands*, 95–107; Lewis, *Jews of Islam*, 154–91.

17. *American Jewish Yearbook* 70 (1969): 273–88.

18. Charles S. Liebman and Eliezer Don-Yehiya, *Religion and Politics in Israel* (Bloomington: Indiana University Press, 1984), 119–37.

14. The Situation of the American Jew

Michael G. Berenbaum

July 14, 1989, was the two hundredth anniversary of the French Revolution. For Jewish history, the French Revolution represents the beginning of a two-century struggle for emancipation—i.e., the achievement of equal rights for Jews within the nation state. In France, the battle for emancipation achieved unequal results. Jews became French citizens, yet even a hundred years after the revolution the Dreyfus trial demonstrated that Jews could not receive basic equality under the law.[1] In nineteenth-century Germany, emancipation was regarded as an imposition of the French and hence a source of resentment.

Only in twentieth-century America has emancipation been fully achieved. Unlike any other Diaspora Jewish community since the emancipation, American Jews can enjoy a public life without concealing religious identity. For the past two decades, the public life of American Jewry has focused on Israel.

The Six-Day War of June 1967 represented a watershed in American Jewish history, inaugurating a twenty-year period in which American Jewish life was Israel-centered. The centrality of Israel reflected itself in the philanthropic life of American Jews. During the Six-Day War and the 1973 Yom Kippur War, funds donated to Israel by American Jews increased geometrically, and the threshold of giving established during wartime fervor became the new baseline for community campaigns. Israeli dominance also reflected itself in the institutional life of American Jews. Scores of organizations based their appeal on how much they were doing to sustain the fledgling state. Non-Israel-oriented institutions, such as the American Jewish Committee or B'nai B'rith, took on an ardent pro-Israel agenda. The Reform and Conservative movements started their own Zionist groups, and Jewish camps developed summer programs in Israel. The numbers of pilgrims to Israel increased dramatically, and the heroes of the Jewish people became generals and political leaders (Moshe Dayan, Golda Meir) rather than men and women of intellectual or spiritual achievement. By 1983, the role of Israel had become so dominant that Amos Oz, Israel's most prominent writer, could proclaim to the leaders of the American Diaspora gathered at the General Assembly of Jewish Federations that in the drama of current Jewish history, Israel alone is on stage. "You are the audience,"[2] Oz told American Jews. Few disputed his claim.

This Israel-centered chapter in American Jewish life is drawing to a close. While Israel will continue to enjoy strong political support from American Jews, it will no longer dominate American Jewish consciousness. In part, the reasons are political.[3]

The decade of the eighties was less heroic for Israel. No raids on Entebee fired the American Jews' imagination. The Yom Kippur War, in which Israel was attacked on two fronts on the holiest day of the Jewish year, gave way to the 1982 War in Lebanon, a war of aggression and not self-defense. The Jonathan Pollard spy case demonstrated that Israeli intelligence was prepared to exploit the loyalties that American Jews feel for Israel in a sloppy, inept operation.[4] The unending struggle of the Arab intifada, which pits armed Israeli soldiers against a relatively unarmed civilian population, produced ugly images in the media. Despite Jewish protests of exaggeration and distortion in the news, reports generally reflected the situation on the ground. Furthermore, the generational transition in Israeli leadership from founders to followers, from pioneers to aparatchniks, weakened Israel's mythic hold on American Jewish consciousness.

On several key issues, such as the "Who is a Jew?" debate and the struggle for Soviet Jewry, there has been a near break between American Jews and Israel. When the confrontation reached its crescendo, Israel was forced to back down and accept the American Diaspora on its own terms. On the "Who is a Jew?" issue, the Israeli religious parties sought to delegitimize Diaspora Jewry's religious leadership by refusing to recognize the conversions, marriages, and divorces performed by non-Orthodox rabbis, thus challenging the core of Jewish identity in the Diaspora. American Jewish leaders refused to allow the Jewish state to demean the integrity of American Jewish identity. Israeli leadership saw Soviet Jewry's struggle as a Zionist issue with *aliyah* (migration to Israel) as its goal. American Jews perceived it as a matter of human rights and free choice; with the new opportunities provided by *glasnost*, American Jews will fight for Jewish cultural rights in the Soviet Union and not only for the right to leave.

In both of these communal skirmishes, Israel lost influence, and its leadership was demonstrated as inept. These lessons have not been lost on American Jewish leaders.

Israel's overall political situation, which seemingly changes by the hour, has an underlying and rather unpleasant stability. Writing for *The Jerusalem Post*, columnist Allen Shapiro said: "only a confirmed anti-Semite could believe that the people of Israel has the leadership it deserves."[5] Hirsch Goodman, the *Post*'s influential military correspondent, recently wrote: "Israel is at the height of its military power and geo-political influence precisely as it is at the nadir of its political leadership."[6] American Jewry is not blind to the dearth of Israeli political leadership and the paralysis that has resulted from two successive national unity governments, which were neither national nor unified and could barely govern. Each election, each peace proposal, each change in PLO pronouncements leaves Israel further divided.

A heroic Israel has given way to an impotent political leadership that can neither attract wholehearted American Jewish support nor sustain the mythic weight that a generation of American Jews imposed on Israel when they sought a vicarious basis for their own existence. Israel has lost none of its urgency, none of its necessity as a haven and homeland for the Jewish people, but merely its mythic sufficiency to carry the burden of ultimate meaning for Jewish existence in America, and perhaps in Israel as well.[7]

Yet the reasons for the loss of American Jewry's Israel-centeredness are more than political. Increasingly, it seems that the Holocaust, the undigested trauma of the Jewish people, has left Israel scarred. Despite the prowess of Israel's army, its regional supremacy, its role as an occupying power, and a fifteen-year alliance with the United States, Israel continues to perceive itself as an isolated victim standing alone against overwhelming odds in a hostile world. Even the intifada, in which the Palestinians have suffered ten times the casualty rates of Israelis, has not diminished Israel's sense of itself as a victim of history, and not as an actor. Over time, this perspective will become ever more difficult for less beleaguered, self-confident, empowered American Jews to share.

The intifada has also given rise to the type of extreme or bigoted thinking that had previously been unacceptable among the Israeli populace because of the memory of Diaspora victimization. Thoughts are now uttered by recognized political leaders that would have been unimaginable five years ago. Two examples may suffice: a prominent rabbi in Judea publicly asserted that Jewish life is more valuable than Arab lives and hence that the punishment for taking an Arab life should not be severe. Israel's Ashkenazic chief rabbi later reminded his colleagues that "all men are created in the image of God,"[8] yet no one in the audience who heard the rabbi's original remarks took issue with this violation of Judaism's most basic teaching. Similarly, the Israel Defense Forces chief of staff Dan Shomron recently remarked that the intifada can only be contained by a political solution or by large scale deportations.[9] He presumed that since the latter would be unacceptable (an echo of a not too distant past), the former would be the only possible solution. Shomron may have miscalculated the weight of public opinion.

I am confident that these radical, unacceptable, and to date, minority opinions in Israel will remain confined to a recalcitrant minority, even if culturally significant and politically influential. Yet the struggle to combat these views, the very engagement in such radicalism, is spiritually debilitating and alienating for both moderate Israelis and mainstream American Jews.

Structurally, American Jewry is presently less in need of spiritual nurturance from Zion. Day schools, seminaries, graduate programs in Judaica, and communal service training seminars now provide a cadre of trained professionals for the American Jewish community, people at home as Americans and as Jews. While Jewish professionals may study for a while in Israel or travel there for conferences and sabbaticals, there is no doubt that their home is in the West. In fact, some of Israel's most successful programs and academic achievements are the product of American-trained scholars who went on *aliyah*.

The links between Israel and America Jewry are deep and enduring, but American Jews cannot sustain a Jewish life in deferment. Jewish options cannot be restricted to another time or place. Increasingly, American Jews have become assertive and nonapologetic about their choices.

Over the past decade, a new development has taken place in America that may reverse the nature of Jewish communal life since the emancipation. When Napoleon offered equal rights to Jews, his terms were explicit: to the Jews as individuals, everything; to the Jewish community, nothing.[10] That is, Jews could achieve equal rights as citizens of the state, but Jewish communal interests were generally ignored. The poet Judah Leib Gordon articulated the Jewish response to emancipation: "Be a Jew in your home and a man in the street."[11]

For generations, Jewish entry into the larger society required the abandonment of parochial attitudes, practices, appearances, and agendas. One could enter the public domain as a citizen of the state, a professional, an artist, or a scientist, but not as a Jew. If one's Jewishness became publicly apparent, it was usually a handicap. Thus, ever since the emancipation, Jews who sought to enter the mainstream of political, intellectual, or cultural life learned to minimize their Jewish identity, conceal it, or deny it altogether. For example, Sigmund Freud feared that psychoanalysis would be stigmatized as a Jewish science and in fact burned his manuscript on Jewish humor. Freud particularly cherished the participation of Carl Jung because of his non-Jewish origins.[12]

Even in America, with its tradition of tolerance and pluralism and the absence of state-sponsored religion, Jewish identity was regarded as disadvantageous. Thus, Walter Lippmann, the distinguished journalist of *The New Republic* and one of America's most influential writers, could comment on every event, but not once did he mention the Holocaust for fear of exposing a parochialism he regarded with shame. Lippmann's behavior was not atypical.[13] In fact, Lippmann blamed the Jews for anti-Semitism. "The rich and vulgar and pretentious Jews of our big cities are perhaps the greatest misfortune that has ever befallen the Jewish people. They are the real fountain of anti-Semitism."[14] At elite universities, such as Harvard or Yale, "joining the club" was a matter of adopting the refinements of the dominant WASP culture and not calling attention to oneself as a Jew.[15]

For the first time, in the past decade American Jews were not reluctant to engage in American life as Jews. For example, Elie Wiesel and Jacob Neusner have both achieved international prominence as Jews working directly with Jewish material. Contrast Neusner's Jewish identity with that of Harry Austyn Wolfson, the Harvard philosopher who was the most prominent scholar of Judaica in academia for forty years (1920–1960). Wolfson also wrote anti-Judaic diatribes under a pseudonym for Harvard's Jewish journal! Of his Jewish identity, Wolfson wrote: "Some are born blind, some deaf, some lame and some are born Jewish."[16]

In political life, an identical process has occurred in which Jewish affiliation and leadership has in no way hampered political ambition. When Stuart Eizenstat was appointed chief of domestic policy for President Jimmy Carter in 1977, he was the highest ranking practicing American Jew to serve in the White House. A decade later, no one even commented on the religious identity of President Ronald Reagan's chief of staff, Kenneth Duberstein, an ethnic New York Jew.

This new political leadership does not hesitate to affirm its Jewish identity or to advocate Jewish interests. Three examples may suffice: Eizenstat was careful to exclude Iranian Jews from the anti-Iranian presidential orders during the height of the hostage crisis. An observant Jew, Eizenstat hosted the president for a Passover seder.

Princeton Lyman is widely credited with initiating the State Department participation in the rescue of Ethiopian Jews. As a mid-level bureaucrat, he did not believe that advancing a partisan cause would hamper his career advancement or that playing it safe would endanger his career. He skillfully exploited the State Department's memory of inaction to facilitate departmental approval for the rescue. Similarly, Ronald Lauder did not feel inhibited by his religion in dealing with the election of accused Nazi war criminal Kurt Waldheim as president of Austria.

In the past, Jews in political life were cautious about their religious background. If elected, they served from districts with large Jewish populations but were timid about asserting a partisan agenda. In the 1980s, Jewish members of the House of Representatives came from Bozrah, Connecticut; Wichita, Kansas; and Dallas, Texas. They represented districts where the Jewish population was less than one-half of one percent. Politicians such as Sam Gejdenson of Connecticut (born in a displaced persons camp in Eschwege, West Germany, the child of Holocaust survivors from Lithuania), Ron Wyden of Oregon, Dan Glickman of Kansas, reflect dramatic changes in American Jewry. They have accepted their own Jewishness as a natural part of their identity and wear it as a badge of honor. They take pride in their ethnicity and their support for Israel is nonapologetic and direct. They respond directly to critics. Barney Frank, another Jewish Congressman from Massachusetts, responded to one of his colleagues who called America a "Christian country" by asking: "if this is a Christian country, what is an overweight Jewish boy from Boston doing up at 5:15 in the morning presiding over the House of Representatives?"

Rudy Boschowitz of Minnesota—a refugee from Hitler's Germany—proudly called himself "the rabbi of the Senate" because of his leadership on Jewish issues. In 1988 Joseph Lieberman from Connecticut was elected to the Senate as an observant Jew, and out of courtesy for his personal religious practice, the Senate Majority Leader has agreed, whenever possible, not to schedule votes on the Jewish Sabbath. Frank Lautenberg had served as national chairman of the United Jewish Appeal before running for the Senate from New Jersey in 1982. Howard Metzenbaum was chairman of the Union of

American Hebrew Congregations' Social Action Commission before he was elected to the Senate from Ohio.

In the arts and literature, in academia and business, Jews now feel fully at home in America. As Charles Silberman has shown, it may be inappropriate to argue by anecdote, yet the accumulation of anecdotal information can illustrate irrefutable trends. Silberman himself cites an event at Harvard as an example of Jewish acceptance. In 1979 Harvard Hillel moved its quarters. The last day was marked by a procession of the Torahs from the old building to the new. The Dean of Harvard's faculty, Henry Rusovsky (himself a refugee from Nazi Germany) was the featured speaker. He said:

> Today Hillel is moving from the periphery of the campus to its very center. Today let it be said that Harvard welcomed us [in the post-World War II era] with open arms as students and teachers. What is perhaps more remarkable is that we have succeeded in transforming ourselves from a group of individuals into a community; that is really what is being celebrated here today.[17]

The United States Holocaust Memorial Museum is yet another example of American Jewry's movement toward the center of national life. The Museum was built with private funds donated by the American people, but its creators and builders were primarily American Jews. The Museum takes what could have been the painful and parochial memories of a bereaved ethnic community and applies them to the most basic of American values. Located adjacent to the National Mall—surrounded by the Smithsonian Institution and the monuments to Lincoln, Jefferson, and Washington—the contents of the museum are designed with its neighbors in mind so that the Holocaust museum will emerge as an American institution that will speak to the national saga.

Such a mainstream undertaking could not have occurred a generation ago. American Jewry would have been too timid, too ghettoized to share its memories. This museum could not have been built by survivors alone, but it was not built without them. Ours is the first generation to stand at a distance from the Holocaust and the last to live in the presence of survivors. The Jewish content of the Holocaust will not be compromised, as some survivors (Elie Wiesel among them)—products of a different generation—feared.

The American Jewish community is a potent political force, able with the help of allies to achieve its political goals: to support candidates helpful to Israel and defeat those who are not; to convince the Congress and successive administrations that aid to Israel is in the vital national interest; and to encourage special efforts on behalf of oppressed Jews in the former Soviet Union and Iran or Ethiopia. This achievement of power is silhouetted against the background of powerlessness and defeat of but one generation ago. American Jews, in the words of Michael Kinsley, live like Episcopalians and vote like Puerto Ricans. They still feel unusual when they are considered part of the "white majority" in the United States.

Israel has contributed much to the renewed pride and self-assertiveness of American Jews. Most Jewish political action—as opposed to political action by Jews—is oriented toward Israel. The American Israel Public Affairs Committee (AIPAC) has come to play an increasingly important role. Its briefings affect Jewish support for political races. Even though AIPAC claims "neither to rate nor endorse candidates," it does publicize voting records with regard to Israel and prioritizes the races each campaign year. It has also spurred the development of pro-Israel Political Action Committees (PACS).

PACS are required by law to operate independently and without coordination, yet the pro-Israel/Jewish PACS are part of an informal network, whose members often play key roles within other Jewish organizations. Politically inclined Jews gravitate toward AIPAC. Given the centrality of American aid to Israel—which is almost ten times the sum contributed by American Jews—and the lure of mainstream American political figures, AIPAC's success has threatened to overwhelm Jewish defense and philanthropic agencies. Over the past several years, AIPAC has recruited key staff members from other Jewish agencies and has thus taken over their major contacts. American Jewish political operatives have also started to play tough, targeting for defeat elected officials perceived as hostile to Israel.

Yet increasingly, American Jews are less willing to support the politics of annexation and extremism. In 1988, thirty-six traditional friends of Israel in the United States Senate, including such prominent pro-Israel Senators as Daniel Patrick Moynihan (NY), Lautenberg (NJ), Boschowitz (MN), Levin (MI), Metzenbaum (OH), wrote an open letter to Prime Minister Shamir advocating that Israel be willing to trade land for peace. Many of the Senators were running for reelection. None lost significant Jewish support. In the waning days of the Reagan administration, the American Jewish community did not fight American negotiations with the Palestine Liberation Organization; they were still struggling with the Israeli government on the "Who is a Jew?" issue.

Threats of renewed anti-Semitic outbreaks have not silenced American Jews. On the contrary, in the aftermath of the Holocaust, anti-Semitism is regarded as the price to be paid for continued Jewish existence; such bigotry is impervious to Jewish behavior—modest or bold, timid or assertive. Thus, Jews feel less inclined to appease anti-Semites.

The second major influence on Jewish public life has been the civil rights movement, which forced the American people to accept diversity and allow ethnicity as an acceptable public identity. Black pride engendered Jewish pride. Black studies on the campus encouraged Jewish studies; and if Blacks were breaking the barriers at elite universities, Jewish quotas were soon dropped. If James Baldwin could write of the Black experience without being forced into an intellectual ghetto, Elie Wiesel could write of Jewish experience during the Holocaust. The broadening of the American mainstream and the open partisanship of Blacks, women, and Jews promoted greater freedom for artists to enter the mainstream without denying the particularism of their concerns.

Anti-Semitism has also decreased for American Jews. It poses few barriers in admission to colleges, graduate and professional schools, and in career advancement in industries that had previously been closed to Jews (such as banking or insurance). The creation of meritocracy has facilitated the rise of Jews to prominence in economic and professional life. For example, up until the late 1960s, no Ivy League university ever had a Jewish president. Since that barrier has been broken, Princeton, Dartmouth, Columbia, and the University of Pennsylvania have all had Jewish presidents. Yale maintained a quota on the admission of Jews until the late 1960s, but less than a decade later the Yale corporation offered its presidency to a Jewish Harvard man. Silberman reports that when Henry Rusovsky turned down the presidency of Yale, his wife asked him if he didn't feel an obligation to accept since he would be Yale's first Jewish president. Rusovsky answered: "I felt we were beyond that. Twenty years earlier that would have been a compelling argument, but not now."[18] Instead, he became the first Jew to turn down the presidency of Yale.

If the rule of emancipation was "be a Jew in your home and a man in the street," the opposite may be the case for some segments of Jewish life in contemporary America. Many American Jews "are Jews in public"; they serve as presidents of national organizations, head philanthropic campaigns and chair major Jewish activities, yet they lead private lives fundamentally devoid of Jewish content. It is doubtful that such public roles without inner congruence can sustain another generation. The offspring of such leaders will either develop a personal dimension to their Jewish commitment or more fully assimilate. American Jews will either choose high intensity Jewish identities, or their Jewish identity, devoid of content, will wither away. American Jews today can choose from an unprecedentedly wide array of Jewish options; intellectual, religious, political, or cultural. They can participate in a wide range of Jewish alternatives, or they can opt out of that civilization without penalty. The challenge for contemporary Jews is to find a way to be a Jew in the home that is congruent with one's public position and with the totality of Jewish experience.

Three theorists of modernization may provide insight into the function the inner life must play for American Jews. Benjamin Nelson has argued that modernization is the movement from brotherhood to universal otherhood.[19] Jews, John Cuddihy wrote, have resisted this final stage of modernization and have maintained a remnant of brotherhood.[20] Peter Berger, the distinguished conservative sociologist, has written of the role of mediating institutions—the church, the neighborhood, the family, and the community—in bridging the gap between isolated individuals and overarching, alienating superstructures. Jewishness will find its continued place in the private life of American Jews in the niche between the atomized individual and the depersonalized larger world. It will endure if it succeeds in becoming a meaningful mediating structure. The breakdown of the family in both its immediate and extended forms has intensified the need for intimate community, and a Jewish structure could also stem the tide of family disintegration by supporting the threatened family unit. Divorce, mobility, patterns of separation (children leaving for college, senior adults moving to the sunbelt), and prolonged single life mean that the family no longer plays the vital role it once did. The family itself, as the most basic structure of the society, is itself in desperate need of strengthening, and the institutions that bolster the family will have much to offer contemporary Americans. Furthermore, in a world increasingly dominated by Gesellschaft (transactional relations) people are in greater need of Gemeinschaft (communities based on organic kinship and shared symbols).[21] Experientially based rather than ideologically, a Jewish mediating structure will permit individual growth in a repersonalized environment.

Orthodoxy already provides the single most powerful mediating structure. Because Orthodox Jews must walk to the synagogue, Orthodoxy in America is neighborhood-based. It has become repersonalized with the *shtiebl* (prayer house) replacing the traditional large synagogue, and the parochial school reinforcing the sense of community. *Shtiebls* provide a sense of community, and since they are not professionally led, they allow for full participation in the service and in religious life for a well-trained male leadership. However, Orthodoxy continues to deny women a public role in the synagogue, which makes this form of traditional Judaism unattractive or unsatisfying for the majority of American Jews living in a world that has enfranchised women in so many other aspects of public life. In addition, Orthodoxy's certitude of ideological conviction—rare in the contemporary world—comes at an enormous cost: the bifurcation of consciousness and a retreat from the larger world. It is unlikely that more than a small but ardent minority of American Jews will be able to accept the complex network of restrictions and rigidities associated with this way of life.

Within the liberal Jewish community, the *havurah* has become an accepted appendage of many large synagogues. Like the *shtiebl*, the *havurah* provides a strong sense of community and individual participation. Reduced in size, it allows for intimacy and growth. In the words of Martin Buber, the domain of "I-You" is particularly needed in a depersonalized setting where "I-It" relationships are increasingly competitive and fragmented. The *havurah* is participatory and generally egalitarian. Even Jewishly under-educated liberal Jews grow in competency as they learn to participate in services. While some contemporary Jews may be Jewishly illiterate, this generation is the best trained, most highly educated generation of Jews in history; thus, such groups are uniquely equipped for self-directed study. The deed, the experiential expression of life cycle events or seasonal rhythms— far more than faith or philosophy—becomes the center of Jewish life. Thus, for example, the building of a *sukkah* (a temporary hut for the fall harvest festival) has proliferated in American Jewish life, not because of a return to the law but because it can be built by the family at home with the full participation of each member and can then be used for eating and entertaining guests.

The intellectual life of the American Jews has also enjoyed unprecedented growth. Scholars now teach Judaica on hundreds of campuses. They write quality books of Jewish interest and content each year. An entire literature for learning and self-discovery, for spiritual growth and historical inquiry, has developed in the English language. It is now possible as never before to become a literate Jew without sacrificing one's intellectuality or the quality of learning that one experiences in the professions. Study groups, both formal and informal, have multiplied.

Ironically, the proliferation of Judaic scholars has robbed liberal rabbis of their traditional role. Two generations ago, the college-educated English speaking rabbis were among the best educated of Jews; for the accented immigrant congregants, such rabbis also served as representatives to the Gentiles. Similarly, a generation ago the non-Orthodox rabbi was the most Jewishly educated of his flock, competent in his field as were the professionals in his congregation in theirs. However, professors of Judaica now often replace rabbis as the repository of Jewish wisdom. Many of today's congregants, products of elite universities with Judaically competent faculty, have studied with the men and women who are writing the books the rabbis are reading. While Christian ministers have been gaining power and political influence, rabbis have been losing power to avowedly secular leaders and to secular learning. Yet the desire for continuing education has only intensified.

Since the average American Jew will spend the first quarter of his or her life in intellectual training (more than eighty-five percent are college graduates), the process of education is unlikely to end with the choice of career. Especially after the final years of academic investment when many people begin to experience the limits of where they will grow professionally or find the alienation of the workplace overwhelming, Jewish learning can provide a significant path for spiritual growth.

Education for young philanthropists, for example, begins with an eight or ten-week training session held in the homes of individual members. "Young Leadership" insists on a sustained time commitment in order to become part of the group. Similarly, synagogues have introduced scholar-in-residence study weekends as the highlight of the programmatic year. In Washington, D.C., the Foundation for Jewish Studies has invited distinguished academics to spend semesters in residence giving scores of lectures and classes. To the surprise of many, hundreds of busy professionals included study as part of their weekly calendar of appointments.

A generation ago, American Judaism was characterized by three religious movements: Orthodox, Conservative, Reform, as well as a Reconstructionist branch of the Conservative movement. Orthodoxy enhanced its position by retreating from the modern world in its pursuit of the past. Conservative Judaism saw itself as normative, as the historical evolution of a tradition that had accommodated to a changing world. Its scholarship probed the historical meaning of a text, its status in a particular time and place. For decades the Conservative Jewish Theological Seminary scrupulously avoided the question of meaning in preference for a value-free "scientific" method of inquiry. Prepared to deal with historical evolution, Conservative Judaism was ill-equipped to grapple with revolution, to deal with a world without precedents, without norms. Responding to the question of historicity, the movement had little to say to the next generation that explored the issue of meaning.

Reform Judaism understood covenantal Judaism as the moral demand for social justice and an ethical world. *Tikkun olam* (mending the world) became its central ideology. Yet over time, the secular world offered the arena of social action; the civil rights movement, the antiwar movement, the crusades against hunger and poverty, the peace movement, and the human ecology movement became the outlet for such passions. One could fulfill such a covenant without reference to the covenant; one could be a good Reform Jew, according to this approach, without a religious framework.

Reconstructionist Judaism was, to use Charles Liebman's term, "an elite formulation of the civil religion of American Jews."[22] It gave voice to how Jews actually behaved. Its founder, Mordecai Kaplan, explained that American Jews lived in two civilizations: a Jewish civilization with its own language, culture, norms, values, art, music, and literature; and an American civilization. The two could be juxtaposed and reconciled without reference to the transcendent. Kaplan's religious naturalism interpreted everything in this-worldly terms. The task was to demythologize Judaism and make it relevant to the scientific categories and humanistic language of American culture.

For more than a generation, Kaplan's writings of the thirties and the forties dictated the course of his movement. Kaplan's views dominated as long as he was alive. In that Kaplan died in 1983 at the age of 102, his work certainly enjoyed a long life span. Within five years of Kaplan's death, the movement shifted ground, naming a neo-Hasidic, liberal, mystically oriented scholar as president of its seminary and thus titular head of the movement. The appointment of Arthur Green (a rabbi ordained by the Conservative movement and the founder of the *havurah* movement) represented a turn toward the transcendent. Ironically, Buber may supplant Kaplan as the spiritual godfather of the Reconstructionist movement—and for good reason.

In the post-Holocaust world, the metaphors for speaking of God must be changed. Traditional covenantal language cannot describe the divine-human reality, and metaphors for power and sovereignty have been debased. God as king with Israel as subjects connotes authoritarian rule to people rooted in democratic values, and the agrarian model God as the shepherd with the Jews as his flock leaves us the sheep who went to the slaughter. Similarly, parent-child images lead to infantilization, and most adults today seek to achieve a degree of autonomy and independence rather than the subservience and dependence that characterize traditional liturgy.

A generation ago, Kaplan thought that scientific categories would provide new meaning. He was clearly wrong. His conservative colleagues thought that historical categories would be adequate to sustain tradition, but in revolutionary times history is hardly consoling.

Religious language will be recaptured only by using the interpersonal as a model for the transcendent. The metaphors for speaking of God and tradition will be personal; what Harold Schulweis has described as predicate theology, reversing Feuerbach's notion that "that which in religion is the predicate, we must make the subject," Schulweis argues that "that which in religion is a subject, we must make the predicate."

The aim is not to prove the existence of the subject, but to demonstrate the reality of the predicates. For subject theology, faith is belief in the subject and atheism is the denial of its existence. For predicate theology faith is belief in the reality of the predicates and atheism is their denial. The critical question for predicate theology is not "Do you believe that God is merciful, caring, peacemaking?" but "Do you believe that doing mercy, caring, making peace are godly?"[23]

A recent article by S. David Sperling provides a second example of relational approaches to the divine. Writing on the oneness of God, Sperling suggested a rereading of the most basic affirmation of Judaism, *Sh'ma Yisrael Adonai Elohenu Adonai Ehad* (Hear, O Israel, the Lord our God, the Lord is One). Sperling suggested that the text be reread, *Adonai Ehab*, love the Lord.[24] Metaphysical unity is to be replaced by existential embrace. A distinguished Bible scholar, Sperling is certainly not proposing a textual correction of Deuteronomy; he knows how the original source reads. Intuitively, however, Sperling understands the requirements of contemporary religiosity. It is not divine essence but the quality of the relational that is paramount.

In the future, the religious needs of American Jews may not be satisfied by the assurances of Conservative Judaism that history will provide norms and meanings; in the wake of the Holocaust and the difficulties of contemporary Israel, no clear sense of meaning emerges. Nor can the demythologizing of Reconstructionism be persuasive when a desacralized world has proved lethal and vacuous. Remythologizing and a return to the sacred world may be required after everything has been devalued, and remythologizing will begin from the interpersonal and move toward community before it encounters the transcendent.

After tragedy and triumph, the inner life of American Jews cannot but be informed by the momentous events of the recent past. Jews will remain engaged in history, involved with power, and in quest of a spirituality congruent with their complex memories of loss and rebirth. No simple innocence can be feigned.

How do we build on the ashes of Auschwitz? Slowly, tenderly, humanely. With humility, perhaps with hope.

Modern art has developed the collage—fragments pieced together to form a whole whose parts can be in tension, in opposition; the pieces may clash, they may lack coherency, or they may strike a tenuous balance. American Jews are creating just such a collage that will be uniquely their own. It may be too early to understand more than the fragments.

NOTES

1. Hannah Arendt, *The Origins of Totalitarianism*, (New York: Harcourt Brace, 1966) 89–123; Richard Rubenstein and John Roth, *Approaches to Auschwitz* (Atlanta, GA: John Knox Press, 1987) 66–68; and Arthur Hertzberg, *The French Enlightenment and the Jews: The Origins of Modern Anti-Semitism* (New York: Columbia University Press, 1967).

2. Amos Oz, An Address to the General Assembly of the Council of Jewish Federations' Meeting in Atlanta. Despite Oz's strong dissent from the Lebanon War and his criticism of the contemporary Israeli policy, he

reiterated his Zionist critique of American Jewry in speeches throughout the United States.

3. By margins of more than two to one American Jews endorse a generally "dovish" position on Israel, yet this does not directly impact on their basic support for Israel. See Leonard Fein's *Where Are We: The Inner Life of America's Jews*, New York: Harper and Row, 1988, chap. 6.

4. See Wolf Blitzer, *Territory of Lies* (New York: Harper and Row, 1989).

5. *The Jerusalem Post*, November 6, 1986.

6. *The New York Times*, July 11, 1989.

7. In a review of Thomas L. Friedman's book *From Beirut to Jerusalem*, Martin Peretz wrote: "As a boy Israel made him [Friedman] proud, stiffened his spine, filled him with a tribal feeling. Like most tribalists, he thought his tribe was perfect. It wasn't until he went to Israel in the 1980s, he says in a startling confession of naiveté and ignorance that he "discovers that it isn't the Jewish summer camp of his youth." This discovery simply busted his Zionist heart. "I was myself a passionate child Zionist too," Peretz wrote, "but I knew very few others whose Israel was so unrealistic, so unnerving, so unflawed as Friedman's. Those I knew grew up." *The New Republic* (September 4, 1989), 37.

8. See "Chief Rabbi Speaks Out," *The Jerusalem Post* (International Edition), June 6, 1989.

9. "Force Can't End the Uprising," *The Jerusalem Post* (International Edition), June 24, 1989.

10. See Arendt, *Totalitarianism*, 29.

11. Judah Leib Gordon, "Awake My People," *Hakarmel*, 7, no. 1 (1866).

12. David Bakan, *Sigmund Freud and the Jewish Mystical Tradition* (New York: Schocken Books, 1965); Paul Roazen, *Freud and His Followers* (New York, London and Scarborough, Ontario: New American Library, 1971); John Murray Cuddihy, *The Ordeal of Civility: Freud, Marx, Levi-Strauss and the Jewish Struggle with Modernity* (New York: Basic Books, 1974), 77.

13. See Stephen J. Whitfield, "From Public Occurrences to Pseudo-events: Journalists and Their Critics," *American Jewish History* 72, no. 1 (September 1982), and Ronald Steel, *Walter Lippmann and the American Century* (New York: Vintage Books, 1981).

14. "Public Opinion and the American Jew," *American Hebrew* (spring 1922).

15. See Dan A. Oren, *Joining the Club: A History of Jews and Yale* (New

Haven and London: Yale University Press, 1985); and Marcia Graham Synnott, *The Half Opened Door: Discrimination in Admissions at Harvard, Yale and Princeton, 1900–1970* (Westport and London: Greenwood Press, 1979).

16. H.A. Wolfson, "Escaping Judaism," *Menorah Journal* 7, no. 3 (August 1921). See Hillel Goldberg, *Between Berlin and Slobodka: Jewish Transition Figures From Eastern Europe* (Hoboken, New Jersey: Ktav Publishing House, Inc., 1989), 37–62.

17. Charles Silberman, *A Certain People* (New York: Summit Books, 1986), 101.

18. Ibid.

19. Benjamin Nelson, *The Idea of Usury: From Tribal Brotherhood to Universal Otherhood* (Chicago: The University of Chicago Press, 1949).

20. Cuddihy, *Ordeal of Civility*, 3–14.

21. Ferdinand Tonnies, *Community and Society* (New York: Harper Torchbooks, 1965).

22. Charles Liebman, *The Ambivalent American Jew* (Philadelphia: The Jewish Publication Society, 1973), 43–87.

23. Harold M. Schulweis, *Evil and the Morality of God* (Cincinnati: Hebrew Union College Press, 1984), 122.

24. S. David Sperling, "The One We Ought to Love," in *Ehad: The Many Meaning of God is One*, ed. Eugene Borowitz (Port Jefferson, NY: Sh'ma, 1989), 85.

15. The *Havurot* in American Judaism

Riv-Ellen Prell

The modern era has been characterized in part by the possibility of a radically voluntaristic Judaism. How this voluntarism has shaped both the Jews and the Judaism of modernity remains one of the central questions in the social scientific study of Jewry. In this paper I propose to explore what may link together some of these apparently different Judaisms by understanding what in the larger culture shapes them. I suggest that we might explore the meaning of a "postmodern Judaism," rather than a modern one, and I look at the American countercultural *havurah* to understand how that postmodern age began.

In the modern and postmodern ages, we inherit our religious traditions like heirloom china, antique furniture, or old family stories. They are ours to polish and to treasure, to store away and forget, or to actively use. They never function precisely as they did for our parents, grandparents, or anonymous ancestors to whom they once belonged. But often, stubbornly and persistently, they remain ours, sometimes in fashion and sometimes not. We do not value them as we might objects purchased in an antique store. Rather, the beauty and perhaps even the meaning of Judaism, is inevitably linked to a past that remains forever opaque to us.

Embodied in this Judaism is a peculiar tension between an implied promise that prescribed words and actions are eternal, and that they are able to represent a personal history of development and choice. This tension expresses the inevitable if obvious fact that our "inherited" traditions are constantly remade, claimed and fashioned in an ever-changing manner. Judaism is always about memory. But the form Judaism takes expresses different definitions of what and who are remembered. Different ages, different social positions, and different cultures have been at the center of how Jews formulated their memories. The voluntarism of modernity has made memory an increasingly individualized activity. Unmoored from socially dense relations, individual memory operates differently than the more collective prescribed sort.

Liberal Judaism has formulated memory in a particularly complex way. Its founders and spokespersons were committed to shaping a Jewish memory in close relationship to the culture in which they lived. As such, they were eager to speak for all Jews, to find just the right balance between what was to be remembered and what was to be inspired by life in the United States, in particular. In the early twentieth century, virtually every generation of American Jewish religious leaders aspired to create *an* American Judaism, a single encompassing framework for all American Jews.[1] They failed to anticipate that American Judaism would always rest upon a base of plural Judaisms. What is possibly the most American about American Judaism is precisely this pluralism, which reflects both a similar Protestant pluralism and lay-domination of religion in general. For Jews in the United States, memory was to be continually contested. How a sacred Jewish past was to be interpreted and how its impact upon the present was to be formulated were linked to the denominations that took root and flourished in American soil. Not just the Jewish systems, but the links between them, must be understood in light of negotiating memory which became the foundation for differentiating one denomination or interpretation of Judaism from another.

What American Jews remember surely affects their behavior and how they act as Jews. The negotiation of memory and the pluralism of American Judaism are linked to patterns of Jewish observance that are minimal. Steven Cohen's research demonstrates that American Jews' personal religious behavior appears to move in one direction—toward laxity.[2] Memory, then, operates at a different level from behavior. If maintaining a sense of one's self as a Jew is not reinforced ritually, memory must be produced elsewhere. The Judaisms of America must resort to cultural or institutional forms. Symbols, rallying phrases, pedagogical theories, or formal ways of organizing Jewish experience all allow us to "read" how Judaism constructs "meaning" at various points in the twentieth century, and what questions and issues people look to Judaism to answer.[3] Even if what underlays these system-level expressions is a decreasing level of observance, the terms in which observance is enacted might best be interpreted through understanding those expressions. Memory, then, is contested and reinforced in a plural Jewish environment in the United States. It is increasingly located within the individual, but formulations are made available through the emerging Jewish institutions of the twentieth century.

Aesthetics and American Judaism

My own reading of American Judaism suggests that it is largely, although not exclusively, constructed by a particular generation in response to specific social and cultural issues surrounding its members. Judaism is not perceived by these men and women as entirely invented. Most of them bring a series of familial associations, religious training, and ideas about religion in America. These feelings and ideas are a bedrock on which Jewish participation is constructed. Although continuity remains a central issue, American Jews seem more eager to forge that continuity with their ancient ancestors than with their contiguous generation.[4] What differentiates various generations of American Judaism is what memory evokes for them. For the founders of Conservative Judaism, for example, immediate familial memories were embedded in religious lives. For third and fourth generation

Jews religious life was created in synagogues and camp settings which did not depend on personal memories of observance. Continuity and memory are cast in different relations in subsequent generations.

American Jews often find themselves in the position of salvaging Judaism from those who have been corrupting it through either excessive liberalism or excessive rigidity. Quite apart from theological conflicts however, American Jews have sought out a Judaism consistent with their own sense of what it means to be, for example, a member of a particular social class, a nonimmigrant, a resident of a "hometown," or preeminently a member of a generation. These social identities have shifted throughout the century, but the link between identity and the practice of Judaism remains consistent. Most often links are expressed through decisions about not only what *mitzvot* to observe (an explicitly halakhic decision), but how to observe them, which may have no specific halakhic implications.

How a man covers his head in a synagogue is a good example of this process. Street hats, uniform paper caps, personally embroidered knitted *kippot* and large bright *kippot* purchased in Israel have all spoken to these social definitions, enforced often by community standards of acceptability. Different head coverings have defined for the entire community social class identity. Uniformity spoke to aspirations for middle-class American aesthetics and mores. Knitted or Israel *kippot* spoke to individualism, rejection of conformity, a redefinition of beauty, and Israel as the location of Jewish values. These debates occurred quite apart from the larger theological debate among Reform Jews that asserted covering one's head had no place in a Western Judaism, a position no longer uniformly held among Reform Jews.

These apparently small gestures, acts of decorum and minute expressions of difference, have loomed large in allowing Judaism to symbolize and express the self, that all important actor of the twentieth century. Precisely because American culture allows and even requires religion to be voluntaristic, aesthetics become an important way to articulate identity and belief. One seeks to "feel" Jewish in a surrounding in which one finds oneself expressed. This process was as true for immigrants as it is for contemporary Jews. It follows that what is beautiful and important to one generation has rarely been appealing to the next. Rabbi Edward Gershfield's poignant remarks to the Rabbinical Assembly in the late 1960s made this point:

> Our services of readings in fine English, correct musical renditions by professional cantors and choirs and decorous and dignified rabbis in elegant gowns arouse disdain and contempt in our young people. They want excitement and noise, improvisations and emotion, creativity and sensitivity, informality and spontaneity. And they are "turned off" by the very beauty and decorum which we worked so hard to achieve. Of course the youth do not want to go into the reasons why these aspects of our life had been created . . . We seem doomed to having to watch our youth relive the same self destructive impulses that we have seen long ago, and thought could not happen again.[5]

Gershfield describes the absence of continuity between the generations and phrases this discontinuity in explicitly aesthetic terms. Indeed, he notes the absence of continuity between the generations and conflict over how best to "remember" Judaism in a contemporary setting. I emphasize these aesthetic forms, then, to understand how much of American Judaism has structured and represented the experience of American Jews. Jewish memory has been tightly linked to negotiating participation in American society. I suggest that it is those constructions we should study because American Judaism is a voluntaristic phenomenon which is dependent on aesthetic expressions for both articulating and verifying one's life as an American Jew. These aesthetic considerations provide insight into the larger cultural matters that link Judaism to American social identity, placing American Judaism into the social class, generational, regional, and other contexts of this society.

Cultural Formulations of Postwar American Judaism

As we stand poised to enter the 1990s how might we assess the cultural expressions of American Judaism of the last decades? What is postwar memory for American Jews? What are the generational expressions of Judaism, the cultural formulations which articulate both the dramatic breakdown in cultural consensus in the United States and the reformulation of American religion in response to it? Understanding something about practice patterns of American Jews leads us to inquire about the communal forms of Judaism which respond to them. These communal forms include our analysis of the postwar suburban synagogue, the rise of federations, Jewish feminism, the development of denominations since World War II, and the increasing viability of Orthodoxy and Hasidism.

In particular, a small but I believe significant organizational form of American Judaism, the *havurah*, has something to teach us about American Judaism.[6] Although there are many synagogue *havurot* in existence today which developed in the middle to late 1970s, I have in mind the more avowedly anti-synagogue *havurot* of the early 1970s. They were a transitional phenomenon created by the postwar generation of Jews in the throes of the counterculture. Their vision of Judaism constituted a critique of the synagogue and a revision of the organization of American Judaism. Members of those early *havurot* have since moved in all possible directions—to Orthodoxy, to religious communities interested in "spiritual renewal" and mysticism, to mainstream synagogues, to small *minyanim* that coexist within larger synagogues, and out of Jewish practice as well. Those initial *havurot* were created to explore alternate possibilities for Judaism rather than to create one fixed form like a denomination. In retrospect, they seem to me to have signaled the start of a new era of American Judaism. They were willing to remember what other generations rejected. They sought a new formulation for Judaism. They are as much a product of the Six-Day War as the burgeoning success of the federation movement and the centrality of Israel to American Judaism.

They appeared to signal a "return" to American Judaism, although they were a rather different phenomenon from the *baale teshuvah* movement.[7] What the various *havurot* revealed was the extent to which the denominations could no longer speak for American Jewish experience. Too closely aligned with the American suburbs, the reaction to immigration, and the desire for a homogenized and mainstream American experience, the Judaism of denomination and synagogues was being reevaluated. Its ethnicity was not very "ethnic." Its approach to religion appeared to be too passive because of the dominance of the professional staff and the lack of education and commitment by the laity. Its scale was too large, yet insufficiently global. The *havurot* of the seventies indicated a shift in American Judaism in the medium of a postmodern American culture; decentralized, ephemeral, plural, and diverse, and highly focused on aesthetics.

Countercultural *Havurot*

Havurat Shalom was founded in Boston in 1967 with funding from the Danforth Foundation in St. Louis.[8] Arthur Green (later head of the Reconstructionist Seminary), then a recent graduate of the Jewish Theological Seminary, envisioned an alternative seminary for Jewish study which would embody those principles of the counterculture most opposed to hierarchy and interested in spirituality and contemplation. This seminary had no denominational affiliation and was committed to Jewish study, including nontraditional subjects such as mysticism and pacifism. At the end of a year, the first participants dissolved its seminary mission, and the group became a *havurah*, a nonresidential community committed to study and Sabbath prayer. Shortly thereafter, *havurot* were formed in New York, Philadelphia, Los Angeles, San Francisco, Chicago, and elsewhere. Each differed from the other, but all shared the conviction that they practiced a type of Judaism and shared study and prayer experiences which were available nowhere else. After a decade of thriving, most closed or their membership or mission were dramatically altered. They identified with no American Jewish denomination because none struck the balance they sought. Liberal groups sacrificed too much tradition. Traditional groups were too rigid and unwilling to make changes in Jewish law that seemed self-evidently necessary—primarily, the right of women to participate equally and identically to Jewish men.

The founders of these groups were critical on two counts of synagogues of all denominations and the American Judaism they represented. They deplored the bureaucratic and anonymous organization of the synagogue that atomized the community into leaders and followers. They argued that the synagogue encouraged passivity by making its members consumers of a Jewish experience rather than participants in it.

In *havurot*, members believed that they participated more actively in their own religious lives. Only as actors did they believe they could create what they thought of as "authentic Jewish community." However, they placed demands on their Judaism as well. They were not Orthodox Jews precisely because they were unwilling to cede all authority to an inherited tradition. They wanted Judaism to reflect themselves. Jewish texts and traditions were subjected to close scrutiny and discussion not only about gender equality, but about issues of war and peace, justice, vegetarianism, and doubt and belief. In the 1970s *havurot* founders sought a marriage between New Left politics and normative Judaism, producing a transformation of each.

The *havurah* was first and foremost an *organizational form* of American Judaism. It founders and members made no attempt to create a coherent theology or to produce a new or revised liturgy. It might be more accurate to characterize their preoccupation with organization as counter-organizational. They rejected formal leadership, coherent structure, and theological or liturgical consistency. The *havurah*, in this sense, was inspired by the New Left. As Kenneth Kenniston wrote about its organizational strategy,

> Indeed, within the New Left there is a certain anarchistic strain that opposed *all* large scale institutions in favor of small face-to-face groups. If there is a hidden utopia, it is the utopia of small groups of equals, meeting together in mutual trust and respect to work out their common destiny.[9]

There was no need for committees, consistency, or coherence in the *havurah* vision because the like-minded were assumed to share a similar approach. Elaborate governance and structure were therefore unnecessary. Indeed, *havurot* shared with the New Left the counter-cultural supposition that no one would need to encroach on another's freedom, yet harmony would prevail. This was no more true in *havu-*

rot than in the New Left, but both spoke to what Kenniston rightly labels a utopian premise. Michael Fishbane wrote about this tension when he was a member of *Havurat Shalom:*

> The responsibility for acting on the basis of the totality of what we had learned and felt made religious development deliberate and idiosyncratic. The diversity of issues with which we wrestled was integrated into the person of each one of us; each of us in our tensions was a Jewish "possibility" (certainly not an authority) for the others.[10]

This powerful statement of freedom and autonomy, voluntarism and obligation, and fundamentally, individualism and community responsibility is manifest in the *havurah* organization. Nothing about the organization was designed to be coercive, no definitions or limits were insisted upon, and members maintained an open-ended sense of possibility in religious life. Integration occurred in the person, not in the organization. Ideally, the organization remained flexible. It did not represent religious life, but enabled it.

Synagogues appeared to be permanent. Their buildings and organizations were massive and elaborate. One member of the New York *Havurah* suggested that synagogues represented a sense of permanence and control that newly acculturating Jews required to convince themselves of their own permanence in the U.S. *Havurah* members required no such signs of permanence. To the contrary. Their ambition was to challenge American culture and the Judaism of their parents in order to fashion an alternative life for themselves. Organization or counter-organization provided that alternative. *Havurot* members usually sat in circles rather than pews. Their Sabbath dress reflected informality and "folk" styles in contrast to the decorous formality of the synagogue. They rotated responsibility for leading worship and reading Torah, and rejected permanent responsibility or formal leadership. They did not worship in the style described by Rabbi Edward Gershfield. They tended not to use the guitars and "throw-away liturgies" inspired by the underground church of the 60s. However, he did anticipate the extent to which *havurot* would challenge the aesthetic and cultural formulations of Judaism that so closely reflected the postwar middle class, and that some of its children would find intolerable enough to refuse to allow themselves to be defined by it.

The postwar children of *havurot* recalculated what was to be remembered. Unlike any preceding American generation they sought to emulate nineteenth-century European Jews. Other generations had revered and sentimentalized those people and that place. But those generations drew an impassable boundary between themselves and European Jewry. Their aesthetic formulations rejected European and immigrant Jewry. The *havurah* generation, in its own romanticism, cast itself as "neo-Hasidic." Its members wanted intense communal ties of a sort, and vibrant spirituality. They did not wish to become Hasidim, but they saw them as their inspiration. Their Judaism could find no model in contemporary American Jewish life. The larger Jewish counterculture wanted to remember Jewish radicalism as well. This generation used memory to disentangle themselves from the middle-class affluence of their parents and grandparents. Nevertheless, they encountered the counterculture through their Judaism. The counterculture rejected American society. Judaism could be their alternative if it could be unharnessed from their parents. And it could, if those buried treasures of mysticism, radicalism, and community could be unearthed from a Jewish past hidden from them in America.

Consensus and Reformulation

Havurot, then, signaled a change in American Judaism. They were created by a newly forming adult generation that, as Steven Cohen noted, would reject virtually the entire Jewish infrastructure of the previous generation.[11] This generation wanted to do things in a different way, despite the fact that its members were far less different from their parents than their parents likely had been from the preceding generation. Shared American birth would not alone define the institutions of American Judaism. This newer generation's deep identification with the counterculture led them to criticize their parents for their "abandonment of Judaism" and identification with mainstream white America. They were comfortable with partial and inconsistent observance despite their sense of themselves as "traditional." Their tradition was a "sensibility," a "style," or an approach which differentiated them from Conservative and Reform synagogues.

The *havurah* founders' critique of American society was closely related to that of the New Left. This widespread analysis of American culture constituted an attack on America's involvement in the Vietnam War, in the treatment of American minorities and the distribution of resources, in understanding the family in general, and gender roles in particular. In the wake of this critique, by the mid-1970s, America had undergone a complete breakdown in what is generally called "cultural consensus." A shared view of the society and its best interests could no longer be articulated, and even its beneficiaries and partial beneficiaries, middle-class youth, white women, and some professionals no longer supported this consensus. Frances Fitzgerald understands the 1960s to have been a switchpoint in this change from consensus to a newly negotiated culture.[12] The counterculture, in retrospect, seems to have been more involved in destroying the consensus than in formulating new visions or a new organization of culture.

Havurot participated in the process of breakdown and reformulation in two ways. First, *havurot* expressed a renewed identification with ethnicity in which Americans were anxious to disassociate themselves from the power and oppression of the white majority.[13] Second, *havurot* might be seen as evidence of an overall resurgence in religious participation, and its link to political activism on the part of more fundamentalist Jews and Christians who had previously resisted it.[14] Although *havurah* members were participants in a liberal rather than fundamentalist religion or politics, their very link to religion would have been unlikely in the 1960s.

As I discussed above, the early members of *havurot* also set about communicating their alternative vision of Jewish community in a new way which emphasized aesthetics and organizational forms. Both their approach and their issues are reflected in other American Judaisms of the 1980s. Mark Pinsky's 1986 front page *Los Angeles Times* article, for example, discussed both *havurot* and small orthodox communities attached to a single rabbi. He called their shared concerns a desire for a "Judaism of scale." Separated in every other way in their Judaisms, they shared a desire for community and more personal visibility. Similarly, Jewish feminists, some of whom were associated with early *havurot* and many of whom were not, often eschew denominational identification. Although they are far more explicitly concerned with liturgy and theology than the *havurah* "movement," their ease with maintaining a "sensibility" while altering Halakhah are parallel. Finally, even the development of the Federation movement which went far beyond collecting philanthropy to defining Jewish identity and experience, seemed to understand the Jews' desire for a different type of activism.[15] *Havurot* and federations understood that American Jews were securing and constructing their identities in a new generational way that depended more upon emotion and experience than evoking childhood memories.

Scale, the creation of experience, and the reformulation of memory, an abandonment of consistency, an interest in local level activity, as well as global organization, such as federations and other international organizations linking Israel and the U.S., all express the characteristics of the postmodern age that followed the breakdown of cultural consensus. The historical and social processes that turned American men and women to religion, to new settings for practicing new types of religion, to enshrining experience and identity within religion, may well describe, if not entirely explain, what is at stake in the Judaism for the 1990s. *Havurot* articulated these concerns and anticipated many more that would come. Judaism may be a great deal more polarized than it was in the 1970s. Like the postmodern age, *havurot* seemed ironically to pursue tolerance and compromise within a rejectionist and rigidly liberal organizational model. Their members' vision of sensibility and tolerance seems to have given way to greater stridency than they might have imagined. That inevitability is for others to understand. My more modest task has been to suggest that with the wisdom of hindsight one can find in American Jewish experiments models for generational formulations of Judaism that reveal the relevant social processes that structure those constructions.

The modern era began with the sacred world contracting. The self, voluntarism, pluralism, and individual choice framed twentieth-century American religion. As a result Judaism, in particular, was forced to transform itself from a culture to a religion. It became a crucial medium for representing and enacting an identity that included social class, minority status, gender, and generation. In the theories of most early social scientists, the voluntarism of modernity was to lead not only to the contraction of the sacred, but to its eventual demise. As religion was increasingly removed from authority and social power, it took on new functions and symbolic meanings that were particularly difficult to abandon as the scale of society became more massive and bureaucratized. With the breakdown of cultural consensus, American religion turned out to be able to formulate, if not unify, conflicting forces in sacred terms. But Judaism, like Christianity, was not to remain the same. Without understanding the postmodern turn in American culture, it is difficult for us to make sense of the apparent contradictions in what appears to be the Judaisms of the 1990s. Methodologically, we are better able to study these changes by understanding the need to locate American Judaism within American culture.

As we look closely at memory in Judaism, we find of late more distance from the adjacent generation and more interest in an imagined Judaism. Menachem Friedman has argued that the destruction of European Jewry is responsible for the development of Judaism within yeshivot in Israel.[16] Judaism no longer exists in communities which can act to curb its rigidifying impulses. The yeshiva creates a peer and artificial community where Judaism is lived in accordance with halakhic study disconnected from sacred objects with family histories and memories. New memories are created about a community to which there is no more access. Postmodern life is above all characterized by the lack of continuity, and the creation of new memory. In a general way the Judaism of the 1990s will share memories born from severed communities which create new ones. Their continuity is mythic. They reject a past which they have been denied. These new communities redefine gender, social status, and Jewish identity in dramatically different ways than those which preceded them. The calculation of memory reveals the cultural underpinning of American Judaism.

NOTES

1. Lawrence Hoffman, *Beyond the Text: A Holistic Approach to Liturgy* (Bloomington: Indiana University Press, 1987).
2. Steven M. Cohen, *American Modernity and Jewish Identity* (New York: Methuen, 1983); *American Assimilation or Jewish Revival?* (Bloomington: Indiana University Press, 1988).
3. The anthropologist Clifford Geertz is largely responsible for introducing the notion of behavior and culture as text-like and amenable to "reading" or "interpretation" (197). Geertz seeks to capture "inscribed discourse" in the flow of everyday life and behavior. This discourse is not only persistent, but reveals what he defines as "cultural" phenomena, the key constructions of human experience developed by particular groups. I suggest that how Jews organize their Judaism is one of the best ways to understand American Jewish culture. Judaism is not all that ties Jews to their culture. One might argue that Judaism is not *the* most salient expression of that culture, but it certainly is an important perspective on it.
4. Werner Sollers' original and imaginative study of American ethnicity has a particularly useful discussion of the metaphor of generations in American history. He argues that from the Puritans to the present Americans have tended to see the second generation as descending and the third generation as reinvigorating the truths of the first generation. Sollers also demonstrates that virtually all writers on the subject count themselves as third generation despite their date of arrival. Few claim themselves to be second generation. He ably argues that the "generational hypothesis" is simply one more version of an American ideology committed to the relations between "consent" and "descent" as the symbolic underpinnings of participation in American culture. See Werner Sollers, *Beyond Ethnicity: Consent and Descent in American Culture* (New York: Oxford University Press, 1986), 208–36.
5. This quotation was cited in Marshal Sklare, *Conservative Judaism, An American Religious Movement* (New York: Schocken Books 1955), 280–81.
6. My interest in *havurot* is in part based on participant-observation research I conducted in a group in Los Angeles in 1973–75. My much

fuller discussion of this group, and my analysis of the links between *havurot* and American Judaism may be found in Riv-Ellen Prell, *Prayer and Community: the Havurah in American Judaism* (Detroit: Wayne State University Press, 1989).

7. The first full-length treatment of this movement can be found in Janet Aviad, *Return to Judaism: Religious Renewal in Israel* (Chicago: University of Chicago Press, 1982).

8. See James Sleeper and Alan Mintz, eds., *The New Jews* (New York: Vintage Books, 1971); and Jacob Neusner, ed., *Contemporary Judaic Fellowship in Theory And Practice* (New York: Ktav, 1972), for collections of articles on the founding of *havurot.*

9. Kenneth Keniston, *Young Radicals: Notes on Committed Youth* (New York: Harcourt Brace and World, 1968).

10. Michael Fishbane, "Have You Sold Out: A Symposium," *Response Magazine* 10 (1976): 58–60.

11. Cohen, *American Modernity*, 1983.

12. Frances Fitzgerald, *Cities on a Hill: A Journey through Contemporary American Cultures* (New York: Simon and Schuster, 1986).

13. Anthropologist Michael Fischer has written with particular insight on the ethnicity of the 1970s and 1980s. His analysis of autobiographical writing of Blacks, Hispanics, and Asian Americans emphasizes the contrast between their understanding of their ethnicity and that of social scientists of ethnicity of the 1950s and 1960s. In addition, Fischer demonstrates the extent to which ethnics influence one another's self-perceptions in a dialogical relationship between groups, rather than a separation from them. Fischer has also reflected on his own Jewish ethnicity in this regard. See Michael Fischer, "Ethnicity and the Postmodern Arts of Memory," in *Writing Culture*, ed. James Clifford and George Marcus (Berkeley: University of California Press, 1986).

14. See Robert Wuthnow, *The Restructuring of American Religion: Society and Faith since World War II* (Princeton: Princeton University Press, 1988), for a discussion of this phenomenon amongst Christians.

15. See Jonathan S. Woocher, *Sacred Survival: the Civil Religion of American Jews* (Bloomington: Indiana University Press, 1986).

16. Menachem Friedman, "Life Tradition and Book Tradition in the Development of Ultraorthodox Judaism," in *Judaism Viewed from Within and from Without*, ed. Harvey Goldberg (Albany: State University of New York Press, 1987).

16. The End of Patriarchy in Jewish Conversation

Sheldon R. Isenberg

In premodern times, there was clearly an official Jewish conversation. In a sense it was about everything, but everything was spoken about in relation to Torah. The hermeneutical conventions were more restricted in the halakhic dimension and less restricted in the aggadic, which included not only Midrash, but also philosophy and mysticism. The conversants were rabbis, men whose consciousness was shaped by the traditional Torah disciplines. Women and other men not so trained, perhaps less efficient memorizers, perhaps more intuitive, were excluded systematically. (The legendary exceptional women more than proved the rule.) Moreover, the conversants crossed centuries. In talmudic and midrashic collections the earliest Tannaim and the latest Amoraim continually engage each other, comment on each other, supplement each other. For the traditional students of the Talmud, there is no sense that the voices of tradition cease with their bodily death.

Rarely do we find explicit inclusions of non-Jews in premodern Jewish conversation, but the Judaism recorded in the Bible shared a basic cosmological horizon with its ancient Near Eastern neighbors, while Rabbinic Judaism swam in the cultural ocean of the Greco-Roman and medieval cultures. Similarly, as Jews have become sharers in contemporary society, they converse within modern and post-modern mental and spiritual assumptive frameworks. The voices of Judaism and the conversations they constitute have mutated accordingly. This paper presents some marginal (and woefully un-systematized) observations about what happens to the voices and conversations of Jews as they pass from the traditional to posttraditional worlds.

Today there is no comparable single over-arching Jewish conversation. Rather, the model is more like Wittgenstein's "language games": there is a "family"—an extended family—of overlapping conversations, with no hierarchically superior conversation containing all the rest. Nor are these conversations limited to the halakhic, the Torah-trained men. In fact, these conversations are not necessarily limited to Jews! We participate in a larger human conversation as we never have before, for there has never been such a conversation, such a world-wide circulation of information.

While, to a great extent, traditional Torah is no longer the universal medium of exchange, nevertheless elements of the fractured Jewish mythos seed the poems, the novels, and the speculations of contemporary Jewish authors. At the individual level, Jews may participate in Jewish conversations, but rarely do they choose to participate *only* in a Jewish conversation. The nature of posttraditional life is such that we participate in a multitude of communities in our fractured lives.

I want to extend the meaning of Torah by conceiving it as a transformation of the rabbis' Oral Torah. The Oral Torah was and is a conversation about everything by an intellectual, spiritual, male elite, cast as commentary on the Jewish Bible—a conversation that lasted for centuries and still continues within traditional communities. The words of the participants in that conversation are valued as, and claim the authority of, revelation. To the vast majority of posttraditional Jews that conversation is unknown. But the discussions continue in a very different format. I suggest that it is useful to see that set of Jewish conversations about values, truth, God, survival, living Jewishly, and so on, as a further extension of Torah that is being generated as a result of Jews living and talking, thinking and storing their thoughts. The conversation has widened, with a lack of dogmatic constraints. It has connected with many more conversations. Especially in its postmodern manifestations, it is more modest in it claims. Torah has become, for now, "decanonized" in the modern and postmodern conversations.

Since tradition has lost its presumptive authority, the voices of tradition no longer incorporate the whole conversation; rather they serve as one set of participants with whom to agree and disagree, in part and in whole, and against whom to create. The path to truth, wisdom, and spiritual power is not solely through the life of Torah for most Jews.

Modern and Postmodern Judaism: Torah De-canonized

By modern and postmodern I mean those imperfect, yet useful, categories that describe that period (modern) which favors first Enlightenment reason and then scientific method as the sole models for finding and establishing truth, all others being "subjective." This we can describe as the age of scientism and modernism. By postmodern we mean the rejection of scientism from a variety of perspectives, for philosophical reasons, moral reasons, esthetic reasons, theological reasons, etc.

Postmodern philosopher Richard Rorty characterizes the postmodern situation as one in which no conversations are foundational to any others, and no type of conversation (e.g., scientific or mystical or moral) is presumed to have privileged access to what is "true" about the world, about God, about history. This pluralization—and, I would argue, inevitable relativization—of knowledge and values has two major sources. First, the security of those very sciences that provided the modern paradigm has been called into question by both relativity theory and the indeterminacy of quantum mechanics, and second, the conviction that has emerged in post-Wittgenstein philosophy and related cultural forms that all human experience is to some extent linguistically or symbolically determined.

Modern and Postmodern in Judaism

Judaism modernized very thoroughly, accepting the authority of, first, Enlightenment reason and then, the scientific temper. Judaism plays on modern fields. From Mendelssohn through Mordecai Kaplan, Jewish thinkers have attempted to bring Judaism into relationship with modern beliefs about what is reasonable, rational, and real. Biblical studies and Jewish studies in general have joined in the larger academic conversation which in its establishment forms is quintessentially modern. Jewish *Wissenschaft* was an early manifestation of Jewish modernism in that sense.

Even Joseph Soloveitchik can be understood as a modern in a dialectical way when he describes himself as one who must choose to be alienated from the modern world:

> What can a man of faith like myself, living by a doctrine which has no technical potential, by a law which cannot be tested in the laboratory, steadfast in loyalty to an eschatological vision whose fulfillment cannot be predicted with any degree of probability . . . what can such a man say to a functional utilitarian society which is saeculum oriented and whose practical reasons of the mind have long ago supplanted the sensitive reasons of the heart?

Listen to the language: Jewish doctrine has no "technical potential," cannot be "laboratory tested" and its predictive potential cannot be measured by scientific standards of probability. Faith is opposed to the heady objectivism of the modern, not the postmodern, world.

But contemporary Judaism is simultaneously postmodern when scientism no longer supplies criteria of meaning and truth with the result that the modern scientistic conversation is no longer given dogmatic authority. For in the postmodern conversation hall, no conversation has such authority. Posttraditional Judaism includes modern Judaism and postmodern Judaism. In his critique of the modern objectification of humanity and God, Buber reveals himself as postmodern, as does Rosenzweig. The rejection of Enlightenment idealism and post-Enlightenment scientism does not result in a return to Orthodoxy. In fact, freedom from materialistic objectivism can result in relativistic nihilism as well as spiritualism.

Modern and Postmodern Expressions

Judaism's paradigmatic thought-form is midrashic. Rabbinic Midrash interprets and resymbolizes biblical traditions. Posttraditional Midrash far more loosely resymbolizes biblical and postbiblical traditions. In current terminology, Jewish thought has always been predominantly intertextual, in its traditional and posttraditional forms. This characteristic it shares with Christianity and Islam. So what happens in a text-based tradition when the sacred text loses its sacrality, its automatic, dogmatic authority? What happens when it loses its context in a multileveled reality as the tradition mutates into modernity? From inside the tradition, Rabbi Joseph Soloveitchik, as we have heard, poses the dilemma of the traditional "man of faith" who in the modern world must become the "lonely man of faith."

In his almost Kierkegaardian statement, Soloveitchik both points to and simplifies the movement of modernity into and through Jewish consciousness. The individualizing tendencies of modern thought and feeling structures and their concomitant social structures have made loneliness a common characteristic of modernity. For the Jews who have perceived themselves throughout the millennia as an extended family, as the immortalization of Abraham's seed, the loss of the foundational power of the Jewish myth has been a source of both liberation and spiritual devastation.

To be a Jew in the late medieval ghettos of Europe was still to be a believer within a context of believers—even the enemies outside the walls were believers! In that spiritual environment the text had context which was not only natural but also "supernatural." In modernity, we might say, the content and context of text is judged at the scientistic bar. In postmodernity, the very distinction between text and context becomes perceived as arbitrary. The rules for establishing value and truth in any conversation are seen as internal to each conversation. As Rorty argues, conversations are not commensurable.

The Conservative, Reform, and Reconstructionist movements and Zionism have been predominantly modern in that they emerged and developed ideologically at a time when Science (or Objectivism) and Religion were seen as either sole alternatives or apparent contradictions to be harmonized. More recent movements which have developed outside the "establishment" are rather in postmodern modes.

Susan Handelman on Hermeneutical Freedom

Let me try briefly to clarify these cryptic comments by engaging a very significant book by Susan Handelman with the wonderful title of *The Slayers of Moses* and the somewhat misleading subtitle, *The Emergence of Rabbinic Interpretation in Modern Literary Theory*. One of Handelman's theses is that the traditional midrashic playfulness with the biblical text blurs the boundaries between "text" and "interpretation" in ways that correlate significantly with poststructuralist, postmodern literary theory—much of which has been theorized by Jewish critics, from Freud to Derrida to Bloom. The significance of that claim lies in the postmodern obsession with language. How language functions in a community is symptomatic of the structure and functioning of the community as a whole.

Handelman makes very valuable observations about the differences between the process of traditional Jewish interpretation and traditional Greek-based logocentric Christian interpretation. For the Jewish mind, Torah is not a given, fixed text, but an endless unfolding through Oral Torah. The text is generated through the rabbinic conversation. The rabbinic conversation is not only *about* Torah, it *becomes* Torah. Each letter, each word of written Torah must be copied with utter fidelity, for Torah is from Sinai, but each letter, each word, each jot, each tittle cannot be limited in *meaning*. Similarly, the meaning of Jewish living, suffering, dying—of Chosenness and

Exile—are constantly reinterpreted in the narrative, the Aggadah, the story of the covenanted community. In fact, she argues, the unclosing nature of rabbinic interpretation emerges directly from the Rabbis' consciousness of the unclosed, expectant nature of their history, its present always being Exile.

In contrast, says Handelman, the Christian approach is to seek to penetrate through language to its essential referent. In Christ, the Logos, the Word, is incarnate once and for all. So for Augustine, "linguistic multiplicity is a condition of the fall. . . .What Augustine, following the Greek metaphysicians, particularly Plato, seeks is the mode of knowing as being-and-having—not the endlessness of interpretation, but the absoluteness of presence (120)." And so "Jesus is the essential link between signifier and signified because with the doctrine of incarnation the substance and its representation are one and the same" (120). Christian interpretation is focused on the Christ event. The multiplicity of the biblical text is reduced to the uniqueness of Christ.

In fact, this kind of topological reductionism is characteristic of the Jewish and Christian apocalyptic literature, while the Zohar allegorizes exuberantly. I believe that there is more variety in the hermeneutical presuppositions underlying the traditional modes of interpretation than Handelman considers. Nevertheless, the connections she makes are intriguing: the rabbinic mind which wanders from interpretation to interpretation lives in, reflects, and patterns the indeterminacy of Exile, recapitulating the paradigmatic exiled life of the people. In contrast, for Christianity, whose Messiah has come, whose eschatology is at least once realized, such unending production of meaning is intolerable. The Word has come—and gone—and salvation is available to the believer once and for all.

Postmodern epistemology perceives all humanity in exile from any objective truth, from any reality uncontaminated by the indeterminacy of language. As Handelman puts it, just as all Jewish talking can be incorporated in Torah so that there is no Jewish meaning that exceeds the boundaries of Torah, so in modernity all humanity is totally contained by language. In that respect all postmoderns are Jews, all in involuntary exile—whether they know it or not.

Postmodern exile is involuntary because of human nature: we have no direct or privileged direct experience of reality. We cannot avoid experiencing through the veils of linguistic symbolization. Handelman joins other postmodern critics who see in language the key to structuring experience. Language does not mimic reality, it does not refer to something other than itself, it is simultaneously a product of and producer of our experience. It is indistinguishable from our experience, and we have no experience without commentary, without subtitles.

One result of such linguistic indeterminacy is political, as we have seen—no conversation can be foundational to any other, implying that no group of conversationalists should justify having power over any other based on their special access to truth and value. Structurally, the postmodernist pluralistic position on truth and values seems to parallel the traditional Jewish rejection of "image-making" or idolatry. For instance, idolatry includes tying God into a particular material form, whether this be reflected in the Deutoronomic prohibitions against images, or the rejection of the messianic incarnation of a Jesus or a Sabbatai Zevi. To tie the text of Torah to any person or any person's meaning, to one stable, knowable referent, is the equivalent of idolatry.

Handelman emphasizes the congruences of traditional Midrash and postmodern literary theory on this basis. Her comparisons of rabbinic modes of language and postmodern criticism are creative and instructive. But she tends to flatten, if not ignore, important distinctions between traditional and posttraditional perspectives.

The rabbinic Torah, and so the major product of the traditional Jewish conversation, is *canonical*. A canon is always a religious and political expression of a hierarchy. (Conflicts between Sadducees and Pharisees, between Karaites and other Jews, and in the modern period between Reform and other Jews are spelled out as arguments about the canonical status of rabbinic literature.) Certain literature is made elite by an elite. In modernity, on the other hand, Judaism has become by and large de-hierarchized, and in the process the boundaries of Torah have been set in motion. While it is true that there was an enormous amount of exegetical freedom internal to the traditional halakhic and aggadic processes, we must still be aware that there is a crucial difference between a complex plurality of voices *within* the unitary, sacred conversation of tradition and the *plurality of conversations* which characterizes modernity.

The Variety of Posttraditional Jewish Voices

The liberation implicit in the postmodern vision is manifest in the extraordinary diversity of voices that make up the modern Jewish conversation. In the contemporary Jewish conversation the rabbinic voice itself has split and diversified into the various official Jewish branches, but beyond that, as we have already indicated, rabbinic voices constitute but one segment of the conversation, and not necessarily the most sought after. For modernity has enabled nonrabbinic Jewish voices to speak publicly as never before. No longer is ordination the entrance requirement to the Jewish conversation.

Some novelists are recognized as Jewish in form and content, as well as some poets, some composers, musicians, and artists. I have just helped to direct a wonderful dissertation on Jewish American poetry that attempts to deal with the eccentric Jewishness of several American Jewish poets. In addition, the evolution of Jewish studies has generated a vast literature about Judaism from perspectives that seek to be "academic." Moreover, the whole range of Jewish history has been made available in ways that it never has before.

Ironically, at the same time that Jews have, in overwhelming numbers, ceased to live inside Torah, inside Jewish space and time, they have acquired access to more information about the whole historical range of possibilities for being Jewish than has ever been available. Shelves of texts until now available only to a small elite are for sale or loan in translation and with commentary. So the voices of tradition are instantly available simultaneously with the voices of posttraditional Judaism.

At the same time, historical criticism has enticed us to envision Judaism as a historical, developmental process in ways radically different from the rabbinic mythicization of tradition that has, for instance, Abraham putting on tefillin and studying Torah. Our separation from total immersion in the traditional mythos, which is concomitant with the modern de-canonization of Torah, has opened the postmodern midrashic process to all participants in the Jewish conversation. Nowhere are the results more evident than in the transformation of Jewish community and consciousness by women.

The Voices of Women

It may be that this century will be best known for the world wide movement to end patriarchy as a way of life, to end the domination of women and children by men that has been such an overwhelming reality of human societies for the period covered by historical records. Jewish women have been at the forefront of this wave and their efforts have been focused on society at large as well as the Jewish community in particular. From the moment that the constraints that prevented women from participation in cultural conversations (rather than only in family conversations or in conversations with other women) have been relaxed, women have been heard.

It is my impression that Jewish feminists in the seventies and early eighties tended to disconnect themselves from Judaism, often joining in the general feminist chorus that blamed Judaism and Christianity for supporting, if not creating, patriarchy in the West. (E.g., Merlin Stone's *When God Was a Woman*.) But as we have moved through the eighties, we find a vibrant self-consciously Jewish feminism emerging, evolving and changing the structure and content of many Jewish conversations. Indeed, recent estimates are that the seminaries of the Reform, Conservative, and Reconstructionist movements will be enrolling women at rates soon to exceed fifty percent of each class. As their graduates move into temples and synagogues, into positions of authority in Jewish communal institutions and the seminaries themselves, the results for Jewish self-imaging are incalculable. Nevertheless, many Jewish women are insisting on speaking and being heard outside of and beyond the current establishment institutions.

Already women's voices are heard in literature speaking Midrash and thereby reshaping the traditions as they search for mythic validations from the inside, for role models buried in the centuries of male-transmitted Aggadah. One of the earlier and still popular magazines that transmits many Jewish women's voices is called *Lilith*. In the traditional Aggadah, she is a demoness who kills newborn babies. But since she is portrayed as Adam's first wife who was created equal with him and who insisted on equality with him, she was a natural role model from the tradition for Jewish women seeking the depatriarchal-ization of Judaism.

A recent publication, in academic idiom, is entitled *Sarah the Priestess: The First Matriarch of Genesis*. The author, Savina Teubal, argues that Sarah, Rebekah, and Rachel functioned as priestesses in goddess worship inside the Hebrew tribe. Thus the patriarchal period is read as a time of struggle between Jewish goddess-worshipping matriarchy and Jewish god-worshipping patriarchy. The thesis is fascinating, responsibly researched, and creatively argued and fits in well with Raphael Patai's more broadgauged claims about Jewish goddess worship and its survivals through the Second Temple period and beyond.

What interests me in her work is not whether or not her historical reconstruction is "right," but rather her valorizing hermeneutic, her desire to ground women's spirituality in authentic, but hidden, traditions:

> Over four thousand years later, this same despair and this same struggle is being experienced by women in other social and religious spheres.
>
> But we are not alone. Sarah is there, standing on the threshold, waiting to be returned to her rightful place in history. There are still some formidable obstacles to be overcome, but the record of Sarah's life reveals the existence of an alternative system to patriarchy. The social system the three matriarchs defended indicates the presence of a struggle against patriarchy, and of a social structure in which women played a prominent part in religion and culture . . . The Sarah tradition gives us an insight into the potential of women's roles to affirm women. [140f.]

This hermeneutical move is part of a common pattern in postmodern liberation movements. The women's liberation movement is full of attempts to ground their current aspirations in historic or prehistoric *mythoi* including the story of the prehistorical matriarchy—which may or may not be accurate in the sense that if we had been there, we would have seen it. American Indian liberation movements, Black liberation movements, and the most secularized Zionists authenticate themselves by anchoring their history as far back in time as possible. Mircea Eliade was right when he claimed that there is something about human consciousness that will not be de-mythologized! We constantly seek originating role models.

There are voices in modern Judaism that are radically revising liturgy. Decades ago Jews began rewriting the Passover Haggadah. There are Socialist Zionist Haggadahs which tell the story of Passover completely in Marxist terms. The National Havurah Movement and Zalman Schachter's P'nai Or network have been involved in radical revisions of the *Siddur* which are both de-patriarchalizing and "re-spiritualizing" in the sense that members of those related movements have been directly affected by the infusion of information about mysticism, especially Hasidism, through the efforts of Scholem and his students and Martin Buber. But women have been especially sensitive to the sexism of traditional liturgy. Study and prayer, the most esteemed Jewish public roles, were reserved for men. Female consciousness about the need to de-patriarchalize Jewish spirituality has informed all movements for liturgical renewal, even penetrating into the Conservative and Reform establishments—although by no means completely.

There are feminist Haggadahs and there is at least one Jewish Lesbian Haggadah that I have seen. Jewish mothers are celebrating the New Moon as a special holiday. Jewish women are reconceiving and revaluing the *mikveh*, disconnecting it from its primary connection with purification for intercourse with a male. Mothers are litur-gically celebrating their daughter's first bleeding (replacing the traditional slaps) and celebrating each other's menopause.

Esther Broner's *A Weave of Women*, a stunning novel, provides a cornucopia of women's Midrash and liturgical fantasy, including a ritual hymenotomy whose meaning transcends "female circumci-sion." She imagines a ceremony which is equivalent to, but does not imitate, the male circumcision. As the baby girl is welcomed into the community of Jews who are women, we understand how much circumcision welcomes boy babies into the community of Jews who are men. And listen to the last poetical lines of her book as she transforms the *mah tovu*:

> What will happen to them, this caravan of women that encircles the outskirts of the city, that peoples the desert?
> How goodly are thy tents, thy reclaimed ruins, O Sara, O our mothers of the desert (294).

Parenthetically, let me highlight why I believe that the women's movement is perhaps the most important posttraditional movement for Judaism. In speaking about the Holocaust, Elie Wiesel once called the Nazis the "perfect victimizers" and the Jews the "perfect victims." As we look through history it appears that Jews have had apparently limitless opportunities to learn the role of victim. It does not appear that we have had nearly so many opportunities for exercising political power over others. In Israel right now we Jews are learning about how easy it is to fall into the role of oppressor! We are losing the sense of moral privilege that we have so often used to compensate for our feelings of powerlessness.

It seems to me at times that the voice of prophecy today speaks more in women's voices than in men's. Feminist criticism opens us to another dimension, a different reading of our history. For in reality, whether the whole Jewish people was being oppressed or not, there has always been internal oppression along gender lines. Jewish men have always had the opportunity to be oppressors and have often acted it out. We cannot afford it anymore. The survival of Judaism, as well as the survival of humanity, require the end of sexism.

What's the Point?

We could continue with a very long list reflecting the pluralization of Jewish conversations. I'm sure every one of us could add many fascinating examples. There are no authorities, no commonly accepted criteria to set the rules of these conversations. All that is required is someone who will listen to, or someone who will print, what we have to say. The traditional conversation that Handelman describes was, with all its internal freedom and playfulness, circumscribed by credentials, by a chain of tradition—real or imputed—by canonization. The invitation list was clear and limited. The modern family of conversations in Judaism is, as Rorty describes the general condition of human conversations, without privilege or foundation.

A value in the postmodern temper is the softening of boundaries, all of which are perceived to be inherently arbitrary. We are enriched by the important increase in images and symbols for transcendence, including goddess images and maternal archetypes. Religious images, symbols, and symbolic actions function as hooks for the psyche into the mythos that integrates us into our communities and also provide a scale for inner transformation. The male-dominated cumulative tradition needs to integrate the lessons that women who are separating out from and often transcending male-dominated culture are learning. The Torah of Moses requires completion by the Torah of Miriam, as it were.

And we are free now to learn from other traditions, from our experiences in other dimensions. As a small example, notice how Elie Wiesel and Chaim Potok, both very popular Jewish novelists, dip into Christian symbology to represent a kind of suffering for which Jewish symbology has no archetypes. Consider also how many Jews have experimented with meditation traditions from the Far East. Many of them have returned to Judaism looking for a spiritual path in which they have roots. The current intense interest in the Jewish mystical tradition has its source in the dissatisfaction of so many of us with the forms of both traditional and modern Judaism. On the bookshelves of every spiritually oriented bookstore are to be found the mystical and spiritual texts of every human tradition—including Jewish. There is a hunger in a large segment of the Jewish population for opportunities to develop spiritually.

Loss of Transcendence

So modernity and postmodernity have brought a measure of liberation. The erosion of belief, the rejection of dogmatism, are part of the modern temper. Under the traditional conditions of the Jewish conversation, Judaism could not survive. On the other hand, the costs of the loss of a tradition's mythos are not to be taken lightly. The cost is assessed in the coin of transcendence as Soloveitchik sees it. Scientism in its inherent materialism prejudices moderns against the reality of transcendence and the efficacy of means to attain it, while postmodern pluralism tends toward relativism and thus nihilism.

We cannot ignore the fact that contemporary midrashic freedom emerged as a result of Jewish participation in and cocreation of what Soloveitchik calls the *saeculum*-oriented "functional utilitarian society." A major feature of such a society is the ontological truncation of experience. With the limitation of cosmology to a uni-leveled universe, our anthropology, our self-imaging, has been similarly limited. One result is our loss of criteria for qualitative evaluation resulting in what Perennialist Rene Guenon has called "the reign of quantity."

Major expression of the shrinking of our values to the quantitative include not only the devotion of so much of the American Jewish community to material success (certainly understandable in light of the material conditions of the early-twentieth-century immigrants) but more generally the emerging of a Jewish ideology of survival. In the pop-Darwinism that permeates Western scientistic culture, by definition the success of any group of organisms can be measured only by its capacity to survive by reproduction. Moreover, Darwinian evolution, shaped by its rejection of Lamarckean teleology, systematically excludes questions of purpose. If the various, often contradictory, voices of the Jewish conversations can agree on nothing else, at least they agree on the imperative of survival. But survival for what? Modern Jews share with other modern peoples the crisis of identity, for identity must be seen in terms of purpose: who we are must include who we ought to be, who we are meant to be.

A Post Postmodern Vision

Let me end by indulging in some prospective speculation to match speculation about past and present. The dean of historians of religion, Wilfred Cantwell Smith, says that the part of modern Western culture that denies the reality of transcendence is an aberrancy. All human traditions until now have lived in the light of the reality of transcendence. He and the Perennialists agree that the nihilism inherent in the loss of transcendent vision is dangerous. He calls for a conversation among the peoples of the world about religious living, about being human as a Jew, a Moslem, a Buddhist. A precondition for participation in that crucial conversation is giving up the notion that God speaks only to me and through me. We now can and should listen to other sacred conversations.

In the *En Sof* idea of the Kabbalah we may find a teaching that rejects theological idolatry while affirming the multileveled nature of reality. Characterizing ultimate Being as *En Sof* entails the incompleteness of every human formulation of transcendence and ultimately the incompleteness of Torah, insofar as Torah is not only the written text but the continued embodiment of Torah in word and deed. But that means also that along the whole path of the Jewish vision, insofar as one can be identified, there is a point where language fails. The name *En Sof* says that. And that is the case for every human vision. But that does not necessarily imply that visions, words, symbols cannot be more and less adequate, that there are no standards that transcend local conversations. *En Sof* presumes *Sof*. Being is limitation: *En Sof*, the Limitless, the Nothingness, is *oleum* not vacuum.

In a sense, it is the apophatic in mysticism that strikes at the heart of postmodern logolatry. Handelman ignores, I think, that traditional Judaism has always lived within a multileveled ontologically hierarchical universe. Medieval Neo-Platonism affected many medieval Jewish minds. In the Zohar we find that Torah is also multileveled with a reality that transcends the words on the page.

> There is garment and body and soul and soul of soul.
> The heavens and their host are the garment.
> The communion of Israel is the body
> who receives the soul, the Beauty of Israel.
> So she is the body of the soul.
> The soul we have mentioned is the Beauty of Israel
> who is the real Torah.
> The soul of the soul is the Holy Ancient One. . . .

As wine must sit in a jar,
so Torah must sit in this garment.
So look only at what is under the garment!
So all those words and all those stories—
they are garments (3:152a/44f.)!

With limitlessness as the linchpin of the ontotheological hierarchy,
symbols that connect differences are valuable. The symbolism of the
Sefirotic Tree models the manifestation of being in that way. Inherent
to that symbolism is the development of and integration—not the
identification—of male and female symbolisms. But even androgy-
nous images are just another set of images, are not to be taken as idols.
Nor are they arbitrary! There is a difference between a pluralization
based on nihilism and one based on an acceptance that no one symbol
can gather together the Totality. The latter is implicit in the kabbalistic
version of the "great chain of being" which culminated in *En Sof* (*pace*
Handelman).

REFERENCES

BRONER, E.M. *A Weave of Women*. Bloomington: Indiana University Press,
1978.

HANDELMAN, Susan A. *The Slayers of Moses: The Emergence of Rabbinic
Interpretation in Modern Literary Theory*. Albany: S.U.N.Y. Press, 1982.

PATAI, Raphael. *The Hebrew Goddess*. New York: KTAV, 1967.

RORTY, Richard. *Philosophy and the Mirror of Nature*. Princeton: Princeton
University Press, 1979.

SMITH, Wilfred Cantwell. *Towards a World Theology*. Philadelphia: Westminster Press, 1981.

SOLOVEITCHIK, Joseph B. "The Lonely Man of Faith." *Tradition* (1965).

STONE, Merlin. *When God Was a Woman*. New York: Dial, 1976.

TEUBAL, Savina J. *Sarah the Priestess: The First Matriarch of Genesis*.
Athens, Ohio: Swallow Press, 1984.

Zohar: The Book of Enlightenment (Classics of Western Spirituality), trans.
and intro. by Daniel Chanan Matt. New York: Paulist Press, 1983.

17. New Roles for Jewish Women

Livia Bitton-Jackson

Jewish women are experiencing an "unheralded revolution." They are awakening to a new awareness of self-worth expressed in a desire of religio-social equality-freedom to assume roles and responsibilities within Judaism on parity with men. Jewish women have come to realize that, in order to achieve their objective, it is up to them to struggle against a largely unresponsive "Establishment" steeped in traditional norms and attitudes.

While Jewish women in the Diaspora have struggled primarily for changes in Halakhah, Jewish law, which has kept them from assuming equal roles in the Jewish religious establishment, women in Israel, where state and synagogue are not separate, have struggled for equality in politics and economy, as well as religion.

Assuming new roles in the mainstream of Israeli life is considered by women a first and a most vital step in establishing a power base in order to bring about social change, to raise the status of women in all spheres.

"To influence, you have to play the game," says Yael Aran, secretary of the Jerusalem branch of the Labor Party's Young Guard and the Histadrut Labor Federation's representative in the Knesset, paraphrasing veteran Knesset Member Ora Namir's message to younger women: "If you want to influence, you have to get involved."

Women in Politics

Leah Shakdiel is one woman who wanted to get involved in order to influence. A young Orthodox mother and school teacher, Ms. Shakdiel moved from her native Jerusalem to a development town in the Negev so as "to deal with the issue of the nature of Israeli society, of Jewish society," she explained. "In a small place all the problems are very acutely felt, but you do have the potential of making a difference."[1]

Leah Shakdiel entered local politics and in January 1986 was nominated by the town council to the local religious council, the first woman ever to receive such nomination. In Israel, local religious councils provide Jewish ritual and social services for all members of their Jewish communities, such as the maintenance of local synagogues and ritual baths, supervision of *kashrut* (dietary laws), and *sheḥitah* (ritual slaughter) licenses, care of the *mikveh* (ritual bath), payment of local officials, organization of burials, etc. As an Orthodox Jewish woman, Ms. Shakdiel felt this was for her the most natural area of involvement for performing a civic duty and the most direct way to have a social input.

When her nomination was rejected by the government, Leah Shakdiel appealed to the High Court of Justice which then ordered the Ministry of Religious Affairs, the Ministry of Interior, and the Office of the Prime Minister to explain their objections. The new Minister for Religious Affairs, resolved to settle the issue of women's participation in religious councils, appointed in December 1986 an educated Orthodox Jewish woman as advisor on women's affairs in his ministry, to investigate and advise. At present [1988], the new advisor's recommendations await renewed hearings of the High Court of Justice. The Court's rulings in the matter will have a far-reaching impact on the status of women in Judaism, not only in Israel but also in the Diaspora.

Like religious councils, committees that select local rabbis have been made up exclusively of male representatives. This year, the Tel Aviv city council broke with tradition by nominating two women, Haviva Avigai and Lilly Menahem, to the thirty-member board to elect the city's next Ashkenazic rabbi. The women's nominations, however, were rejected by the Ministry of Religious Affairs, arousing widespread controversy. A great number of organizations and individuals back the women councilors in their struggle for recognition of their rights; others argue that the local rabbis have an important effect on the lives of women and therefore it is desirable that women participate in the election of the rabbis.

The traditional objection to the election of women to public office derives to some extent from the view of Maimonides: "A woman is not appointed to the kingship, as it is said, 'Set a king over thee.'"[2] A king, and not a queen. Does this qualifying injunction exclude women from all public offices?

Some rabbinic authorities question the validity of Maimonides' ruling in the context of modern realities. Among others, Rabbi Uziel proposed that twentieth-century women could be entitled, in theory, to elect and be reelected. Although a fresh rabbinic view concerning theory is encouraging, Leah Shakdiel is concerned with the existing gap between theory and practice. She explains: "My personal concern is to fill the gap that exists now in what is already possible by the standards of Orthodox Halakhah and the reality of our lives. I bear in mind that Halakhah exists in history, changing all the time, and my daughter will possibly live in a different world."[3]

Some rabbis base their opposition to women in political positions of responsibility on the traditional Jewish issue of female modesty. They fear, in their words, that political responsibility might threaten female modesty by placing women in the position of having to argue with men in the same forum.

Leah Shakdiel's response is a call for a redefinition of the concept of modesty based on a more comprehensive understanding of relations between the sexes and on an understanding of the notion of responsibility. While explaining her need for self-realization as a Jewish woman she expressed the profound dilemma this need poses in the context of traditional Jewish values: "I need to realize myself as a person. I am looking for my own identity and I'd like to actualize it . . . But when we talk about Judaism we talk about things that transcend the individual . . . like responsibility to your community and your history, to God and to Torah, to your family and to future generations . . ."

Jewish feminists reinforce the argument of individual responsibility *versus* Jewish community values by pointing out that their efforts to promote the public role of women represent a commitment to collective responsibility. "The central goal of politics is to express the interests of the wider public," explains Haifa University political science lecturer, Daphna Sharfman, one of the founders of the Women's Study Program at the university.

International surveys show that the average age of women in politics is higher than that of men. This is most likely due to childbearing responsibilities: while young women are busy raising children, their male contemporaries are gaining valuable professional and political experience.

Family and Career

Professor Alice Shalvi, head of Israel Women's Network and principal of Pelech Religious High School for Girls, believes that until responsibilities for childcare are shared more equally between the spouses, women will not have real equality. "The question is really children, not marriage," Israeli feminist Lisa Blum seconds Professor Shalvi's argument.

In Israel, the difficulties are reinforced by traditional Jewish education. Because Israeli women have been educated to consider marriage and raising children as a first priority, they do not think of politics as a viable career option, nor do they have good role models of women with political careers. To remedy one aspect of this handicap in a dramatic fashion, Ettia Simha, advisor to the prime minister on women's affairs, announced on International Women's Day the formation of a women's lobby in the Knesset to create an awareness of women's issues and to encourage participation of women in all areas of public life.

According to Esther Eilam, one of the founders of Israel's feminist movement, "There are fewer women in politics than there were a decade ago. Managing a career and a family leaves hardly any room for public life for women. Politics is where things are decided and this is the sphere in which women are rarest."[4]

"To advance the status of women in the public sector, I have to give them tools to deal with the issues," Etia Simha explained recently. "This includes dissemination of information and helping them to be more assertive." To this end, Ms. Simha has recently formed an advisory committee of academicians specializing in women's studies.

Simha considers the law of equal opportunities at work, passed by the Knesset at the end of February 1988, "a revolution in Israeli society." The bill provides for equal opportunities at work for men and women, described as "the most important" in its field in the history of the Knesset. According to the law's main provisions, employees may not be discriminated against by reason of sex, marital status, or parenthood. Men, as well as women, may take postmaternity leaves, with the choice of who takes the leave being up to the parents. Similarly, the father, rather than the mother, may decide to leave his job after the birth of a child, in which event he will be entitled to compensation pay. The right to obtain leave from work to attend to a sick child is to be conferred equally on either parent. Etia Simha believes that the key to equality lies in educating men and women to share responsibilities: the younger generation has in many ways taken quantum steps toward that new goal.[5]

The idea of a "paternity leave" and the leave to care for a sick child conferred on either parent, has the makings of a revolutionary gesture certain to exercise a lasting change on women's self-image and career options.

Despite the difficulties, there are some Israeli women in their twenties and thirties who are making their mark in politics. Energetic, well-educated and realistic, they represent the next generation of women politicians prepared to take on leadership roles and affect social change.

Yehezkel Landau, information director of the 'Oz V'Shalom-Netivot Shalom religious peace organization, views the issue of women's new roles in messianic terms: "Israel won't be redeemed without the active contribution of women. While we were building and defending the state, the masculine dimension of our collective personality was primary. But the feminine aspect, which in our tradition is the Shekhinah, must come forth," he declared with feeling.

If women in the public sector have two major problems—time constraint because of family responsibilities and convincing their male counterparts to take them seriously—in religious circles these problems are greatly exacerbated. Besides juggling (what is usually) a large family and a professional job, religious women in politics have to deal with additional limitations. The most formidable among these is the fierce opposition of their male counterparts. The most often voiced objection that politics is a public endeavor, "the woman's place is in the home," and that "the woman has an important role to play in education and other areas of the community, but not in elected positions," was summarized by Knesset Member Avraham Shapira of Agudat Yisrael, with the conclusion: "There is no place for women in political life." To buttress this argument, Knesset Member Shimon Ben-Shlomo of the Shas party quoted King Solomon: "The honor of the daughter of the king resides in the house," with the popular commentary: "That is to say, righteousness for the woman is to be found in the home, raising children. Politics is full of jealousy and lies. It is not modest at all."

In the face of such opposition it is surprising to find a number of Orthodox Jewish women in leading political positions. Viva Sivan, the first female Jerusalem city councilor from a religious party, finds combining family, religious observance, and career not too difficult: "I don't see my religion as a barrier to anything," she observes. "I see Shabbat as an advantage. It makes me turn off politics and turn into family." The difficulty lies with the Orthodox male establishment. "It's certainly not easy for religious women to break down prejudice because the religious community is more conservative," she admits.[6]

Role-Equality in the Synagogue

In 1972, the Hebrew Union College-Jewish Institute of Religion in Cincinnati, Ohio, the Reform rabbinical college, ordained the first woman rabbi in the face of much opposition from among the members of the congregations. In the same year, a delegation of women presented a manifesto to the Rabbinical Assembly, the central organization of Conservative rabbis, declaring, in part:

> Although the woman was extolled in Judaism for her domestic achievements and respected as the foundation of the Jewish family, she was never permitted an active role in the synagogue, court, or house of study. These limitations on the life patterns open to women, appropriate or even progressive for the rabbinic and medieval periods, are entirely unacceptable to us today . . . It is time that women be granted membership in synagogues, that women be counted in the *minyan* (the quorum of ten required for public prayer), that women be allowed full participation in religious services, including *aliyot* (called to the Torah for public reading), serving as Torah readers and cantors, among other responsibilities.[7]

The Conservative women did not ask to be ordained as rabbis. The time of the daring idea had not come yet then. The Reform movement had given expression to a liberal view with regard to women's ordination as early as 1922, when the Central Conference of American Rabbis (CCAR) concluded that "in keeping with the spirit of our age and the traditions of our conference . . . women cannot justly be denied the privilege of ordination."[8]

Storms of protest followed this statement, and a number of women attempted unsuccessfully to reaffirm the resolution by pursuing a rabbinic course of study. Thirty-three years later a committee formed to investigate the issue urged the Reform rabbinical college to admit women to ordination. However, it took another sixteen years for the first woman to become a Reform rabbi.

No wonder that the issue of rabbinical ordination was not included in the Conservative women's manifesto of 1972.

The tradition of exempting women from positive, time-bound commandments was invoked in rabbinic responses to that manifesto. Exemption from *aliyot* was a major, problematic issue, one that was not based on the principle of time-limitation but rather on the talmudic dictum: "A woman should not read the Torah because of the honor of the congregation."[9] Neither the Talmud nor its commentaries explain the enigmatic phrase "the honor of the congregation," causing much speculation and debate, and delaying a rabbinic consensus which would reverse the exemption.

Many believed that the phrase was a veiled reference to women's "uncleanness" during their menses, as a period during which they would be prohibited from touching the Torah scrolls. This, however, is a popular misconception: rabbinic authorities have accepted as binding Rabbi Judah ben Bteira's ruling, according to which "The Torah is immune to being rendered unclean by contact."[10] The most notable among the rabbinic Responsa dealing with the issue of *aliyot* for women is that of Rabbi Meir of Rothenburg, a leading fourteenth-century German-Jewish scholar, stipulating that in certain exceptional cases women may be called up to read the Torah. Rabbi Rothenburg's decision has been cited in a number of legal codes.

Rabbi David M. Feldman, member of the Conservative Law Committee charged with the task of reviewing the halakhic implications of women's liturgical roles, refers to another basic consideration relating to the issue:

> The most formidable problem, from a strict halakhic point of view, is that of sex segregation and the attitudes and practices associated with it . . . This is illustrated by the incongruous suggestion of Professor Meir Friedman, written as a Responsum to the President of the Jewish community of Vienna in 1893. If you want to institute, or re-institute, *aliyot* for women, he wrote, it goes without saying that a special,

covered stairway should be set up, leading the women, unseen, from and to the ladies' gallery. The problem reflected here—'mixed-pew' usage notwithstanding—is not at all simple of resolution. Sex equality is one thing, the halakhic concern with sexual distraction is another.[11]

Many Orthodox women, in their eagerness to assume active roles in the synagogual services and thus achieve spiritual fulfillment, took the initiative in setting up separate prayer groups. They felt that the *mehitzah*, the partition in the synagogue, not only separated the women from the men but removed the women from the center of the "action." They saw the *mehitzah* as an instrument designed to keep women beyond the religio-social pale. The women's prayer groups, organized into the Women's *Tefillah* Network, have faced firm opposition from numerous circles. Many rabbis, including leaders of Yeshiva University, categorically condemned the practice of a women's *minyan*, a public prayer service which requires a quorum of ten men. Rivka Haut, a founding member of the movement, defends the practice on a halakhic basis: "We are not a *minyan*," she explains. "We do not say any of the prayers for which a *minyan* is necessary, such as Kaddish. We operate solely within bounds of Jewish law, under the guidance of an Orthodox rabbi."

Despite rabbinic censure and various handicaps placed in its path, the Women's *Tefillah* Network continues to function. It coordinates the different prayer groups through regular contacts and biannual conferences. Scheduling for the prayer meetings has become standardized for all groups: the services take place once a month, on the Sabbath when the blessing for the New Moon is recited in the synagogue.

Rabbinic opposition consolidated the women's resolve. Rivka Haut voices the seasoned wisdom of having come of age: "This experience has taught us that we cannot turn to the rabbis for guidance, since the rabbis are not really hearing us. We tried to establish a dialogue with them—which they refused to enter into. In the long run, they probably helped us because they taught us that we have to turn to each other."

The rabbinate's refusal to allow the assumption of new roles by women within Judaism exposes a much more fundamental problem. It is the problem of synthesis between tradition and modernity. In the words of a modern Jewish thinker, Jewish spiritual leaders "do not have the conceptual models yet for dealing with the confrontation between Judaism and modernity. There is a conspiracy to prevent modernity from entering Judaism."[12]

The above statement appears to echo Leah Shakdiel's sentiments expressed in a *New York Times* interview half-a-year earlier:

> I think the issue of women's status in Judaism goes hand in hand with a whole range of issues which fall under the general headline of how Judaism deals with modernity. I personally do not believe that you can take one issue—like women's status—and just start trying to rectify it by demanding that a woman be allowed to be the next chief rabbi.[13]
>
> Ever since the industrial age, the major challenge to Judaism has not been other religions but Western modern secularism. But Judaism has not yet accomplished the task of facing secularism to its full extent, and, as a result, it has not faced up to the issue of the status of women. I see my task less as trying to promote women's right in Judaism per se, than trying to get Judaism to adapt itself to modernity. I am working for a synthesis between Judaism and modernity within which the status of women will naturally take care of itself in a way consistent with both aspirations of women and interpretation of Jewish law.[14]

According to one assessment, in "Israel women's search is less for spiritual fulfillment than for social justice . . . In Israel, women feel they must face the nuts-and-bolts issues of human dignity before they can spare the energy to organize around spiritual concerns."[15]

Women activists believe that the issues of human dignity are pivotal to Jewish ethics. "We are working in Judaism's best interest," Pnina Peli declared at the First International Conference on Women and Judaism. "We do not seek to be better feminists; we seek to be better Jews, to get the best, rather than the least, of what Judaism has to offer."[16]

In 1983, the Union for Traditional Conservative Judaism was founded to counter a "liberal" trend in Conservatism that culminated in the decision to ordain women as rabbis.[17]

The Rabbinical Assembly, the Jewish Theological Seminary, and the United Synagogue of America, three major institutions of Conservative Judaism, issued in March 1988 a joint statement of principles which "paid tribute" to the expanded role of women in the Conservative movement. Simultaneously, the document acknowledges the fact that women's roles as rabbis and cantors have not as yet become an integral part of the movement's functioning due to opposition by a number of Conservative leaders.

The statement makes reference to the existing controversy over women's roles in religious ritual: "Many believe that women should be encouraged" to serve in a ritual capacity in the synagogue, adding: "while others believe that women today can find religious fulfillment within the context of traditional practice."[18]

Women as Cantors

The Conservative branch of Judaism recently began ordaining women as cantors. The chancellor of the Jewish Theological Seminary, Ismar Schorsch, declared that the decision was "in full accord with Halakhah," and referred to it as "the culmination of a century-long evolution of the status of women under the law." Rabbi Schorsch's opinion is, however, representative of the views of the liberal faction within the Conservative movement. The Union for Traditional Conservative Judaism, formed specifically to protest the ordination of women as rabbis, expressed forceful opposition also to this move.

Harold Jacobs of the National Council of Young Israel, an association of nearly three hundred Orthodox synagogues, voiced the Orthodox view on women's ordination as cantors when he declared: "Our tradition provides ample opportunity for the participation of Jewish women in communal life. Confusing the roles of men and women by ordaining women cantors for the Conservative movement further weakens the fundamental bonds that hold Jewish family and Jewish community together."[19]

In the Reform movement, women as cantors have become a familiar phenomenon. The Hebrew Union College Cantorial Student

Ensemble and Community Choir is composed of men and women. Musical director and conductor Carol Davidson explains: "In America, it's already an established fact that fully fifty percent of those studying *hazzanut* at HUC are female. Religious pluralism does not stop at the *bima*."

As with other women-related activities, the HUC choir is made up of members from the entire spectrum of religious observance. "In our group we have both secular and religious members," Ms. Davidson explained. As to the Orthodox members, "the only concession we have made—and we are glad to do so—was the substitution of '*Hashem*' for God's name. A love of singing good Jewish music does wonders for reconciling religious differences."[20]

Women as Scholars

Torah learning, a primary *mitzvah* for the Jewish male, is attracting more and more women. Jewish women of all backgrounds are leaving their babies with sitters and engaging in Jewish scholarly pursuit. They study Jewish law with the various commentaries, Jewish philosophy, and even *ta'ame ha-mikra*, with the accents used in chanting the Torah, traditionally a subject exclusively for study by men. In response to the demand, seminars for women's study, or *kollelot*, have been established in the United States and Israel, where special arrangements are made for married students and young mothers. Fulltime married women receive a stipend, just like men, and nurseries are attached to the halls of study. Each student makes up a personal plan of study—formal classes augmented by independent preparation of the text. A basic objective at most academies is to teach women how to carry on independent study of the text.

In some classes in Torah subjects, women and men study together and the women actively participate even in Talmud classes. In the past, women had been excluded from the study of the Talmud: all religious educational curricula had included the study of Mishnah and *Gemara* for boys, and the study of Bible for girls.

American women introduced the phenomenon of the independent

study group called *havurah* and the traditional study partner called *havruta* which offer the option of informal yet serious study of different Jewish scholarly texts outside the academy. Dozens of *havurot* in Manhattan, Los Angeles, Jerusalem, and Beer Sheva coordinate the study of Jewish sources with the help of *Luah Limud*, a monthly calendar and diary published by the Union of Orthodox Jewish Congregations of America, containing a daily portion of Mishnah and commentaries in English. Shirah Leibovitz, a professor of civil engineering at Ben-Gurion University, a mother of five and an ardent student of talmudic texts, refers to the *Luah Limud* as a source of inspiration: "All over the world people are learning the same section in Tractate Shabbat this month," she explains. "It's a wonderful feeling to know I'm part of it. Some working women find time during their lunch break; young mothers might study together over a cup of coffee while their children nap."[21]

One group of Orthodox and secular women has been studying the Bible in English at a private home in Beer Sheva once every two weeks for over fifteen years. In another home a class in Hebrew on prayer meets every Sabbath afternoon. Ma'ayan, an institute for Torah studies, has five *shi'urim*, Talmud classes, for women. The *Habad* movement sponsors classes for women on the study of the *Tanya*, the basic text of *Habad* Hasidism. At Makhon Rahel in the Old City of Jerusalem, every Monday morning 20–25 housewives are engaged in four hours of Talmud study in the community center's study hall, while their infants sleep in baby carriages parked in the anteroom. In Mevasseret Yerushalayim, a settlement outside Jerusalem, some thirty women attend three consecutive morning classes on the Torah portion of the week, Jewish laws, and philosophy. Makhon Lieberman in the Judean Hills operates full-day classes in Jewish studies with a special emphasis on Mishnah and Gemara. Director of the institute, Hannah Safrai, explains: "Today women who want to understand Torah must study Talmud as well, since it is the basis of all Jewish learning. Modern women who are capable of running government offices, businesses, educational institutions and can hold any other position as well as a man, can hold their own in this field, too." Rabbi Hayyim Brovender, head of Mikhlelet Bruria, a women's academy in Jerusalem originally established for the *ḥozrot bitshuvah*, "returnees to Judaism," explains the curricular choices at his institution with the same argument: "We integrate the Oral Teachings with the Written Law, for without one the other is incomplete."

Drisha Institute for Jewish Education on Manhattan's Upper West Side addresses itself, according to Rabbi David Silber, founder of Drisha, to "women's great need for serious Torah study and the Jewish community's great need for educated Jewish women to effectively face the challenges of our complex society." By combining methods of secular graduate study with those of traditional yeshivot, women are trained to handle independent, in-depth study of halakhic and non-halakhic Jewish texts full-time, from Sunday to Thursday. By arrangement with the Board of Jewish Education, Drisha students can take series of seminars that qualify them for a license as teachers of Judaic studies.[22]

Sarah Japhet, head of the Hebrew University's Institute of Jewish Studies, occupies one of the most important and prestigious positions in academic Judaic studies anywhere. She had to struggle against society's unspoken and often unconscious prejudice toward women on her way up the academic ladder. Judaic studies had traditionally been dominated by male scholars. She explains her own reason for hesitancy at first: "It's a matter of almost unwitting career decisions. Even today, a woman looks for a job in her chosen profession that will allow her time to devote to her family . . . Most men, on the other hand will think first and foremost about their professional lives."[23]

Even the Hebrew University's Talmud Department, though traditionally averse to appointing women to its staff (apparently a throwback to the days when Talmud was exclusively a male domain) now has a woman instructor.[24]

In April 1988, a unique meeting of women took place in Jerusalem. It was convened by the Council of Women's Organizations in Israel, an umbrella organization encompassing all the major women's organizations in the country. The meeting, called the "Jewish Women's World Leadership Forum," stated its objective as the establishment of a "parliament of Jewish women leaders the world over."

The uniqueness of the occasion was manifested by the harmony of purpose uniting diverse groups of Jewish women, the first such gathering anywhere. It revealed a new sophistication on the part of Jewish women, a new awareness of their roles and responsibilities not only as Jews but as women confronting present realities.

Heads of major Jewish women's organizations came from all parts of the globe, representing, among others, the Association of United Synagogue Women in the United Kingdom, B'nai B'rith, Conservative Women, Emunah, Hadassah, Herut Women, Israel Association of University Women, International Council of Jewish Women, Israel Bonds Women's Division, Israel Women's Network, Jewish International Women Worker's Organization, Keren Hayesod Women's Division, Liberal Women's Organization (ANALI), Naamat, ORT Women, Soroptomist International of Israel, Women's International Zionist Organization, and various Temple Sisterhoods. They came from Argentina, Australia, Belgium, Canada, Finland, France, Germany, Israel, Japan, Mexico, The Netherlands, New Zealand, Peru, South Africa, Sweden, Switzerland, United Kingdom, Uruguay, United States, and Venezuela.

The delegates represented the full spectrum of Jewish religious and cultural affiliation, and they discussed issues that echoed an entire range of Jewish concerns. They dealt with the many facets of the question of Jewish women's leadership in local congregational structures, religious institutions, Jewish educational systems, and Zionist organizations. They also discussed the search for identity within the context of universal and Jewish ethics, tradition and commitment to Israel.

The set of proclamations and resolutions issued at the conclusion of the three-day forum revealed the existence of common denominators and a wide basis for an operational consensus. The women declared:

> We affirm our commitment to Jewish identity, tradition and to the centrality of Israel in Jewish life.
> We strive for—a democratic society in Israel based on mutual respect and freed from any form of discrimination;—the highest standards of education including the humanities, science, engineering and

technology;—a sound and independent economy;—cooperation with the other countries in the region.

We, Jewish women in Israel and in the Diaspora, should engage in an open and free dialogue about matters of common concern and stress the importance of tolerance and respect for divergent opinions.

Israel strives for peace through dialogue and negotiations. As women we have a vested interest and a special role to play in this process. We therefore call upon women in Arab countries to participate with us in a dialogue for peace.

1. We recommend that the women's organizations should be in the forefront of the following three fields of activity:

   a. Fight against assimilation, intermarriage and the influence of cults through Jewish and Zionist education.

   b. Help and support for Jewish communities in distress to ensure their spiritual survival.

   c. Commitment to Israel's future and its quality of life.

2. In order to bring closer the ties between the Diaspora and Israel, women's organizations should encourage:

   a. Aliya

   b. Frequent trips by their members and their families to Israel

   c. Young people to spend longer periods of time in Israel for study and for work

   d. Families to celebrate festivities in Israel.

3. To strengthen Jewish unity and understanding of each other, we recommend that the Hebrew language be studied and spoken by all Jews wherever they are so that they can be part of the Israeli culture.

4. Jewish and Zionist education is a priority in the home and we recommend to strengthen and to ensure the continuity of our people through both formal and informal programs.

5. It is our duty to know and teach Jewish heritage and Jewish history in all its diversity.

6. As Jewish women leaders, we must respect Jewish tradition at all times.

7. To further education and Jewish identity as well as Zionist ideals, we recommend for all Jewish organizations in a community to hold periodical meetings devoted to these subjects.

8. We urge women's organizations to give priority to the combatting of anti-Semitism and to the better understanding of the Holocaust.

9. In order to advance the status of women and of Jewish women in particular, women's organizations should cooperate in the spirit of mutual respect, understanding and equality to further our common goals.

10. Women's organizations should initiate programs to educate adults and children from the earliest age to accept equality in all spheres of life.

11. Innovative programs should be initiated to enrich Jewish women's self-esteem and their involvement and participation in all fora of national and Jewish spiritual life.

Will women indeed assume roles of responsibility and leadership in order to carry out their ambitious agenda? In my view, whatever the future holds, the very language of the resolutions indicates a sense of readiness born of a new self-awareness of ability, a major step toward achievement.

NOTES

1. *The Jerusalem Post*, December 27, 1987.
2. Ibid.
3. Ibid.
4. *The Jerusalem Post*, September 18, 1987.
5. *The Jerusalem Post*, March 8, 1988.
6. *The Jerusalem Post*, February 7, 1988.
7. Cited by David M. Feldman, "Woman's Role and Jewish Law," *Conservative Judaism* 26, 4 (1972): 29–30.
8. "Report of Committee on Ordination of Women," *CCAR Yearbook* 66 (Philadelphia: Central Conference of American Rabbis, 1956), 90–91; cited by Sally Preisand, *Judaism and the New Woman* (New York: Behrman House, 1975), 62.
9. *B. Megillah*, 23a.
10. *B. Berakhot*, 22a.
11. Feldman, "Woman's Role and Jewish Law", 29.
12. *Hadassah Magazine*, April 1987, 23.
13. *The New York Times*, Sunday, October 12, 1986.
14. Ibid.

15. Susan Grossman, "Revolution with a Difference," *Hadassah Magazine*, April, 1987.
16. Ibid., 23.
17. *The Jerusalem Post*, March 29, 1988.
18. Ibid.
19. *The Jerusalem Post*, February 7, 1987.
20. *The Jerusalem Post*, April 20, 1988.
21. *The Jerusalem Post*, May 17, 1983, 8.
22. Livia Bitton-Jackson, "Drisha—A Unique Opportunity," *The Jewish Press*, June 13, 1986, M31.
23. *The Jerusalem Post*, May 17, 1987.
24. Ibid.